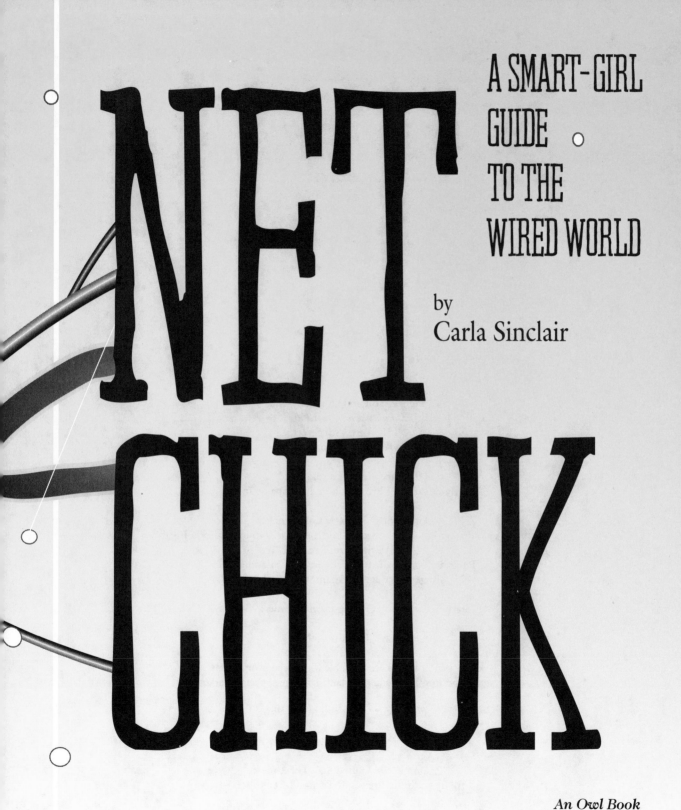

NET CHICK

A SMART-GIRL
GUIDE
TO THE
WIRED WORLD

by
Carla Sinclair

An Owl Book

Henry Holt and Company • New York

Henry Holt and Company, Inc.
Publishers since 1866
115 West 18th Street
New York, New York 10011

Henry Holt® is a registered
trademark of Henry Holt and Company, Inc.

Published in Canada by Fitzhenry & Whiteside Ltd.,
195 Allstate Parkway, Markham, Ontario L3R 4T8.

Library of Congresss Catalog Card Number: 95-81183

ISBN 0-8050-4393-4

Henry Holt books are available for special promotions
and premiums. For details contact: Director, Special Markets.

First Henry Holt Edition—1996

Designed by Georgia Rucker and Margo Mooney

Printed in the United States of America
All first editions are printed on acid-free paper.∞

1 3 5 7 9 10 8 6 4 2

ACKNOWLEDGMENTS

Last summer would have been a bitch on wheels if it hadn't been for my adorable and patient husband, Mark Frauenfelder, to whom I give my biggest thanks. As well as putting up with my stress-laden and anti-social behavior for 4 months without complaining, he cooked for me, brainstormed with me, designed my Website, and even painted my toenails when I asked him to. What a guy! He's so supreme.

I also want to thank Gareth Branwyn and Colin Berry. Even though they were going through the same hectic times finishing up their own books, they unselfishly let me kvetch to my heart's content about my slack-free days. And, having gone through this before, they knew exactly what to say.

Other thanks go to my agent Karen Nazor, my editors Debra Williams Cauley and Ben Ratliff, and my designers Georgia Rucker and Margo Mooney. Laura Curtis, Ron Gompertz, Shalini Malhotra, Tasha McVeigh, Jonathan Steuer, and Lance Volland also get a high-five.

Oh, and I can't forget my mom, Jackie Bly, and my sis, Melissa Bardizbanian, for letting me sneak some of their gorgeous photos in here. See if you can guess who they are. And then I can't leave out my dad, Joe Bardizbanian, and my step-dad, Mel Bly, or they'd get jealous.

Thanks everyone!

contents

by kristin spence

Section Editor, *Wired* magazine

I was a trouble-making tomboy weird-kid, growing up. And, well, not much has changed. It's probably a big reason why the Internet appealed so strongly to me. I had an inter-esting and, I've since come to realize, unusual child-hood. My mom was a teacher, my dad a nuclear physicist, which meant computers, technology, and vast possibility were as natural to me as skinned knees and mud under my fingernails. It also meant that watching TV was a barred activity in our house. Substituting for the "boob tube" were easels, paints, Erector sets, books, musical instruments, records, and a great deal of the great outdoors. Early on, I also realized that I didn't much like girl-toys, or girls for that matter. Boys were simpler, straightforward…plus, Hot Wheels, Tonka trucks, and dirt bikes were a helluva lot more appealing than the torpid world of…(shudder)…Barbie. I much preferred following my dad around, "helping" him fix our cars or work on the house.

All of these things worked to only heighten the fact that I wasn't like most of the kids around me—especially the girls. Funny enough, the older I got, the less I wanted to fit in. I straddled the worlds, so to speak. A grrrl in a world of boyz, embracing digital technology in Gaia's natural world.

Luckily, my formative years were spent careening around the hills of Berkeley, so I never really felt uncomfortable or apologetic about who I was. (Okay, okay…I'd be lying if I said that existence in the twisted, Lord-of-the-Flies underworld of kiddom didn't take its emotional toll. I frequently came home crying, exhausted after a day of persecution and humiliation.) But fate always seems to provide some hidden method to its madness: little did I know just how much all of this would perfectly prepare me for life in the male-dominated, high-tech, digital world.

It's obvious our context has changed. Though we are still suffocating in a patriarchal society, the days of Donna Reed, "M-R-S degrees," and pining for that ring-mounted rock have passed like a bad martini hangover. Instead, we women are now the diamonds. Each of us is unique, self-possessed, multifaceted, clear (focused, directed), beautiful, rough or polished, and tough-as-nails strong. Better yet, even if you're stranded in the most intolerant pocket of the world, you can now move freely within a community as tolerant and diverse as the Berkeley of my youth.

The community I'm talking about is, of course, the Internet. Some describe the Net as a vast ocean of resources, complete with surfable waves of information. Others call it the new Wild West (a pretty accurate descriptor, as cyberspace is still populated mostly by men and runs basically on mob law). But I like to imagine the Internet more as a bizarre universe of idiosyncratic planetoids (think STAR TREK TNG meets PEE-WEE'S PLAYHOUSE set in Mad Max's aggro, post-apocalyptic world and you're getting close). In this wide expanse of deviant life-forms, you'll find Websites spotlighting such reprehensible geezers as Newt Gingrich and Rush Limbaugh sitting right alongside pages dedicated to alternative energy sources. Amnesty International gopher holes lie just across the cyber-plain from Build-a-Bomb BBSs.

Obviously, regardless of how you envision it, this is where it's all happening—and where it will continue to happen. The momentum propelling information technology forward is steadily strengthened with each new innovation, each new Internet subscriber. So wait not, fair grrrlie: hie thee to a modem connection and get thine ass online! This ain't a passing fad; this techno stuff is real, and, in case you haven't heard it from Madge, you're already soaking in it.

But connecting is only a small part of a much larger picture. Let me interject a cautionary word before you rabidly immerse yourself. Like any radical movement, the Digital Revolution is dense both in meaning and implication. The societal topography of your world will soon be unrecognizable—everything is changing: your classroom, your workplace, your home, your cafe. So the next time a friend asks you, "So what does this mean to me? What's the big deal, anyway?" you'll have a few things to tell them.

The big deal? Cyberspace is a world ruled by knowledge, driven by communication. Never before has there been the possibility of such a level playing field in such an immediate medium. Think about it: Here is a medium in which your physical identity—your age, sex, racial heritage—is no longer the focus. Hell, it can be a complete mystery if you want it to be. The beautiful thing that then happens is that the attention is shifted to your ideas—your thoughts, your language. Guyz (or whoever else) are forced to address your mind, not your chest. Now think about this: The root forces driving this medium—communication, community, and creativity—are inherently feminine. They are things women innately excel at. Plainly put, this means we were built to do this.

Studies have shown that women come to technology with quite a different set of expectations than do men. We perceive a computer as a tool, not a toy. This becomes incredibly compelling when you realize what a powerful tool is a computer with an Internet connection. It's all about communication, power, equality. That's the big deal. And the reason why every woman owes it to herself, and to her community, to get wired.

Granted, much needs to be done to ensure that the Internet is indeed planed to its level potential. We have a long way to go towards ensuring that those who can't afford technology can still gain access to it. Many other dangers also lurk in the wings. For one, the U.S. government is already attempting to legislate and compromise the freedom of this new medium before the majority of Americans have even connected. As it stands now, Congress doesn't even have direct Internet access. The implications are sobering. Our government is laying down the law on something our constituents—and citizenry— have yet to understand. Nothing new there, but it speaks to the fact that the time has come to stretch your virtual limbs, learn their dimensions, cry out before the full range of your voice is silenced.

That said, there are a few things I hope you'll keep in mind as you're out there cruising around. Going back to that Wild West metaphor, the Internet is indeed still populated by an overabundance of men. While plenty of them are perfectly nice guys, the medium remains quite clannish. It is the ultimate patriarchy. Rosie Cross pretty much nails it when she depicts the Net as burgeoning with "boring conservative righteous sexist bloody men who really need to get a life." Be prepared to get flamed and flamed hard. Be prepared to fight your way into the treehouse without the secret password. It ain't pretty out there sometimes. As a result, the immediate temptation is to flirt with the idea of grrrl-only Internet providers, conference areas, CD-ROMs, games, magazines. While it is always tremendously affirming and empowering to hang with your own posse,

such a ghettoization of the Net would be a tragic step backwards. I am by no means suggesting that femme spaces be abolished or unfrequented. I applaud them. I'm merely bringing up the issue of balance—an issue that will be of increasing importance as we move forward.

It appears that our lot is to be the pioneer women of this medium. Hardily, like our female frontier predecessors, we should stand strong and firm, remembering that we are actively plowing the way for the grrrls who will follow us. As Magdalen so aptly explains, "The Net's really about screaming." It's also about convergence—integration: the integration of a wide range of people and of the sexes. For, as in analog society, our spiritual health—and ultimate evolution—depend on finding and cultivating a balance, both within ourselves and in the world around us.

Carla Sinclair has here worked to foster just such a balance. This isn't some schmarmy telling of the trials and tribulations of yet another perky Cybergrrl. Nor is it a flaccid catalog of the best online places to get advice on hair and makeup. This is a book for women of the digital age—for and about women with sharp intelligence and humor, who are living the balance of their feminine and masculine energies. Here you'll meet some powerful role models—women with something to say, and women who are already making it happen, paving the way. The author has infused each page with her own irreverent, strong yet girlish sensibility, and always seems to unconsciously find the humor in any situation. Internet books come a dime a dozen these days. I almost wholly despise them, actually (with a few singular exceptions). But here's a title that Tank Girl no doubt has stuffed into her gun turret.

If I were to leave you with anything, I would leave you with this: read, experience, experiment…seize your power. Scream wildly, unabashedly, and unashamedly. But straddle the worlds; remember your connection—not the line connection, the bits whizzing through your ISDN line, but your connection to the very earth and nature that sustains us all. For balancing this—male and female, digital and natural—is our ultimate challenge.

As grrrls, and even troublemaking tomboy weird-kids, it's funny to think that our day in the sun may finally, actually be dawning; yet here we are, basking not in the light of our nearest star but in the incandescent glow of our computer monitors. I've always loved irony.

Kristin Spence
August 1995
San Francisco, California

NET
CHICK

Welcome!

oosen your bra straps and take a deep breath— you're about to embark on the most sumptuous, estrogenic journey ever taken through online culture. Thousands of smart, opulent, and entertaining salons await you in cyberspace, and this book will escort you to the best of them. On your way, you'll meet some of the sharpest, baddest, raciest Net Chicks who've helped shape the feminine energy now flooding the Internet.

Last spring, I finally got my very own connection to the World Wide Web, the booming new region of Cyberland, where people combine bright pictures, sounds, videos, and text to create their own virtual playgrounds that the rest of us can visit. Up until then, my only means of getting on the Web was by nudging one of the *Wired* folks (the magazine was upstairs from my office) to scooch away from their desk for a few secs while I checked something out. I was extremely anxious to surf the Web from my own turf and anticipated a whole slew of vibrant electronic pages that would bring me the latest on everything that interested me: new zines, fashion, gossip, the latest in health news, book reviews, astrology, travel ideas, women's issues, *Melrose Place* updates . . . but first I needed some hints as to where the most happening Webspots were. So I scurried down to a well-stocked bookstore and asked the nerdiest looking clerk if he could recommend the best Internet guidebook for chicks. "For chicks?" he asked, with a dumbfounded stare. He suddenly became irritated, as if I were challenging him with a preposterous request. He didn't think there were enough girls online to warrant such a book, but he was sure I'd find something suitable in their large selection of Net books.

Not enough girls online? This guy was obviously clueless. First of all, I had just heard a statistic that said America Online and Prodigy each had close to 40 percent female membership. That would mean almost two million women using those two services alone. And, even if I hadn't been informed of the numbers, I knew that at least half of my friends were now online, and most of the women I admired—and there are a lot of them—were pioneer grrrls on the Net.

While leafing through the store's three jam-packed shelves of Internet guides, none of which pointed to intelligent or glamorous grrrly Websites, a thick steam began to ooze out of my pores. How dare that nerdboy think there weren't enough of us chicks interested in the Net. And how dare he be right about the merchandise: I couldn't find one book, out of what looked like hundreds, that pointed to anything I would have found in *Sassy* or *Mirabella*.

Totally deflated, I went home and halfheartedly decided to see what I could find on my own. At least I could expect some cool stuff on music and comix—I had already visited those types of sites via others' modems.

After looking up words like *travel* and *art* in the various search engines and finding a couple of semi-amusing pages, I remembered an email message I'd received from an Australian woman, Rosie Cross, with whom I had been corresponding for some time. In the note she had told me about a Webzine she was starting called *geekgirl*. My stomach fluttered while I quickly rummaged through my old e-letters. I was psyched to find not only *geekgirl's* address but also some information about another online magazine called *Urban Desires*.

I thought about the discouraging words that bookstore dweeb had spewed as I tapped the long Web URL (address) into its proper space. But before I had time to glower over his rotten-ass assumption, I was looking at an adorably femme screen full of women talking about cyberfeminism, overcoming computer phobia, and the empowering feel of a modem, and even an interview with alien-abduction Schwa artist (and friend) Bill Barker, who mentioned my zine, *bOING bOING*, in his conversation. That did it. I was hooked. After *geekgirl*, I moseyed on over to *Urban Desires*, and the vivacity emanating from their pages almost knocked me over. Wow! So much color and fashion and mod humor and inspiring articles. The best thing about *Desires* is that it goes on forever—I don't think I ever have read the whole thing.

Like any cool Website, *Urban Desires* links you to other happening spots, which link you to even more hip stops. By following this domino trail, I came across a bunch of women's "Personal Home Pages," Websites created by chicks who use the space to share their photos, memoirs, gossip, likes and dislikes, art, and favorite links. Nosy by nature, I loved these personal sites the most.

I'm not sure what led to what, but within a matter of months I had the equivalent of an address book's worth of Websites saved in my Netscape program. Was I the only one who had garnered such a large collection of grrrlish URLs? And with so many over-the-edge chicks creating lavish parlors on the Net, and even more hip women just surfing for the gems, as I was, shouldn't we all know how to find each other? Most importantly, who were these bold, brazen women staking a claim in cyberspace? I wanted to find out.

Hence *Net Chick*, the only guide to stylish, post-feminist, modem grrrl culture.

WHO ARE NET CHICKS?

This isn't like *The Preppy Handbook*. Being a Net Chick is not about following a particular dress code or wearing a special badge. It's not about what model of car you drive, what brand of cereal you eat in the morning, or what area of the planet you inhabit. None of that kind of stuff is important or even relevant to being a Net Chick. Being a Net Chick is about having a modem. It's about being a grrrl with a capital R-I-O-T. It's about using your keyboard to navigate through the thousands of worlds floating in cyberspace. It's about becoming empowered by your access to and knowledge of the Internet. It's about communicating.

Just as you don't need to know how the wiring of a telephone works to talk on the phone, you certainly don't have to be a technical expert to be a Net Chick. No way. What you *do* need is a sassy-ass attitude and a sense of adventure. Net Chicks realize the power of the Internet. They aren't afraid to explore the digital jungle, finding that this medium actually facilitates communication and offers unlimited avenues to new information and entertainment. They don't buy into the myth that the Net is a male-dominated area. Because it's not!

Okay, so maybe the world of computers used to belong to men, but that was only because women gave it to them. How can a machine that allows someone access to hip magazines, social interaction, sex advice, grrrl music, video clips of fashion shows, shopping, resources for women's issues, and private, chick-only salons with names like BITCH and FemXPri be something that's just for men? That's so ridiculous!

Thank goodness for the progressive chicks who saw through this myth, whipped out their machetes, and cleared the way so that the rest of sisterhood could easily enter the digital world. Some of these more popular leaders include:

- St. Jude (co-author, with R.U. Sirius, of both *How to Mutate and Take Over the World* and *The Cyberpunk Handbook*, and former managing editor of *Mondo 2000* magazine; one of the first computer hackers)
- Stacy Horn (founder of ECHO, a bitchy, savvy online service loaded with chicks, and author of the upcoming book *The Electronic Mask*)
- Linda Jacobson (author of *Cyber Arts* and *Garage VR*, and a former editor at *Computer Life* magazine)
- Lisa Palac (producer of *Cyborgasm* CD, author of forthcoming *The Edge of the Bed*, and former editor in chief of *Future Sex* magazine.)
- Ada Lovelace (one of the very first computer programmers, who worked with Charles Babbage in the 1840s programming the first proto-computer, the analytical engine)

But the Net wouldn't be any fun if it weren't for the huge community of Net Chicks (a.k.a. Webgrrls, geekgirls, Voxxen, you, me, etc.) who make the Net such an amazingly cool and radical place. We grrrls have infiltrated every nook and cranny of cyberspace. You'll find us zooming down every lane on the Net, blasting through chat rooms and newsgroups, cruising through online shopping malls, participating in panel discussions, and creating incredibly hot pads (Websites, or virtual rooms) where people can drop by (if they dare!) to play with us.

The Net is for women to do what they want with it. You're a Net Chick whether you use your modem for email only or whether you go all the way and take advantage of the Net for communication, information gathering, business transactions, entertainment, and, most important, self-expression. The more there are of us warriors who stampede through this digital playground, the more exciting it will be for all of us. The Net can only continue to be an awesome place for chicks if we are there. It's time to roll up your sleeves and learn how to play with (and without!) the boys.●

jorja

BENEFITS OF THE NET: WHAT'S IN IT FOR ME?

I've already mentioned some of the scintillating delicacies you'll encounter on the Net: fresh online magazines, stimulating conversations with others, sex stuff, new music, online fashion shows and shopping, resources for women, and private grrrl clubs. What more could you hope for? Glad you asked! Here's a list of why I'm so attracted to the Net, and I'm sure that once you cruise the Net, you'll come up with a bunch of other bennies to add to it.

DIVERSITY

With thousands of newsgroups (ongoing conversations found on the Net) and hundreds of thousands of Websites, the online world literally has something for everyone. And if, per chance, you're into some offbeat groove that isn't represented somewhere on the Net, it's easy and cheap to create your own online site.

INTERACTIVITY

Television, radio, and publishing are all one-way media. They pontificate about this and that while you passively sponge it up. (I love all three of these media, so I'm not knocking them! Just using them as examples.) With the telephone you get more interaction—a dialog exchange. But the Internet is the most interactive of them all. First of all you get live chat rooms, where individuals from all ends of the earth can gather in one virtual spot and gab with each other (assuming they all speak the same language). You can also respond to newsgroups, shop online for anything from corsets to feminist books to computer toys, and even help shape the storyline of an interactive *Melrose Place* type of soap opera taking place on the Web, called *The Spot* (see Chapter 5). Of course, if you just want to be a mouse potato, that's okay too. You can tiptoe through the Internet, if you're so inclined, and enjoy the fruits of others' conversations and Web projects without saying a word. It's fun to snoop, and no one will ever know!

RESEARCH

For students and data seekers the Net can be a savior. If you need specific information immediately and can't leave your office or home, don't panic. Instead, tap into the various info resources on the Internet. Every major newspaper, most magazines, and research papers can now be accessed with your modem through commercial database services like Nexus Lexus or Dow Jones New Retrieval. But there are far cheaper ways to search for information as well. Many times you can get what you need just by using a gopher (an Internet search tool) or by searching the Web. Also, if you're conducting a survey, the cost to send out questionnaires is the same whether you're sending one or millions.

CHEAP DISTRIBUTION!

Using the Internet is the cheapest way to get ideas, art, and information out to the public. Everybody has equal access to the same global soapbox. You can publish an electronic journal just as easily as Condé Nast can and with the same inexpensive distribution capabilities. You have just as much power to produce a digital "TV series" as ABC has. You can affordably exhibit your art project to the same international masses as Leroy Neiman can. Everyone's on equal footing, no matter what kind of shoe you wear. In fact, one could conceivably display a Webzine to millions of people for only twenty dollars a month. Compare that to the hundreds of thousands of dollars major paper magazines pay for the same exposure.

I'm not saying the Net is flawless. I've spent many a distressed night wondering why my computer crashed when it got to a particular site, or hating my modem for not downloading the Web pages fast enough (until I got my speedy ISDN line). Back in the early anarchistic days of radio I'm sure people had the same types of frustration when their favorite program was suddenly flooded with static or when a pirate show crossed an "established" channel, causing chaotic noise for hours. But those pre-FCC days also represented a time when anybody's voice could be heard as long as they owned a low-cost transmitter (and many folks did back then). The airwaves belonged to everyone. I hope that most people would agree that the random static was well worth the complete freedom of expression.

An anarchistic means of expressing oneself to the masses has returned. Whether we want to tap into just a fraction of the Net's potential—like sending email, participating in chat rooms, and perhaps shopping online—or take full advantage of its many benefits, the Internet is a way for us to instantly communicate with each other, and to express ourselves to the world. How could anyone pass that up? •

The Net

WHAT'S IN THE BOOK?

Every online service (America Online, CompuServe, Prodigy . . .) has its own private "amusement park," and they each have their special attractions. For example, if you're a member of AOL, you get access to the online version of *Elle* magazine. CompuServe members can enjoy "WorldsAway," a graphical chat room that allows its members to interact with each other as animated cartoon characters. As titillating as some of these digital diversions may be, however, I'm not including them in this book (with the exception of a few that I couldn't resist). The reason for this is simple: a member of one service can't tap into the arena of another. If you belong to the WELL you won't be able to enjoy AOL's *Seventeen* magazine forum.

So, while I set out to explore the femme side of the Net, I concentrated my search for hot sites on the World Wide Web only. I wanted to cover territory that everybody could relish. Granted, not everyone has a connection to the Web, but more and more services are extending themselves to the WWW, and getting a separate Web connection is quite simple. Even more importantly, most Web pages aren't edited by stuffy suits, as material on private services is; the Web is unadulterated, unfiltered, and uncensored. Yahoo!

As I scouted the Web, I realized there were two main types of sites: commercial and independent. Commercial pages exist to advertise products for companies, while independent sites are created by individuals who want to share and show off ideas, information, and art. Of course the independent pages won me over and thus constitute most of the Websites covered in *Net Chick*. However, I have nothing against a mersh site if it also entices you with something besides their merchandise, such as links to inspiring sites or useful information that isn't related to their wares.

The Body Shop is a good example of a company with a hip Website (see "You've Got the Power," Chapter 8). I was captivated for hours reading about endangered species, women's issues, and preening tips in this colorful zone. So commercial doesn't necessarily mean rank, as you'll see when you check out the sites listed within these chapters.

Other goodies in the *Net Chick* grab bag include my collection of worthwhile newsgroups, computer-related tips (from me as well as other chicks), and enlightening essays from a few of my wired friends.

The most thrilling aspect of writing this book was being able to use it as an excuse to talk with some of the most vibrant women of the online world. In every chapter you'll meet the gals who are involved with cyberculture and how it relates to sex, style, the media, entertainment, recreation, health, employment, and political issues. These trailblazing Net Chicks are inspiring not only because they've transformed what was once a boys' club into a co-ed soiree (and for those who don't like it, too bad!), but they've also redefined what it means to be a grrrl who owns a modem: She no longer hides her grrrly traits but flaunts them as a symbol of strength and power.

If you'd like to join the gang but feel awkward about your lack of Internet knowledge, don't go away! Just jump to the back of the book to the "ABCs" chapter, which explains the basics of getting on the Net without any overwhelming nerd jargon. You'll be in-the-know in no time! And to tell you the truth, you don't even need to understand the world of computers to dig what the following pages have in store for you.

Well, what are you waiting for?
Turn the page already! •

B ack in the early '90s a new buzz-word was fervidly vibrating throughout the media: CYBERSEX. The concept of having virtual sex—that is, doing the nasty with robots or with other humans long-distance using computer-controlled sex devices—titillated reporters of all ranks, from the alternative press to the mass media like *USA Today* and CNN. Even my zine, *bOING bOING*, was swept into the hype, dedicating a full issue to the topic (we went so far as to throw a hugely successful gala called CyberSex at a club in Los Angeles, complete

with a futuristic fetish fashion show and a virtual reality sex game). I should be cringing, but I can't—I had too much fun reveling in the craze!

I think the psychedelic cyber rag *Mondo 2000*, when it was still in its black-and-white stage, was the culprit of the cybersex rage. Without actually terming it "cybersex" (I still think *bOING bOING* was the first to name it as such), *Mondo* featured a tantalizing piece on the future of technology and sex called "Teledildonics: Reach Out and Touch Someone," by Howard Rheingold. In it, Rheingold sheds light on what virtual sex *could* be like in a decade or two, when, through teledildonics, individuals in lust could slip on lightweight "bodysuits" covered with intelligent tactile sensors before jacking into cyberspace, where they'd meet their "date" for the night.

In theory, yes, virtual sex could work. But with today's, or even tomorrow's, technology? We journalists were so pumped up by Rheingold's thrilling look at the extreme end of virtual reality that most of us didn't realize (or simply chose to ignore) the high level of sophistication this kind of machinery really entails. Hence, just about every major publication picked up on the new techno-term and ran with it, many of them frantically phoning magazines like *Future Sex* and even *bOING bOING*, trying to find out who was making these body suits and where they might be able to see a prototype. *What bodysuits*?!

And then the ethical questions rolled in. Was it cheating if a married person "slept" with someone else in cyberspace? Would the potential danger of virtual rape be great? Would sexual harassment exist online? I even went to a salon where the main topic was cybersex, and these questions provoked fiery spitting debates.

Slowly, however, the realization that cybersex was more of a vision than a near-reality overcame us all. Just as we were settling into our newfound sense of rationality, another buzzword torpedoed into the limelight, only this one isn't erotic or whimsical, it's just plain idiotic: cyberporn. Give me a break!

Yes, you may find nudie pictures on 1 to 2 percent of the Internet's World Wide Web (And guess what? Some people like them!), but you'll also find that you can get much more porn at your local newsstand. Obviously it's not going to go away. But the Congresscritters are all up in arms (most of whom I'm sure haven't even been on the Internet) and now want to censor the Net. As if! You can't censor something that is catered to and created by a large percentage of users outside of the U.S. Do they really think countries like Italy, Australia, and Japan are going to kowtow to our moral dilemma?

What irks me most about the hysteria over cyberporn is also what bugs me about online sexual harassment woes: The "victims" want the government to make things all better for them, even if it's at everyone else's expense. Get out of here! Instead, why not shred the stupid victim banner and take charge of the situation, Net Chick–style. If adult material on the Net isn't suitable in your household, just censor your own computers with software like SurfWatch and Net Nanny. It's easy, and it'll solve the whole cyberporn matter in seconds! If you feel you're being harassed online by a jerk, just get an email software program like Eudora that will filter the jerk's messages right into the trash!

Eradicating the word *victim* from your vocabulary is what being a Net Chick is all about. Once you're victim-free, you get all of your power back. And then you can enjoy what may have once been an uncomfortable situation for you.

This chapter, "Sexy," doesn't deal with today's already-old-news illusory cybersex problems. Instead, it points you in the direction of sex-positive women, entertainment, and communication that revolves in and around the Net. This includes a stimulating conversation with former *Future Sex* editor Lisa Palac ("I'm still trying to convince women that it's okay to have sexual fantasies, and it's okay to look at pornography with your own eyeballs . . ."), as well as a look at sexy—and romantic (there's a difference!)— spots to visit on the Internet. You'll also hear from my friend, Marjorie Ingall (who's a freelance writer for fashionable chick magazines like *Mademoiselle*), who tells us how her online relationship with a *Wired* boy turned into a full-on romance.

Although teledildonics in its literal sense doesn't yet exist, computers are still a great tool for heavy flirting and human bonding, a way to access adult stuff like erotic art and literature, and an alternative vehicle to buy sexy toys you may feel funny about buying in person. Tune in, turn on, make out!

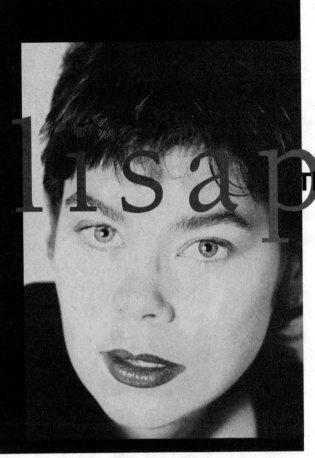

lisapalac

It's hard to believe Lisa Palac was once a staunch anti-porn activist, but she says she used to protest anything X-rated, believing it to be "inherently degrading." Then she saw her first pornographic movie, discovered it turned her on, and her whole life took a 180-degree turn. Since then, her positive pro-sex feminist message has spoken to hundreds of thousands of people, and she's been able to use technology as a way of getting her words across.

"The Cybersex Chick"

When I first met her in 1993, she was already editor of Future Sex, the only magazine solely devoted to the fusion of sex and high-technology. I noticed in the premiere issue of FS that even as Palac promotes the advantages of digital love ("There's nothing like a good dose of high technology to get the erotic imagination popping"), she always makes sure to incorporate human elements—consciousness, sweat, feelings, emotions—into her work. ("The most popular demand for tomorrow's sex world is this: intelligence.") It was great to see this balanced, femme take on sex in a mainstream publication, and it was about time.

After leaving Future Sex in '94, Palac went on to produce parts One and Two of the Cyborgasm CDs, which are anthologies of sex skits and monologues, each story told in "3-D audio" by a different artist. I listened to them and was amazed at how real they sound! (Not to mention how sexy.) Palac also has a book coming out with the same title as her second CD: The Edge of the Bed. She says it's very autobiographical and uses pop culture as the hook. In the near future she hopes to direct a movie—an erotic thriller—"something funny and filthy and psychological." Woo! I can't wait!

What inspired you to get online?

> I was editing *Future Sex* and heard a lot about being online, so I just thought, "Man, I have to get with the program. I have to be online, I have to have email!" It also came about at a time when I had just gone through this break-up, and I thought going online would be a great way to get back into the groove of things, to find a different group of friends. I was hungry for intellectual debate.

Phyllis Christopher

> **How did you feel being a woman on the Net back then? Or even now?**

> Well, it's interesting. I've never experienced any kind of sexual harassment. I've never had anyone be condescending to me—not that they haven't flamed me or anything, but I don't think it was because I was a woman. I never got the sense that I was being picked on because I was a girl. I know that some women have those experiences, but I've just never had that, and I don't know if it's because my reputation precedes me. I think it's the subject matter I deal with, what I do for a living. Sex and technology are two male-dominated fields, which never scared me away, so there was no reason to be scared away by too many boys online. I mean, there are always too many boys. Wherever I go, it's always too many boys.

> **When you were little did you have many hobbies that were boy-oriented?**

> Well, I was just very curious, very adventurous. I never felt like there were things that I shouldn't do because I was a girl. I remember in our neighborhood, when we were teenagers and turned thirteen, a lot of the boys started smoking pot and going to rock concerts. It was a very boy thing to do. Only one other girl in the neighborhood, her name was Carol, would go with me to all the shows. We even played embarrassing air guitar at parties—something that girls never did! We were derided for it, it was horribly humiliating. I'm so glad people didn't have video cameras back then. So I've always been attracted to that fast loud rock 'n' roll lifestyle that has traditionally been a male kind of thing. And most of my friends when I was younger were men, although now that's really changed. Most of my friends in San Francisco are lesbians.

> **Maybe some of that has to do with doing *On Our Backs*.**

> Yeah, it probably has to do with that, and I think most of the people in San Francisco who are doing progressive sex entertainment are women, and I certainly tend to gravitate towards those crowds. So most of my friends are women, and most of them are lesbians. I just realized that the other day.

> **What are the advantages of being a woman on the Net, if there are any?**

> You can kick ass online!

> **What do you mean by that?**

> I just think my verbal skills are really pretty good. I don't make a habit of going around saying things to people or about people that I wouldn't say to their face, but I can take out a lot of rage and a lot of hostility online, and I can get really mad at people and fight well with people, whereas in real life I would just turn red and get choked up.

Early '80s

Hard-core anti-porn feminist.

> You don't have as much time to think in real life.

> Yeah, and being online gives you that delay to plan your attack.

> Now a man could've given me the same answer, so are there no benefits to being a woman online?

> I'm not sure how to answer that. To me the biggest advantage is that it's really broadened the network of people that I know, and I can get a lot of feedback on my work. I can talk to other women about their ideas on sex and sexual politics in a way that maybe face to face they might be uncomfortable doing. So I think that's really interesting, that people will often be more candid online.

Advantages of being a woman online . . . hmmm . . . I think of it in terms of *human* advantages, and all the advantages as a human being that you can get from communicating in this way, which is really unprecedented— being able to reach so many people and to exchange so many ideas with so many different kinds of people.

> I bumped into you at Cafe Centro [San Francisco] last year and you were laughing about all of the people who would call you at *Future Sex* wanting to know about teledildonics and asking when the "body sex suits" were going to be available. What are some of the biggest misconceptions about virtual sex?

> Well the biggest misconception is that it exists! It's fake! We made it up! That's the biggest misconception—that there's going to be some kind of virtual reality 3-D cybersuit thing you're going to put on and have sex with. I mean, give me a break. We have to remember here, as far as women are concerned, there is such a high percentage of women who still don't know where their clitoris is or who have never had an orgasm. So you can't really expect me to go hog wild over some VR sex suit idea when I'm still trying to convince women that it's okay to have sexual fantasies and it's okay to look at pornography with your own eyeballs, and it's okay to think about somebody else besides your boyfriend even while you're having sex with him! That's where we're starting from. From a male perspective—now I know not *all* men think this way—but the whole VR sex suit concept is pretty much a guy's idea, because a guy's been there, done that, they've had their blow jobs and they've had their oral sex and anal sex, and hell, let's stick it in a Jell-o bowl, you know? What else can we do with it? Let's invent a suit! So I think that's where the difference is. Women want to have sex in the here and now, like right now,

1986

Starts sex zine called *Magnet School*.

1988

Has her first erotic story published in a book titled *Herotica*, edited by Susie Bright.

here, in this moment, and not in some sort of computer-generated environment.

> **Okay, instead of saying *virtual sex*, what if we say *computer sex*?**

I think I call it *digital* sex because (otherwise) people think the sex is coming from the computer or that the computer somehow is a sex toy, like a vibrator. But even a vibrator is just a tool, and the computer is just a tool. What's most interesting to me, the most fascinating thing of all of the technology, is being online. It's truly the most exciting thing, because you're interacting with real people and it's really uncensored, at least it still is now.

When people use those search engines on the Net, *sex* is the most common word that people type in. And sometimes you'll be very disappointed, because you'll type in *sex*, and you'll come up with "The Sexual Mating History of the Gadfly," or some ridiculous arcane academic term paper on something that you're not interested in. And then most of the sex stuff on the Web is just pictures of naked women, which serves its purpose, and that's fine and all, but people expect sex to be *different* on the Internet. So far all I see as being different, in the positive sense, is that because people can be anonymous they will often give you the real lowdown on what they're thinking and feeling in all areas of sex. It also means you get some liars, too, and you get people with that teenage adolescent mentality who just want to say as many dirty words as they can. But for the most part it's very uncensored and it shows you what's really going on in people's minds when it comes to sex, and of course it's really difficult to talk to people face to face about that kind of stuff.

It's always been difficult for people to connect and to meet each other, and modern society certainly has special conditions that make it increasingly more

HOT SITE: Cyborgasm Home Page
http://www.iuma.com/Cyborgasm

*W*oo! Stim out to the hot sound samples from all three *Cyborgasm* CDs. Then, once you've calmed down, take a behind-the-voices peek at those involved: Palac, Susie Bright, Carol Queen, Alice Joanou, Dennis Matthews, and the rest of the cast. For an even better look, slaver through the "Adults Only" (yeah, right!) photo gallery. If you've gotta have a copy (or three) of your own, you can order *Cyborgasm* online. Yum!

difficult for people to hook up with each other. People are driven to succeed, they work long hours, going out at night alone is dangerous. There are lots of reasons. So the online medium is a really successful way to get to know people's minds, which is often what they say they want. Of course then they see their faces, and it usually doesn't work out, but I've been lucky.

> **How have you been lucky?**

> Oh, my big online love affair, yes, well, it's happened to me. I've met several people online and one in particular whom I've fallen madly in love with, and we met face to face, and at that point I was so in love with him it really wouldn't have mattered [what he looked like]. We were both really honest and good communicators and we talked about a lot of things, and we talked over the phone.

> **Did he already know what you looked like?**

> Yeah. A lot of people already know who I am, which, let me tell you, is a drawback! It's like, I couldn't get laid if my life depended on it sometimes, because everyone thinks, "She must have done it all, I'll never measure up."

> **God, I thought it would be the opposite for you.**

> Well, you would think! I've come all this way now to say, "Hey, you know what? I really like sex! I really like it! Okay? I'm not going to play a game, or say no when I really mean yes. I mean, I really like it." And then everyone runs in terror in the opposite direction.

So I think meeting people online is really fun, and I think it's a great alternative to the bar scene. Once you leave college you just don't usually make those rounds anymore, and if you've exhausted the supply of young single available people in your immediate work group, it's difficult. I've had some great online experiences.

> **Are you still going out with that guy?**

> Well, he lives in New York and I live in San Francisco, so that makes it a little difficult. But we do keep in touch, and I would say I love him deeply, and he's really changed my life. He means a lot to me. It's really one of the most amazing things that's ever happened to me.

> **It figures something like that would happen to you.**

> I'm a lucky girl! *(laughs)*

> **Tell me about your *Cyborgasm* CD.**

"Hey, you know what? I really like sex! I really like it! Okay? I'm not going to play a game, or say no when I really mean yes. I mean, I really like it."

Phyllis Christopher

> It's recorded with a bona fide virtual reality-based technology that records sound in three dimensions, or the way human beings really hear sound. So when you put on the headphones it is mind blowing because it sounds like this is happening in the same room. When you hear someone walking up behind you, and then whispering in your ear, you could almost *feel* that person's breath, I mean, it's really a trip. So when you combine the intimacy of that experience, even if it's just someone opening a can of soda by your ear and listening to the fizz, when you combine the intimacy of that experience with the intimacy of sex, it's a pretty powerful combination.

> **What's been the response to it?**

> Overwhelmingly fabulous! After the first CD we got this licensing deal with Time-Warner Audio Books. I couldn't believe it, because this is X-rated. It's *X-rated*. It's not like, "Honey, hold my hand on the beach while we walk in the sand and kiss." I'm like, "It's hard core!" And they said, "Oh, no problem." So we just released the second one which is called *Cyborgasm 2: The Edge of the Bed.* . . .

> **I thought that was the name of a book you were doing.**

> That is also the name of my book. You know, it's such a great title! (*laughs*)

> **It's wonderful!**

> I'm going to use it for every project I do from now on. (*More laughs.*) There are a lot of great people on it: Susie Bright, Alice Joanou, Dennis Matthews who's an actor, Joe Gore who wrote a lot of the music and is now playing with PJ Harvey and has played with Tom Waits. So there are a lot of people—not necessarily sex people, but people from all areas of the entertainment world—who came together to make this record, and that was really exciting. The stigma of, "oh it's pornography, sorry I can't contribute" was erased. And because it's audio, and there are no pictures, I think it's a very good introduction to pornography for women.

> **So you have one more CD to go.**

> One more.

> **What's this one going to be called?**

> I think I'm going to call it *Heavy Breathing.* Because everyone's always asking [in mock dumb-jock voice] "Oh, what's this album, heavy breathing?" Huh, like an hour of that would be very dull. The psychology of sex is what's very exciting to me, and everybody has different fantasies, and sometimes just the way a woman says "panties" could throw someone over the edge. You never know what's going to work.

1989

Moves to SF and starts working on lesbian sex magazine, *On Our Backs.*

1991

Gets hired as editor of *Future Sex* and meets Ron Gompertz at the same time. They start producing *Cyborgasm. The New York Times* calls her the "Queen of High Tech Sex" and all hell breaks loose. She is forever known as the "cybersex chick."

1994

Lisa hosts
Generation Sex,
a San Francisco
radio show
about sex and
pop culture.
She then gets
a book deal to
do *The Edge of
the Bed*, about
sex and pop
culture.

> **When you were growing up was it your goal to do what you're doing now? Or did it all just randomly happen?**

> I was just having this conversation with a friend of mine the other day, about how mad I get when I hear from successful young people, meaning younger than myself, who *always* knew that they wanted to be a writer, or who *always* knew they wanted to be a filmmaker, and oh, they would just do anything it took, and now they're that thing, and now they're incredibly successful and they're making millions of dollars and they're younger than me and I hate them.

I went to see *Tank Girl*, and it was so much fun. It was such a girl movie. And I thought, you know, I wonder how my life would be different if when I was a young girl I could go see girl-girl buddy films like this, where girls had adventures, and they got into trouble, and they were happy, and they were angry, and they could get their anger out, and they could be sexy, too.

> **And also a hero, which is unusual.**

> Yeah, all of these things. I just wonder how much further along I might be.

I never knew what I wanted to do. I wanted to be a ballerina, then I wanted to be a doctor, and everything in between. I always sucked at sports, so I knew sports was out. But there were always lots of things I wanted to do, and when I finally went to art school and was going to study filmmaking, I got swept away in this whole anti-porn campaign. . . .

> **Oh really?** *Anti*-**porn? Wow, I didn't know that.**

> Yeah, I was a little anti-porn feminist, everyone's favorite story.

> **Tell me the short version of the story.**

> Well, I didn't have any exposure to pornography at all except that it was bad and dirty and for men. Then when I grew up, the next round of exposure that I had to it was from a feminist point of view. Certainly not all feminists think this way, but I was living in Minnesota, and Catharine MacKinnon and Andrea Dworkin were there, teaching at the University of Minnesota. It was their anti-porn politics, which is that pornography is inherently degrading, there's no way you can look at this image and get anything positive out of it, it's the reason why women are second class, and if we could just eliminate pornography we would eliminate oppression, and men and women would then be equal, and the fight for economic rights and the right to abortion and all those kinds of things would fall into place. Then when I saw my first porn movie after having been this defiant snot-nosed little anti-pornographer, well, I just had a very different experience. And I had a boyfriend

who, as they say, was into porn, and he was a very nice guy, and we had great sex, and so eventually I was able to masturbate and have my own orgasm and have sexual fantasies, and I never had them before I started looking at pornography. Never had them. It radically changed my life. So then I had to start writing about it. Writing was cheaper than making movies. So I started hooking up with other writers, and that's how I ended up doing *On Our Backs*, and then doing *Future Sex*. I never imagined I would do these things. I never imagined I would be writing a book. Never imagined I would be spending a career talking about sex.

> **And you really do represent the sexual-tech side of pop culture right now. You're everywhere!**

> Yeah, I'm like the cybersex chick. And it's so funny, because technology as a whole doesn't really do a lot for me. It's not like I look through MacWarehouse and go, "Ooo! Ooo! What can I buy!?" I couldn't give a shit! But it's a tool. Any way that I can get my message out there is really important to me, so I want to understand it, and I want to keep on top of it for my own business reasons. Also, the only way women are going to have a presence in cyberspace is to just be there. They have to be there.

> **What's next?**

> *The Edge of the Bed* is a very autobiographical book, the past ten years of my life, and pop culture is the hook. I've also been doing some research into things that I've always had questions about and really never had the time or the reason to go to the library, but now I do. So I'm working on this book, and it's very scary for me, very frightening, probably the most difficult thing I've ever done, because it involves spending a lot of time alone, and putting your thoughts down on paper in this immortal sort of way. So it's really a big deal, and I'm really terrified of it, but I am also really looking forward to it. I just keep on imagining my book release party, and that keeps me going! After this I don't know. There's some interest in doing another radio show, a national show, and I would like to direct a movie. That has been a goal of mine, to direct a feature film, something that is an erotic thriller. Something funny and filthy and psychological. Then I can have babies. •

1995

Cyborgasm part 2 is released.

1996

Publication of *The Edge of the Bed*.

Sex and romance go together well, but if I could only choose one, romance seems so much sweeter. I'm a sucker for exotic flowers, wild Valentine's Days, and passionate love letters. Make my heart flutter, treat me like a queen, and I'm yours forever. Other romantics will appreciate what I've found:

AFRICAN WEDDING GUIDE
http://www.melanet.com/melanet/wedding/

Want an African wedding but need help? If so, this is an excellent place to start. Representing the customs from a variety of African groups, this guide offers ideas and tips on all aspects of the wedding, including the matron/maid of honor, bridesmaids, dancers, drummer, chieftess/chief, clothes, and traditional customs. You can also learn the meaning of fabrics and how to select them, how to say a religious prayer in Swahili, and the meaning of the African symbols of life ("water: represents sincerity, the eternal force of life and cleansing away of all bitterness"). Lots of pretty, colorful photos compliment this site, which is frequently updated.

THE WORLD WIDE DATING GAME
http://www.cid.com/cid/date

Sounds like a cross between *The Dating Game* and *Love Connection.* Here's how it goes: Each game has one player who asks three contestants five questions. The audience—anyone who's plugged in at the time—votes on the answers they like best. Then the player chooses a "winner" based either on the audience's choice or on her/his own gut instinct. You and the prize must pay for your own date. Students Eve Andersson and Aurelius

SEX CHAT SURVEY

Identity Switch Test
For some reason I'd never gone into an online chat room posing as someone else. I'm not sure why. I guess my reluctance to take on a new identity stems from the fact that I'm a very candid person. Thus, pretending to be someone else would be difficult since I'd probably give myself away.

But I recently decided to conduct an experiment to compare what it was like to be a girl or a boy in a chat room. Of course in order to do that I had to create new identities. I decided to go into AOL's "Flirts Nook," first as LOLLY, and then as ZACH. I timed it so that each got one-half hour in the nook. In both cases I began with the same introductory line, but then ad-libbed from there. Here are the results:

I started off by typing, "Hi Gang!": ZACH—No response. I felt like a geek. LOLLY—Tons of immediate "Hello!"s and Instant Messages (private messages sent from admiring boys). I felt popular!

ZACH—Was forced to take initiative and finally started up a conversation with a chick.

LOLLY—Never took the initiative, since I was too busy trying to keep up with the conversations and Instant Messages that were being thrown at me.

ZACH—Was afraid to flirt too heavily, since I didn't want to seem like a dick. Instead, I had a nice, friendly, but not-too-sexy conversation. No one ever Instant Messaged me.

LOLLY—I began to flirt right away, since that was the point of being in the room. But then one of the Instant Message writers became too obnoxious. I blew him off and decided to stay in the crowded room only.

ZACH—Although I had a great conversation with this girl (we talked about music, Colorado, my job as a bike messenger), I noticed that the guys were a bit hostile with each other. I was afraid to say anything to them.

LOLLY—The guys were great—really nice and fun to talk to—but when I asked one of the girls how she got her name (better not mention it here), she was such a bitch! I decided just to hang with the guys.

In conclusion, as ZACH I did feel more in control than I did as LOLLY, but I also felt like making friends was more of a struggle. As LOLLY I was swept off my feet—like I had just entered a wild party—but I didn't take anyone too seriously. As ZACH I felt like I really connected in some way with my newfound friend. In all honesty, I can't say which was more fun. Or more awkward. You interpret it. Or better yet, try the identity switch test yourself! •

by Max Reid from Loveplex

Prochazka are behind this love arena, and they ask that you fill out their application only if you are single and serious about finding romance on the Net.

THE LOVE PORT
http://www.amore.com
Their intentions are to bridge the gap between genders, and I have to admit, it borders on being corny. But I did find myself engaged in a couple of interesting items here: "10 Biggest Mistakes Men Make in the Bedroom" was on the mark, and the surveys, presented with charts, were interesting. The Port also has a supposed "Sex Goddess" named Natasha who will answer all of your questions about romance, though she wasn't there when I knocked. You may want to see how keen you are with their sex trivia, or check out the videos for sale.

LOVEPLEX
http://www.gigaplex.com/wow/love/
What a funhouse full of romantic nuggets! I'm not sure if it's pure camp or text book, but I felt like I was back in my 12th grade sex-ed class while watching the plex's mini-movies (QuickTime) on love, relationships, marriage and family. If you're still confused about your sex life after video-viewing, mosy on over to Suzie and Chick's sex advice forum, where you can get group therapy or have a private session. •

H⊙T SITES:
XX + XX

Although sex and romance are a couple of the hottest subjects on the Net, not all of these sites are where girl meets boy. No ma'am! If you're a girl who digs other girls, take a gander at these low-testosterone but high-temperature E-zones:

CAFE QUEER

http://www.interport.net:80/~sorel/
cafe-queer.html

Grab a latte and groove to the jukebox in this offbeat New York cybercafe. Originally created in 1994 on Mindvox (and still there), this is a hangout for both girls and boys who want to converse about dildos, coming out, extra-large girl-clothes for big boys, butches and sissies, and anything else that's queer-injected. If you're feeling shy, test your personality, read lyrics from the jukebox tunes, and listen to Leathermom. Once the latte hits, you'll be chatting with the best of them.

THE LOVEGRID

"The Shocking Photo Expose of the Lesbian Barbie Scene."

http://gecko.desires.com/1.2/art/
docs/lovegrid.html

Woo! Barbie shows her other side! Here you get an impressive image map of twenty icons to click on, each one revealing this blonde babe in an erotic scenario. These images are surprisingly quick to download. It's obvious that a lot of creativity and artistic talent are behind these displays, which are beautifully photographed by Maria Vullo. Sometimes a naked Barbie is frolicking with her lesbian girlfriend, while other scenes show Barbie interacting in full S-M gear. Go girl!

--more-->

CYBER QUEER LOUNGE

http://cyberzine.org/html/GLAIDS/
glaidshomepage.html

You must prove you're eighteen years old or older with a notarized application before you can join this exclusive club. Once you're in, it may take days to get out if you want to experience everything offered here. A small sample of what you'll find includes special chat rooms, reading rooms, personal ads, a Beverly Hills love psychic, "Cosmetics for Queers," and the latest from Queer Press International, *Seattle Gay News*, and other newsy resources. Sounds more like an alternative amusement park to me! •

2

Since I've been having a hot love affair

with the same man for the last twelve

years, I haven't had a chance to experience

a budding online romance. But it does

A Puke-Inducing Email Love Story

happen, and I have proof! My friend

by Marjorie Ingall

Marjorie is here to share her soon-to-be

un-personal story of how she and her

boyfriend built their passionate relation-

I was the Senior Writer at *Sassy*. Jonathan was the Online Tsar at *Wired*. Our magazines loved each other before we did; the first issue of *Wired* praised *Sassy*, and six months later, *Sassy* proclaimed its love for *Wired*. *Our* relationship began less propitiously. Jonathan's first email read, in part: **I think your mag is the absolute shit! After a long day of thinking about networks and protocols and Information Providing and bits and bytes and ftps and gophers and URLs and email and email and email, nothing gets me back to the world**

ship through . . . THE INTERNET .

inhabited by living breathing humans faster than a dose of Zits 'n' Stuff or Cute Band Alert. I found this slightly condescending. Still, I offered to have coffee with him if he was in NYC. Lo and behold, two weeks later, he took me up on it. I found him goofy and charming. But alas, I thought, charm alone cannot overcome baggy purple jeans, green Doc Martens, masses of hair, and dangly earrings in both ears. My tastes at that time ran more to flannel. How ashamed I am today.

: ∞ :

Anyway, he had a girlfriend, so I just didn't think of him In That Way. And I just didn't believe people could have real email relationships. I knew of too many scummy, trolling online boys and too many girls who'd felt deceived and duped. I'm of the no-faith school: When you're cyberslimed with mind-numbing regularity simply because you're female, you can't imagine trusting *any* denizen of cyberspace enough to date him. But (fine distinction follows) I could certainly see the appeal of using the Internet to foster an *established* relationship, the way Victorian ladies and gentlemen used letters—to hint, to charm, to seduce, to chat in a deceptively airy, very witty way about nothing (and therefore everything). Still I felt there had to be a real-life foundation first.

: ∞ :

Jonathan agreed. Email can indeed stand as a barrier to real intimacy. **It doesn't translate to real life very well**, he told me later (on the *phone!*). **It's not the same thing as hugs and kisses. It's easier to fool someone in email—even yourself. There's all this slack where you can read**

tips

on Online Dating
from two chicks with experience:

"You can fall really hard on the Net. People say that BBS sex isn't risky sex, but emotionally it's incredibly risky. You have to be careful of what you're looking for. You may fall in love a lot more quickly than you could ever imagine because everyone presents the most perfect sides of themselves, and your imagination runs wild. So you have to be on guard, especially if you're in a place where you're particularly lonely or vulnerable and you're looking to get involved in a relationship."
—*Lisa Palac*

"I'd be wicked wary of any guy I met online. Any male who's trolling for babes on IRC or randomly instant-messaging women on a BBS is very likely either a Beavis or a psycho. However, guys you become interested in because they are regular posters

turn page for more tips!

things into the other person that may not be there, and they can say things they think they mean but don't. Really getting to know another person is hard enough; when you factor in the extra variance of sending and receiving email, who knows if it's real or not?

: ∞ :

But as the streams of data flew through the air, I gradually became aware of how much I was looking forward to Jonathan's letters. I started taking longer to compose each missive, trying harder to be clever, getting petulant when I didn't hear from him for a couple of weeks. However, there was no way I could tell him this. One, he had a girlfriend. Two, he had a girlfriend. And three, he was trying to convince me to
work at

HotWired, *Wired*'s new online venture. No way was I going to go all Sandra Dee on him if there was any chance of us being coworkers. So I said nothing. But when I look back on my email from that period, I can't believe how flirtatious I was, in my own weird way. Clearly I was delusional.

: ∞ :

To: Jonathan
Subject: Re: duuuuuuuuuuuude
From: Marjorie
Date: Mon, 06 Jun 94 17:47:29 EDT

some female hyenas have a phallus.

male secretary birds give female secretary birds a special gift of dung.

the female praying mantis eats the male praying mantis's head during sex. he fucks better with no head because inhibitory centers in his brain send him contradictory "flee!" messages.

i'm doing a story for Sassy called "flirting tips from our animal friends." animal courtship behavior and how teenage girls can adapt it. i'm not sure how i'll use the first and third examples—maybe i'll advise them to visit the Good Vibrations nearest them for a strap-on phallus, thereby emulating the female hyena, and eat their dates, emulating the female praying mantis. yeah, that's the ticket.

let's talk, mr. steuer, and not about praying mantises. mantii. whatever.

: ∞ :

The strain of not telling him outright how I felt was

1

killing me. But he was having struggles of his own over the direction *HotWired* was taking, so I didn't want to burden him any further. We continued to exchange elaborately casual, slightly flirty e-letters. My stomach hurt a lot. On Yom Kippur, I sat in my parents' house in Rhode Island, reading email and crying. I told him only:

i'm zonked. have an easy fast, if you're doing that jew thing.

He replied:

i didn't. i wish i did. i needed it. i forgot. i am lame. confused, exhausted, maybe even depressed. and quite honestly, i miss you. awkward, but true.

: ∞ :

Whenever we saw each other, every few months, the eye contact could have burned holes through steel, but we were as close-mouthed as mollusks. Though I wanted him so badly I was quivering, I knew that a never-to-be-satisfied jones for a boy who lived across the country and had a girlfriend was not healthy. I wrote him:

i don't know whether i'm shooting myself in the foot by saying this, but i feel like you are playing with fire. (cliche.) (i'll continue to critique my own writing in parentheses as a way of distancing myself from the essential emotionality of the material, which is making me feel vulnerable and therefore prone to self-deprecating joking.) i feel like i should've slammed a door on this a lot earlier and didn't.

no, you didn't, and neither did i. and i knew better literally from the moment i met you, in fact. really, i know that sounds cheezy but it's true. i mean, i didn't know *what* would

TIPS *continued*

in forums you read—in other words, because you think they are witty and interesting and insightful—are more promising. Send said boy some email saying, 'what an insightful post on the use of light/dark imagery in the sonnets of Edna St. Vincent Millay!' Strike up an email conversation, confining yourself at first to the ever-fascinating subject of Edna St. Vincent Millay and gradually getting more personal. Make sure he hasn't murdered his family and doesn't sleep with a stuffed Snoopy. Do many normalcy checks. If he passes, you can progress to meeting him in a well-lit public place. You may find him so unbearably barky in person that one face-to-face meeting squashes that little kiss-impulse into the dirt.

"If you find him attractive enough, continue to proceed with caution. Talk on the phone more than online (I think there is something delusional about conducting a relationship *primarily* online—it's unreal, and too much subtext is missing.) Keep it casual as long as you can.

"In terms of how to be alluring, this isn't hard. You're a girl. There aren't that many of them in cyberspace. You automatically get mega-points for having two x chromosomes. Just be funny and you'll be fine. Enjoy the oddness of being judged only by the quality of your ideas and self-expression, not by your looks." •

—*Marjorie Ingall*

Sexy. Newsgroups

Sex and romance newsgroups seem to attract more extraneous noise than any of the other Usenet groups. You'll run into annoying juniors who can't stick to the topics, can't think of anything but XXX gifs and who giggle each time they see the word sex. But you'll run into these same individuals at a bar, in sex-ed class, or at a football game. No need to fret. Plenty of mature, intelligent, sexy people also hang out in these forums, so you can focus on them. Here are the more stimulating groups on sex stuff that I've found:

alt.hi.are.you.cute
So sugary sweet, so . . . cute! Exactly what a flirtatious newsgroup would have been like in the '50s, with contributors discussing in earnest topics like "cute movies," "cute poems," and "penpals wanted." I hope they stay this cute for a long time.

alt.magick.sex
"Magick" seems to be forgotten in many of the topics here, but there are some good discussions on Tantric sex.

alt.motss.bisexual
A spot for people to place personal ads. Not much conversation.

alt.politics.homosexuality
Youch! Fiery debates on sex, morals, and family values. Really gets your blood boiling.

alt.polyamory
Lots of different opinions here on what "polyamory" means, but basically this newsgroup is for those who want to talk about polygamous relationships and multiple sex partners.

alt.romance
This one is so sweet! You'll find lists of romantic quotes, romantic songs, favorite love poems, etc., as well as supportive discussions on topics such as interracial dating and how to get over a broken heart.

happen, but i knew someday, *something* would happen. at least, i knew it as one knows such sorts of things. but enough of my meta-commentary . . .

but *i* feel dishonest, like *i* am cheating on her as a friend. perhaps girls have a different standard of what constitutes cheating, but emotionally i feel i'm doing a bad thing.

this is totally understandable, and i would not blame you at all if this were a (or *the*) primary reason why we decided to table discussions of this sort for the time being.

but i would be disappointed . . .   %:-(

i think continuing to talk with me is not the smartest

thing for "you", since there is chemistry between us beyond that of just buds. <foot shooting follows> if you are truly going to make a commitment to her, i think you should not be talking to me. focus on what you want from your current relationship. you and i can still discuss work and stuff . . .

i wish it were this simple, that i could draw the line so clearly and so easily . . .

*i do have designs on you (quaint phrasing) . . . i just don't know what they are. i . . . ahhhh . . . i am curious about . . . what could happen between us on a physical level. (*that* was clinical sounding.)*

to continue in a totally clinical tone, the possibility of a physical side to our relationship intrigues me as well . . . but under current circumstances, it is unlikely that we will obtain any further empirical data in support of my various theories on this matter. i have not designed any particular experiments at this time, and would prefer not to consider this subject further, mostly because it makes me squirm in my seat.

*i mean, do you have that boy-need to be attractive to all available women? i know you are a flirt—as am i— but with you, i'm not just whistling Dixie. i don't know for a fact that *you're* not. so think carefully about what you want—and have—from anna before putting it at risk by continuing to talk with me. and be fair enough to me to shut the door hard on the way out, so i don't maintain any illusions.*

i'm a flirt, but not *that* much of a flirt. i don't feel the need to be attractive to all available women—just the ones to whom i am attracted. in other words, i may be a flirt, but i ain't no Dixie-whistler.

alt.romance.chat
Big hodgepodge of topics in this group, from light pick-up lines to more serious confessions, revelations, and compassion.

alt.sex
Sex in the broad sense of the word. Conversations range from enjoyably raunchy to informative to prurient. Anything goes here.

alt.sex.bondage
All about bondage, of course.

alt.sex.masturbation
A few fun topics here, especially the one where girls swap ideas and techniques.

alt.sex.safe
A '90s kind of group, with talk about condoms, men's birth control pills, masturbation, etc.

alt.sex.wizards

A place where sex prodigies can show off their knowledge. Ask any question and you'll be sure to get lots of answers.

alt.sexy.bald.captains

Silly chatter about, you guessed it, the Captain Stuebings of the world. Actually was set up by fans of Jean-Luc Picard, but lust for any baldy on a ship will do.

soc.singles

Besides lots of personal ads, you'll find topics on recent break-ups, how to deal with loneliness, dating etiquette, and how to kiss. Also some losers who start embittered discussions like "Why are women false and untrue?" and "Why are men so shallow?"

soc.support.youth. gay-lesbian-bi

Confused about your sexuality? Don't know if you should come out? Should you tell your parents? That's the kind of stuff people will help you with here.

uiuc.org.bisexuals

More personal ads.

: ∞ :

For the next couple of months, Jonathan and I barely spoke. I assumed he just had Boy Disease, the malady of jerkiness. Okay, he did tell me that his relationship was in trouble, but I didn't inquire any further. Then he emailed me that he was coming to New York. **i think you should spend all your free time entertaining me**, he wrote. I got mad.

To: Jonathan
Subject: Re: in new york
From: snarly
Date: Fri, 10 Feb 95 21:10:30 EST

i feel manipulated. i know that there is always a temptation to keep one's options open, if i may be so bold as to propose that that is what you are doing. cut it out.

: ∞ :

Soon afterwards, Jonathan's girlfriend called. Make that "former girlfriend." She was hurt and furious. "My boyfriend just told me he's had a crush on you for a year," she said. Afraid that she would be unable to hear me over the sound of my heart slamming, I managed to stammer that I was sorry and needed to process this information. "I trust you to do the right thing," she said. I hung up and bolted for the computer. There was email waiting.

To: Margie
From: Jonathan
Subject: options. open and otherwise.
Date: Mon, 13 Feb 95 01:27:32

yuck. i did not want this to happen. i don't mean to make you uncomfortable here, but i do have a lot to explain, a lot to say. please bear with me at least as long as your interest holds. hopefully to the end.

3

... you (rightly) chided me for flirting, manipulating, and keeping options open. i guess to some extent i am guilty on all counts. when i read your message of friday night, i realized that if i don't want to look back on my relationship with you (whatever it might become) as anything more than a sad series of might-have-beens, then spilling my guts (in which you are now standing midstream) needed to jump to the top of my priority list. hope you got yer waders on ...

as i may or may not have told you before, i have had an e-crush on you from the minute i read your first reply to my first message to you. when we actually got together f2f for coffee in new york last february, this e-crush turned into a real one. this was very inconveniently timed, since it was also the first weekend i ever spent in new york with anna. but such are the occurrences that make life interesting, fun, painful, and sometimes annoying ...

... why do i feel like i am in the middle of a _melrose place_ episode here? oops. i digress. where does that leave us? i dunno ... but at least i

Bed in bianca's smut shack by Jillo

Most women have a hard time walking into a sex shop, either because there isn't a shop for thousands of miles, the place isn't female-friendly, or, most commonly, they're just downright shy. Whatever the reason, if you're a girl who wants some toys and can't seem to get any, don't worry! These online catalogs will fill your toy chest in no time.

EROTICA
http://www.erotica–toys.com/
After getting past several "warning—sexually explicit material" hurdles, I finally got to the goods: sex toys, dolls (boys and girls), leather gizmos, and even a special shaver for those hard-to-get areas, all accompanied by color-ful photos. If you want more variety, they offer their paper catalog for five

--more-->

can honestly say that my flirting is genuine, and that i am not just trying to "keep my options open" in order to leave myself an escape route. manipulation is not my goal here—just communication.

i'm willing to proceed on any course that makes you comfortable.
i'm curious where that course might lead.
i'm committed to maintaining our friendship at all costs.
so let's see what happens. ok?

To: Jonathan
From: Margie
Subject: uhhhhhh
Date: Mon, 13 Feb 95 22:34:52 EST

i'm in information overload. too much data—from you and from her—in one night. i feel like i've ingested masses of caffeine and it's all spinning around in there.

. . . part of my anger at you has been anger at my own ambivalence. tell me, how can someone who says "don't flirt with me, asshole" then call him "beeper boy" in the next paragraph? that's supposed to be the lan-guage of derailment? . . .

i think you and i really need to talk f2f, yes?

He flew to New York. And stayed a week. And we talked. And talked. And talked. And . . . well, we did what people have done since before there was email. (Sorry to deprive you of the gory details.) And we instantly knew this was not just an ASCII thing.

To: Margie
From: Jonathan
Subject: disconnected ramblings from dr. cheezie
Date: Tue 7 March 1995 19.10.56 EST

. . . i don't remember ever feeling this way about someone in the past. since i first started "liking girls" at about age 10, i have been in and out of relationships that were fun, entertaining, intellectually stimulating, sexually fulfilling, desirable-from-a-distance-but-no-fun-close-up, status-inducing, ego-boosting, etc. some of them included brief glimmers of what was probably love, but none managed to sustain it for any length of time.

i dunno what we have here, but i do know that it is different. i think about you a lot. i think about us about as often. when i think about how our relationship is taking shape, i think of something kristin used to say to me—advice handed down by her mother: "start as you intend to continue." it is an encouragement and a warning: on the one hand, a reminder that taking things slowly, as we have from a distance over the past year, is a good thing; on the other hand, a warning not to get too attached or too buried too fast.

the grim reality of the situation is that i don't ever recall thinking i was "in love" before. and i do now. however, the good doktor does not like to make grand pronouncements without substantial empirical evidence. i need a second opinion on this diagnosis. the lab will get back to you with further test results at its earliest convenience. please make sure you have filled in all the circles completely with a number two pencil. make no stray marks on the test form. do not bend, fold, or mutilate. do not remove under penalty of law.

i have said enough. good night.

love—

—j—

bucks. You can order anything online, by fax, or by regular mail. They ship anywhere in the world. Your stuff will reach you in two weeks, and they promise your name will not be put on any mailing list.

BLOWFISH
"Guaranteed Not to Suck"
http://www.blowfish.com/catalog.html
This catalog sells sexy books, videos, safer sex supplies (condoms, potions, and other sperm dams), and all sorts of the usual toys. Stuff soon to come: edibles products, erotic arts and crafts, magazines, zines, comix, and an "impossible to classify" category. You can order their paper booklet, which, besides selling merchandise, also includes "erotic photography, poetry, fiction, and other interesting things." Blowfish has a sexuality information center here as well.

PUSSYWILLOW
"Fine Toys for Naughty Girls and Boys"
http://www.swcp.com/pussywillow/
This "woman-run, woman-sensitive" sex business sells all sorts of toys, leather, books, CD-ROMs, videos, and even has a sale bin for you penny-pinchers. Order online or through traditional venues. As a special bonus, check out the "Pussywillow Photo Corner," where you can see sexy shots of the Pussywillow chicks, including Ms. Willow herself. These photos change monthly.

Pussywillow image by Roy Sandoval

m
o
r
e

--more-->

BIANCA'S BEDROOM

http://bianca.com/shack/bedroom/index.html

This chick Bianca invites you to her little smut shack on the Web. In her bedroom (one of many rooms) she's got a diary and dream book that you can read and contribute your own thoughts to. She also describes each of her oh-so-many sex toys, all purchased from Good Vibrations in San Francisco. If any of them excite you, you can email Good Vibes from this site and ask for their catalog.

When the bedroom has exhausted you, feel free to visit any of her other rooms, like her cafe, bathroom, foyer, movie room, etc., all of which are full of hot raunch. Warning: If you're a prissy church-going clean-cut prude girl, don't EVEN go here. You've been warned! •

: ∞

Since then we've been making American and United rich. The volume of email (never truly voluminous to start with) has diminished radically. Since February '95 we've talked on the phone every night we weren't together, reveling in the getting-to-know-you-ness of voices and clumsy pauses and real-time, stammery, interruption-filled conversation. Email has been relegated to quick notes, flight info, the forwarding of interesting net-clippings (in the way our parents cut out interesting tidbits from the morning paper). Still, I occasionally send him email and pager mail (yes, the boy has a digital pager) mocking how ridiculously wired we still are, sitting back-to-back at our computers in my living room or his office.

To: Jonathan
From: Margie
Subject: hee
Date: Sun 30 Apr 1995 23:39:37

hi! you're in the bathroom! i'm in here! the cat's licking his stomach! i love you!

: ∞ :

These days we deal with the same issues as any couple in a long-term long-distance relationship. The logistics are hard, but I've never been so in love in my life. Sure, I miss the thrill of opening my virtual mailbox, but I feel like I've traded it for something deeper and far more lasting than ether and electronic blips. •

Fin

HOT SITES:
E-rotic Reading

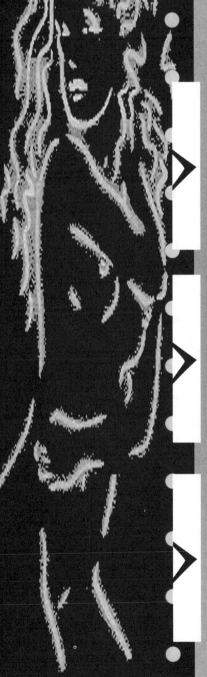

Sometimes reading is the best aphrodisiac, since your imagination gets to create whatever sounds, scents, or visuals it desires to accompany the written words. Although Playboy *and other mainstream sex rags can be found online, I prefer publications that are smaller and more independent, which makes them more personal. And sexier.*

LIBIDO
"Journal of Sex & Sensibility"
http://www.indra.com/libido
Awesome! Everything in here is well-written and highly interesting, and the *Libido* crew finds topics that are fresh. The long table of contents includes the true story of a transvestite Zulu tribesman who unknowingly tricked the American Victorian elite into cherishing him as a her; a piece on homeopathic aphrodisiacs; and a profile on the humorous sex illustrator Francis Madden. Of course there are photos to inspect as well.

From *Yellow Silk*, "The Kiss" by Sigmund Abeles

PARAMOUR
"The Literary & Artistic Erotica"
http://www2.xensei.com/paramour
This is both an electric and a paper zine on "artsy smut," as publisher/editor Amelia Copeland puts it. The gorgeous black-and-white photos are definitely artsy smut in the best sense of the phrase, but I'm not blown away by the rest of the rag. Nothing else was too, well, smutty, and the "upcoming events" have unfortunately already passed. Interesting book and video reviews, however. With such nice design and a seemingly dedicated editor, I do think *Paramour* shows lots of promise.

YELLOW SILK
http://www.enews.com:80/magazines/yellow_silk/
This twelve-year-old paper journal of erotica for both girls and boys is now showing off on the Web. Beautiful photography and paintings fill their pages. But these luscious graphics are all separated from the literature and poetry, since anything text-based must be read from their gopher site (ugh). I hate the way gopher stuff feels on the eyeballs, but too bad. You've gotta check out *Yellow Silk* anyway, if you want to see some A-quality stuff. •

From *Pussywillow* by Roy Sandoval

From *Paramour*, by Andrew Savard

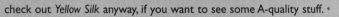

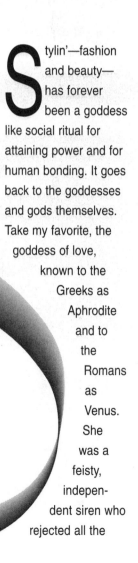

tylin'—fashion and beauty—has forever been a goddess like social ritual for attaining power and for human bonding. It goes back to the goddesses and gods themselves. Take my favorite, the goddess of love, known to the Greeks as Aphrodite and to the Romans as Venus. She was a feisty, independent siren who rejected all the

drooling gods who came slobbering after her. She even dumped her "husband," Hephaestus (a match her father, Zeus, had set up), who tried to keep the goddess by building her a beautiful palace. As if! Aphrodite would be with only the gods whom she desired and would seduce them with her magic girdle, an accessory that would make its wearer irresistible. And she wasn't selfish—she lent the mystical lingerie to her friends as well.

As far as ordinary humans go, attaining beauty as a cultural and social phenomenon can be traced to Ancient Egypt, where hairdressers are repre- sented on frescoes, urns, ceremonial coffins, and elaborate cases that held hair lotions, combs, barrettes, scissors, and shaving tools. Dyes were used to darken hair, and henna was applied to finger- nails and toenails to give them a reddish tint. Beauty shops first became popular, however, in Ancient Greece. Not only were they places to receive facials, hair treatments, manicures, and fragrances, but they also served as a central salon to exchange hot gossip and news.

Throughout the millennia, beauty has continued to thrive as a ritual involving social interaction. As a girl I spent many a night at slumber parties where we sat around and braided hair; as a grrrl, I can't count the number of times I've engaged in heavy rap with hair stylists, masseurs, facialists, and manicurists; and even as a college student I found myself swapping makeup and gossip at Mary Kay parties. So when I first got a computer and plugged in my modem, and for as enthralled as I was with my new communication device, I was disappointed with the lack of parlor talk. It made me realize I was playing with a nerdboy's toy, which was okay by me (I grew up with Hot Wheels and microscope sets), but I was puzzled. Why weren't more women online? Wasn't communication supposed to be a strong female trait?

Within the last couple of years, however, I have noticed a change. Suddenly a feminine aura is flowing through the Net. More and more modems are being fired up by grrrls—I don't need to take a poll or hire a

statistician to tell me that. What gives it away are the style-related Websites and beauty BBS topics that are rushing online (as well as the smart powergrrrl zones, of course). Net Chicks have arrived!

So communication and beauty continue to evolve together. The salon is no longer relegated to a geographical place. We can now converge to talk haute couture—or anything else we women talk about in the shoppe—from wherever we please. In newsgroups and on the WELL I've run into many captivating conversations on primping and style, from how the morning ritual of getting ready can be a peaceful, meditative forty-five minute experience to the thrill of dressing seductively for the night, to the fears that some have of not measuring up to society's standards.

"Stylin'" will let you know where these fashionable online salons are, as well as point you to Websites that serve up a slice of fashion. (Although stimulating talk on fashion and beauty—makeup, hair, skin, etc.— exists on the Net, I was able to find hip Websites only on fashion and not, unfortunately, on the subject of

beauty. So, after I got over the shock, I added a beauty parlor to my online clubhouse on the Web. Come and luxuriate with me!)

What's more, you'll become acquainted with two wired chic-chicks: the almighty hostess of the WELL's pampering Plumage topic, Tiffany Lee "Magdalen" Brown ("I think people have kind of a librarian nerd image of women [who use computers] . . . I personally know a lot of hot babes who happen to be online"); and the metallic warrior-garb designer, Rene Cigler ("I'm attracted to metal . . . I like combining the soft with the hard edges, and I want to cause chaos with the two contrasts"). And finally, you'll get a glimpse at how one visionary sees the future merging of fashion and technology.

Yes, style and beauty can be thought of as frivolous matters (and a goddess should be playfully trivial at times!). But, for whatever reasons, the forums in which these topics are discussed seem to provoke some of the most frank, understanding, and amusing conversations on the Net. If you don't believe me, see for yourself. *Vive la frivolité!*

RENE CIGLER: WIRED ATTIRE

Rene Cigler isn't your ordinary fashion designer. She doesn't know how to sew. In fact, her favorite tools are wires, pliers, a file, rubber car hoses, and thin sheet aluminum. "It's very primitive, the way that I work," Cigler says, in describing her self-taught method of bending metal pieces by hand into shapes and then attaching the pieces together with shiny, pliable wire. But it's this primitive quality, combined with an elaborate and futuristic sense of design, that has landed the sculptures, costumes, and jewelry of this fashion

http://www.emerald.net/grinder/

What sights to behold! Feast your eyes on the dramatic costumes and accessories displayed in Ms. Cigler's gallery (with seductive titles like "Desert Warriors," "Death Valley," and "Chest"). Then, if you have the time to download it, check out her QuickTime video to see her work in action. If you want to know more about this wired woman, read the article (not as good as mine!) and bio about her. Although the big stuff isn't available to us Net cruisers, we can buy her jewelry online. •

renegade onto the sets of *Demolition Man*, the upcoming cyberfilm *ReCon*, and most recently, *Tank Girl*.

Cigler was introduced to Tank Girl in 1989 when she picked up a copy of the British rag *Deadline* (Tank Girl's first home), and remembers an instant attraction. "At the time I had shaved hair and boots that buckled, and I liked shorts and vests, and short white, blond hair, and that's what Tank Girl happened to be about." Cigler became an avid fan of the spunky, ass-kicking punk girl, so when an article appeared four years later in the *Hollywood Reporter* stating that *TG* was being made into a movie, she didn't hesitate to send in her resume. Of course her style was perfect for the film, and she became *Tank Girl's* jewelry designer.

Her aberrantly twisted jewelry and armor-like outfits first caught my eye in 1992 at a CyberArts convention. I was seduced by the glistening metallic plates connected by delicate intertwined wires adorned with coils, spirals, and curvaceous tubing. A couple of friends and I were about to throw a bash called CyberSex at a Hollywood club, and I would have done anything to show up in one of Cigler's luscious metal ensembles. Although I couldn't afford it, I hungered for it.

Cigler thinks her pieces have an element of empowerment that attracts women. "It really wakes people up. It's the whole goddess thing. A certain power comes out of people when they wear these costumes. They're sexy, and they bring out the feminine side of the women who wear them. But it's also something a warrior would wear, or something you'd wear before going into battle."

Besides being one of the only women who create metal props and costumes for Hollywood, it's this goddess-cum-warrior aspect of her work that sets her apart from the

RENE CIGLER: WIRED ATTIRE *continued*

other designers. "I don't think they can quite place the outfits I do. The costumes have an edge. People think it's armor, and then there's this tribal thing, and this future thing."

What she may most accurately be describing are the very intricate headsets she created for *ReCon*, a futuristic film in which the police force (using Cigler's techno-contraptions) rummages through people's memories and takes out incidents that will help solve their cases. *ReCon* was a project she worked on with director Breck Eisner (son of Disney's Michael Eisner) and Peter Gabriel, who stars in the film. She said Eisner didn't have a clear vision of how he wanted the "memory reconstructors" to look, so in her typically enterprising style, she went home and drew up five or six different conceptual sketches. When she presented them to Eisner, he enthusiastically accepted and used them, along with her other ideas for props.

Surprisingly, Cigler isn't into wearing her own gear. "Most people expect to see some artist in a hole creating this stuff. They expect me to be this rough and tough girl, and I'm not." She says although her outfits empower other women, it's just not her style. So what inspires this petite, pale beauty to indulge in what some may call hard-edged materials? She says growing up in Cleveland, Ohio, has been a

Roger Fatica

major impact on her design sensibilities. "It's an industrial area. It's filled with machinery, metal, and corrosion. I like the way things look there. It's beautiful."

The peculiar items Cigler chooses to accessorize her costumes—vegetable strainers and ice-cube tray levers, for example—further demonstrate her fascination and playful creativity with the industrial. "I'm attracted to metal. I don't use plastics. I use everyday objects that are usually only meant for one use, and I reapply them to make you look at them in another way."

I ask her what her philosophy behind her work is. "I design things to cause chaos," she answers, referring to her stained baby dolls with metal wings. "I like combining the soft with the hard edges, and I want to cause chaos with the two contrasts. I want to add a human quality to my work, along with the corroded and stained but beautiful edge. I think the two together create a lot of strong feelings."

As I talk with Cigler about her burgeoning film career, she stresses to me that she doesn't want to be categorized as only a costume or set designer for movies. In fact, she constantly struggles to define what she does. For instance, even while she takes on these jobs for Hollywood, she has a corporate day job as a senior designer at Mattel, which she says gives her the freedom to turn down films that she doesn't find interesting. What's more, she's started a line of products, from keychains to T-shirts featuring images of her sculptures. And as if all that weren't enough, she's also been involved with some extravagant performance art, which received its most public exposure at Lollapalooza.

"This gentleman, Archie Bell, really took to some images I had sent him. They were really powerful, with

Leather bras, corsets, rubber pants, spiked heels ... all accessories that have emerged from the world of bondage and discipline to become statements of style. Or is it vice versa? Interested parties, read on.

A SMALL HISTORY OF UNDERGARMENTS: PART I

http://www.charm.net/~jakec/UG1.html

PART 2

http://www.charm.net/~jakec/UG2.html

Did you know that corsets have been around since the days of Minoans, Tiryns, and Thebes? And that women aren't the only ones who have squeezed into the waist-clamping garment? Part one of this well-researched article covers the use and style of undergarments from 1100 B.C. to 1867. It focuses on how corsets evolved throughout the ages, who wore them, and

--more-->

Hot Sites: Fetish Fashion *continued*

when they've been the most popular. Part two picks up with lingerie from the Victorian age and takes us to the use of underwear as outergarments of today.

These engaging pages come from **Lynda Stratton's Fashion Pages** (http://www.charm.net/~jakec/), which, along with other hip straight fashion articles, has more engaging fetishy pieces: "Corsets," "Decorated Bodies," and "Fashion & Fetishism."

THE FETISH FASHION PAGE

http://login.dknet.dk/~pg/WWW/
fetish.html

A hefty assortment of stylish fetish links.

PAGES OF BETTY PAGE

The rebellious 1950s pin-up queen known as Betty (or Bettie) Page has been a strong influence on today's popular fetish look. Her image embraced many aspects of goddess-hood, from good-girl neighbor to jungle grrrl to Playboy Playmate to fetish femme, the latter being her most famous. But even in her fetish getups, her sweet eyes and smile projected a friendly wholesomeness, free of any kind of guilt or shame. She made it seem perfectly natural to strap on a torpedo bra and wasp-waisted corset, ready to spank her partner with a riding crop. The merging of the girl and dominatrix is what has made her so accessible to the happening chunk of the masses today. Here are some of the Websites dedicated to Ms. Page:

I WAS A TEENAGE BETTY

http://pobox.com/slt/revenge/betty.html

When someone told Bonnie Burton she resembled Betty Page, she took it

--more-->

RENE CIGLER:
WIRED ATTIRE *continued*

these women wearing my costumes, and he was starting this performance for the Lollapalooza tour called Future Culture, which he had been doing with these performers and tribal drummers. So it was a natural connection. The performers wore my outfits and would embody my sculptures and other pieces I made." Future Culture started the tour on one of the side stages, but when the band Ministry came out to play on the main stage, lead singer Al Jourgenson was swept away by the dancers and their getups. He bought some of the metal accessories from Cigler, which he then wore on stage, and he had the whole group of dancers and drummers perform with his band for the rest of the tour.

Sculptures and jewelry came before her costumes. Cigler had been doing sculptures for magazines like Tundra's *Bonesaw* and my zine, *bOING bOING*, and then her work was discovered by set decorator Bob Gould, who used some of her pieces in *Demolition Man* (starring Sylvester Stallone). She had been selling her jewelry to various people during this time. One day she decided she should start making full body outfits, however, because she wanted to make her stuff more public, and as she puts it, "Jewelry can't be seen on a runway."

At the end of one my conversations with Cigler, she begins to ask *me* lots of questions about my upcoming book, my agent, publishers I know. Finally, she tells me she's picking my brain because she'd like to create a book for her next project. With a background in advertising and illustration, she's got stacks of drawings "with edgy images" and would love to incorporate them into

RENE

Hot Sites: Fetish Fashion *continued*

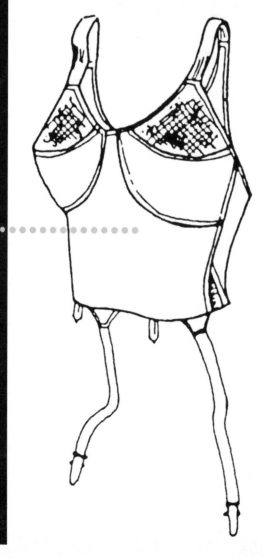

one package. "I illustrate what I see in people—expressions, attitudes—and then I blow them up and put them way out of proportion."

What I like most about Rene Cigler is her sense of exploration. If she wants to see what's on the other side of a wall, she'll just clunk it down with her combat boot. If she sees something that looks hot, she pursues it. She's sweet, she's intelligent, and she's willing to play her way into success. •

to heart. Read about Bonnie's obsession with Ms. Page as she thoughtfully tells us the history of her idol. You also get a photo of Betty and of Bonnie, as well as links to other Page sites. Make sure to jump to Bonnie's Home Page from here, which is full of other good reading material.

DAVE'S BETTIE PAGE PAGE
http://www.fantasies.com/bettie/bettie.shtml
A bunch of pretty illos of Page by artist Olivia, followed by Bettie links.

ATOMIC BOOKS: PINUPS/CHEESECAKE/BETTIE PAGE
http://www.clark.net/pub/atomicbk/catalog/pinup.html
You can get your own Bettie merchandise to cherish by ordering online from Atomic. Examples of the Page wares for sale: a 3-D picture book, various sets of trading cards, and issues of *The Bettie Pages*, a zine by avid Page fan Greg Theakston.

While you're here, you might as well take a look at the other sexy collectibles, like Annie Sprinkle's Post-Modern Pin-Ups and Pleasure Activist Playing Cards, and all of the pin-up art and cheesy chicky magazines.

OTHER PAGE URLS: BETTIE PAGE . . . SUPERMODEL!
http://www.fantasies.com/bettie/super.shtml

THE BETTY PAGE HOMEPAGE
http://www.ids.net/picpal/bphome.html

> "Now is the time for all pro-sex, pro-art, pro-beauty feminists to come out of the closet."
> —Camille Paglia, *Vamps & Tramps*

> *Magdalen, a.k.a. Tiffany Lee Brown, introduced herself online to me and my friends in the WELL's bOING bOING conference in '92. She added insightful wit and an air of flirtatiousness to our topics that charged our E-territory. This newcomer was suddenly charming the hell out of everyone on the WELL, and I seemed to bump into her in every conference I visited. She was sharp, sassy, and cute. I had to like her, in spite of my jealous twitch. Even the name Magdalen was so damn enchanting and, shall we say, goddesslike?*

Homage to Plumage and the Sacred Whore

> *Magdalen soon became employed at the WELL. Not only did she help shape the streams of smart dialogue already taking place, but she also created my very favorite WELL conference, "Plumage." This is a forum where people can trade fashion tips as well as discuss their aversions, fears, and insecurities about the world of style. People who usually talked about the dynamics of their work, political beliefs, or musical passions were now exchanging ideas on corsets, crocheting, and how fashion made them feel. Oddly, this more "frivolous" arena is in many ways one of the more affectionate and human-bonding places on the WELL.*

> *MagTif, as many call her, had immediately made friends with the* Fringeware Review *folks and guest-edited their "Chicks in Cyberspace" issue, garnering herself a permanent spot on their masthead. She also became instant chums with the* Mondo 2000 *crowd, modeling several times in their magazine as the punky, flamboyant, darling creature I had already conjured her up to be. But it wasn't just the Net nerds she had bewitched. A year after playing on the WELL, she appeared in* Time *magazine's cyberpunk cover story. Is she to be the Cyberchick archetype that will be embedded in the minds of future mutants?*

How did you pick the name Magdalen?

> I was reading a book about the archetype of the Sacred Prostitute throughout history, and the main focus of the book was that this was a really beautiful feminine archetype that does not have a place in modern society. It's been pretty much swept under the rug and villainized. The book really affected me. I thought it was incredibly beautiful and incredibly sad. It struck me really deeply. And of course Mary Magdalen was one of the Christian carriers of that ideal.

Barr Nagel

> **When did the Sacred Whore really exist?**

> It's one of the tenets of the Goddess, matriarchal-oriented societies. The Greeks were really big on it. There were temples for certain Goddesses or Gods, or temples surrounding a particular muse, a psychic woman, and they would have the Sacred Prostitutes there. Sometimes it would just be once a year for the sex ritual, or sometimes it would be a place that was very hard to get to, and a man would have to go across the seas and climb the mountain on the island to get to it.

> **Do you think our culture could ever get back to a place where the Sacred Whore exists?**

> I think if our culture somehow evolved to the point where we wanted something like that to happen again, the twisted version Americans have of sexuality and religion would have to disappear. I think there are aspects of the purity and beauty of the ritual that still carry on behind bedroom doors. When you have a really spiritual sexual experience, you're tapping into the same thing that the Sacred Prostitute did a thousand years ago.

> **And what is it that you're tapping into?**

> Hell if I know! (laughs) It's the Goddess or some primordial power. Everyone has their own version of what it is.

> **I think fashion ties into all of this, depending on what angle you're looking at. When I told a friend of mine I was covering fashion in this book, she said, "Oh, but fashion objectifies women. Why are you covering that?" And I have a hard time with that attitude, since I personally love to look at women who wear clothes that accentuate their features.**

> I have extremely mixed feelings about that, but overall I pretty much support the right for individuals to dress however the fuck they want. I also think we're very quick to peg fashion, clothing, and self-presentation as shallow things. Whereas my background is in the theater, and from that point of view, fashion and adorning or costuming yourself is a ritual, and that could be a very important ritual. And to tie back into the Sacred Prostitute, something that I read a considerable amount about was these women who would take pride in the ritual of bathing and scenting themselves, to make this connection between the man and the God. But today fashion doesn't have to just be about tarting yourself up for the opposite sex. I really do believe you can be costuming a character or a part of yourself that you want to let out. Sometimes that can be completely shallow, but I think that the reason fashion keeps working and that there's a huge fashion industry is that we really do see the clothing of people at the same time that we meet them. It's part of the first impression, and it's part of a really intricate ritual of interaction between people.

HOT SITE: Magdalen's Home Page
http://www.well.com:80/Community/Tiff/

*d*o the phrases "raw vein reefer wig" or "tux frees u" mean anything to you? Try shuffling the letters around . . . there you go . . . much better. "Fringeware Review" and "Future Sex" make a lot more sense.

If you like word games, you'll love what Magdalen has concocted—all by hand, mind you. Every link heading on her Home Page looks like gibberish, until you recombine the letters to make words like Buzz, Magdalen, or Tiffany Lee Brown. If you're stumped, just click on one of the bizarre anagrams, which will springboard you to a page with the "answer" at the top.

But the brain teasing doesn't stop with the anagrams. Once you've deciphered all of them, take a keen look at the collage she put together—if you mix up the words of its message with some of the decoded anagrams, you'll get a James Joyce quote. Totally cool, huh?

Of course through these anagrammed links you find out more about MagTif and her friends, and you get lots of photos, too.

> I think fashion is an extension of a person's self-expression, and you can tell a lot about certain people by what they choose to wear. It's fascinating, and it kind of makes me mad when people heedlessly say it's shallow, although for some people it is. It just depends on the wearer.

> Right. There is an element of fun and frippery to fashion, which is part of its appeal. Certainly in the Plumage conference on the WELL, there's a lot of conversation that's very off-the-cuff or fairly witty or fairly insider-fashion-news kind of stuff, and that's part of the fun. Sitting around talking with drag queens is really really entertaining. I think in order to enjoy and engage in that kind of conversation you have to be aware of what you wear, you have to be aware of how other people dress, and how they use that to carry themselves. You also have to be fairly comfortable with the idea of your body. Even if you don't like your body or you think it doesn't match up to some sick ideal of what the media has presented you with, if you get into clothing you're always aware of your body. It's the thing that's filling up the clothing.

> You've modeled in *Mondo 2000*, *Time* magazine, and you've been on the cover of *The Cyberpunk Handbook* —what's made you one of the "fashion icons" of the digital culture?

> (laughs) Well, I basically just looked really weird. When I started using the WELL, I had my head shaved, with a little blob of hair in the back, and attached to it were around thirty hair wraps, which are fake hair things made out of string, and at the end of each hair wrap was a piece of hardware or a chain. So I had this really odd hairdo with a lot of metal in it, and I worked at a head shop, so I pretty much just wore boots and cut-off shorts and a T-shirt most of the time. That's how I looked when I first started meeting people on the WELL. *Time* magazine was doing an article on cyberpunk and they needed someone to be part of the illustration, so St. Jude (from *Mondo*) called me and asked if I wanted to do it, and I was like, "Fuck yeah!"

> **Why did you start Plumage?**

> Mainly there was just a need. There wasn't any conference on the WELL to discuss these things. I used to work for the WELL, and I'd wear all sorts of goofy little costumes to work every day. Someone commented on my clothes and asked, "Why isn't there a fashion conference on the WELL? We think we need one. Why don't you host it?" So I started the conference. We've just been letting it evolve in a natural direction. There's a woman, I think she's a fashion editor at the *San Francisco Chronicle*, and she's been a very big voice in Plumage.

Bart Nagel

She's just having a ball and keeping everyone entertained.

> I was surprised to see that Plumage worked on the WELL. It doesn't seem like the kind of conference they would take to.

> Well, I wasn't that surprised that it worked, because there are so many eccentrics on the WELL who are at least aware of dressing as something that can cement your eccentricity by making it very external and obvious to other people. Or there are a whole lot of geeks on the WELL who want to know how to dress, and they're literally coming in and asking for advice. Those are some of the better topics—when someone comes in and says, "Look, I've been wearing a blue tie and a white shirt and a pair of slacks and a sports coat every day for the last

fifteen years, and IBM says I don't have to anymore. Will you please help me dress?" It's really fun! A lot of times it's the women trying to help the men who ask for help, trying to explain to them how to shop, and it's hilarious to read. I was recently in one of these conversations, and I was telling this guy, "Just go around to these stores and don't intend to buy anything," because he was threatened and intimidated by clothes, he felt so overwhelmed if he went to Nordstroms. So I said, "Just go to shops and look at the clothes like they're little pieces of art. They're just something aesthetic. Touch the stuff and find out what feels good." And we got into this huge conversation, and it was actually a great way of sharing in a very WELL-like tradition. There's really this kind of "take somebody by the hand and lead them through" experience that happens a lot in how people communicate on the WELL. This sort of campfire type of sharing. So that happens in Plumage, too.

Topic #2: is fashion unforgivably SHALLOW?

plumage conf Topic 2: is fashion unforgivably SHALLOW? # 1: shoe addict (miga) Thu Oct 27 94(14:24)

. . . the thing is, there is more to fashion and style than what's in cosmo. Mindlessly imitating whatever is presented in the fashion mags is shallow... but dressing to please yourself or play with your public image' can be an art . . .

plumage conf Topic 2: is fashion unforgivably SHALLOW? # 2: Aqua Net and Lip Gloss (marybeth) Mon Oct 31 94(07:39)

I've been called "whimsical" by more than one source. Wearing the butterfly pants or the dog biscuit barette tells folks right off the bat the sort of girl they're dealing with a lot faster than reading my resume can.

plumage conf Topic 2: is fashion unforgivably SHALLOW? # 3: Madam Satan (magdalen) Tue Nov 1 94(12:31)

I heear that, mb! of course, the reeel fun in all this is that you can completely mindfuck people with these reliable objects and pieces of cloth. "oh look, it's a nice little girlie-girl!" say some of my outfits. "then why does she have that punk rock hair-dew?" and then when you actually TALK to the person, you can blow them far far away with your unexpected depths of wittiness, heights of intelligence, and breadth of knowledge about such obscure subjects as the dynamic values of German wheat beer, market indicators in the emerging stock markets of Venezuela and Indonesia, and the kinetic art movement in Shang Hai.

> **What attracts you to the digital world?**

> I've started wanting to know how everything works and, more importantly, to be able to use and fix things myself. I'm a very typical girl who didn't know anything about electronics and mechanical things—still don't really—but I've developed a little bit of that curiosity that drives little boys to find these things out. I think there's basically this fifteen-year-old boy in me that started coming out when I was about twenty-one. It's part of wanting to feel really independent and very self-sufficient.

Also there's a lot of fear dynamics to meeting people in today's society and especially in urban environments, and the Net still has that aspect of freedom to it where you can meet people and talk to them about whatever the hell you want, and you don't have to worry about them following you home. So that's a lot of what I've been enjoying. The WELL is an extremely special place, it's my kind of place. It's small, wacky, and yet has an intelligent level of conversation.

> **How did you first get involved with the WELL?**

> I had been on the little cafe SF Net in San Francisco, in '92, and I loved it, went totally apeshit for it. But then the conversation, the tone of conversation on SF Net started changing; it became less witty, more politically correct, and just generally kind of boring. I'd been reading about the WELL in different zines for a few years prior to that, so I decided to call them, and had no idea what I was doing, hadn't really been online except this chat board on SF Net. I immediately went into the *Mondo* conference and started posting my eyeballs out, and literally, it just took a couple of weeks before I was completely addicted to communicating in that manner.

> **Do you think there's a certain image people have of women who use computers?**

> I think people have kind of a librarian-nerd image of women. Like, I was watching the news the other night, and this woman who works on the Internet was on TV being interviewed, and she was good-looking and very neat in appearance, but she had this real severe bun, and was wearing glasses and a just little bit

Bart Nagel

of lipstick, and she was pretty, but really looked like the librarian type. That's one image that people have.

Another image comes from guys—especially younger guys that I know—who are always just shocked to meet me, and they're like, "Oh, I always assumed that anyone who says they're a chick on the Net is either a guy, or some big ol' fat ugly horrible nerd girl who only talks about Dungeons and Dragons." I've heard that from an amazing number of nerdy little boys!

I personally know a lot of hot babes who happen to be online. I think one of the more positive images that people have is this sort of over-the-top cyberpunk kind of chick. Somebody like Romana Machado from Stego, clothed in black leather, you know, that whole thing. Usually a little gothic, a little bit over the top, fetishy, tall boots, high heels.

Those are all fun images, and they're all boring by themselves as far as I'm concerned. Mixing and matching is where the entertainment value comes in.

> **How does fashion play a part in the Net world?**

> I think there's been quite a convergence of science fiction and comic type images, and trying to incorporate them into actual fabrics and actual designs has been very popular with the mainstream designers for the last several years. That was a natural thing for a bunch of geeks to come up with, as far as trying to establish any kind of look that they would like.

> **Give me an example of the look you're talking about.**

> Well, the whole over-the-top fetishy look that I was describing before. I think that's a very cartoony look.

> **And maybe the Tank Girl look as well.**

> Right, that's more of where I would fall in terms of a look. It's kind of cartoony, it's fun. The Net is so natural at fostering little subcultures full of people who couldn't find each other before. Little subgroups of various kinds of freaks, and any kind of group tends to come up with its own style of dress. So I think the Net has helped all these little subcultures, whether its the net.goths or the regular dweebs who wear black geeky shirts every day, it's helped these groups find out about each other. There's been a lot of cross-pollination among really marginalized subcultures, and so you go somewhere and there's this really normal guy wearing Dockers and glasses just hanging out, being his nerdy little programmer self, and he's standing right next to somebody who's a hippie, who's standing next to someone looking like a punk, and they all have something in common now just because of the Net. •

I usually surf for E-fashion to get an alternative look at style—something a little different from the ordinary stuff on the newsstands or MTV's House of Style. With people of all ilk putting up their own "fashion" pages, you never know what kind of trends you'll find on the Net. On the other hand, sometimes I just feel like flipping through the pages of Vogue, and if I don't have a copy lying around, I can also find a good amount of gloss online. Here's my collection of jaunty URLs:

HEMP FASHION
"Social Fabric—Plan It—Plant It—
Wear It"
http://www.hooked.net:80/buzznet/
fad/items/hemp/hemp.html

Not only do clothes made from hemp look cool and feel comfy, but they're also extremely planet-friendly. It requires NO pesticides to grow hemp, and compared to cotton, hemp needs less water and fewer chemicals to process into fabric. The drawback? Due to big greedy lobbying corporations, hemp is illegal to grow in the U.S. Thank goodness it's not illegal to buy and sell hemp duds that have been imported from other countries. This site sports a couple of hemp fashion photos, gives you some background information on the discriminated plant, and lists places where you can buy cannabis clothing in the U.S. as well as zines that keep you updated on the hemp scene.

THE FASHION PAGE
http://www.charm.net:80/~jakec/
This is the first "fashion" site I found on the Web, and it ended up being the most awesome. Containing so much more than your ordinary mainstream paper fash rag, these pages give you a stylish angle on shoes, corsets, undies,

Hemp fashion photo courtesy of FAD

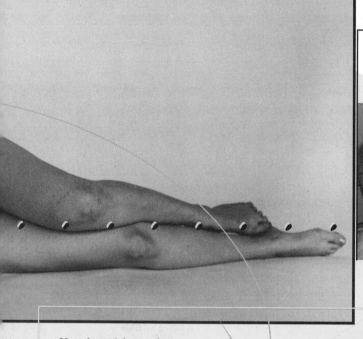

Yep, these girls are glamorous and gorgeous, the kind of chicks you love to hate. Check out these high-fashion hunks, as well as some beautiful wanna-bes who are just starting out. If you stare at your screen long enough, I'm sure you can find a flaw! (Tee hee.)

(P.S. I looked in earnest for male model sites but couldn't find one. If you want to see sexy boys, guess you'll have to create those pages yourself!)

MODELS
http://goldenshears.infobahn.com/models
Wanna be a model? You can check out a bunch of photos from two San Francisco modeling agencies and see what the competition is like. They've created a couple of pretty (of course) image maps of their models. Just click on the babe of your choice and voila, two large black-and-white photos of her will pop up on your screen. Have any darts?

MADE IN ITALY: MODEL AGENCIES
http://www.flashnet.it/made.htm
Hundreds of Italian beauties reside at this site, making it a little slow to download. The agencies represented here are Elite, Fashion Model Management, and Why Not. I don't know if they're advertising their services or just trying to make me jealous. If you're thinking of modeling in Europe, this is a good place to start your research.

BODY LANGUAGE
http://totalny.com/voices/model/vcmdc.html
This promo page for the book *Model* is a bit flimsy (natch). But then this is a model page, and you do get photos and quotes by Cindy Crawford, Christy

make-up, bathing suits, environmentally-conscious clothes, fashion designers, and lots more (for both sexes). Lynda Stretton, who was a pro in the fashion retail and wholesale biz, now dedicates herself full-time to this e-magazine.

WHAT DO YOU EXPECT FOR FREE, VOGUE?
"Fabulous, Yet Friendly, Fashion Tips"
http://www.sils.umich.edu/~sooty/fashion.html
I like this stylish spot because it's so homemade and personable. Its creator, Sooty (a.k.a. Chris), has some "fashion" photos (for lack of a more casual term) modeled by friends. Sooty (Girl or boy? Beats me.) also puts Net people into categories, describing how each group dresses (Ha! Didn't peg me right!) and has links to a bunch of other fashion URLs. My favorite part of this site is the list of "Hints from Models," which is loaded with really funny (spooky-funny) quotes from high-fashion models. Here are a couple:
"Everyone should have enough money to get plastic surgery."—Beverly Johnson
"I would rather exercise than read a newspaper."—Kim Alexis
(YIKES!)

@FASHION
http://www2.pcy.mci.net/fashion/
Oh dear. Here is MCI's take on a fashion site. If this were a magazine it would be super-shiny and attractive enough to look at but utterly void of personality. Fashion is fashion, however, so how important is a voice? Depends on the reader, I guess. @Fashion takes itself very seriously, talking about big designers and the look for next season. It's hosted by the emcee of Canada's FT: Fashion Television, Jeanne Beker. It does have some pretty glam shots, and even if you're not one to follow the mainstream, it *is* kinda fun to see what we're supposed to be wearing. Of course there are no links here to other cool sites.

--more-->

Hot Sites: Threads of Fashion *continued*

SAN FRANCISCO FOCUS' "MOONSTRUCK"

http://goldenshears.infobahn.com/

I was a little surprised to see that this site is created by San Francisco Focus, a magazine usually devoted to social causes. But they said they wanted to launch their site showing something "intensely visual . . . and there is no fashion show on the Internet like this." What they mean is that you can download some QuickTime video clips from the trendy tenth annual Absolut Golden Shears Awards and see some beautiful models prance around on your screen for a few seconds. Kinda neat, but for the amount of time it takes to download, kinda not neat. You do get to see some slick photos of the latest in chic. What I like more about this site is the SF clubs and restaurants they talk about.

DYE IT BLACK FAQ

http://www.dcs.qmw.ac.uk/~bob/goth/dye.faq.html

I always thought a box of Rit was all you needed to color your wardrobe, but my traditional ways have been challenged. Lady Bathory is a dye-shop technician for the theater costume shop at the University of Tennessee, and she practically makes an art out of dying. Here she answers frequently asked questions about blackening clothes. Find out how to determine the fiber content of your garments, the dying equipment you need, what kind of dye to buy, and how to dye velvet. If your clothes are especially delicate or difficult to color, you should also read Lady's How to Dye Clothes Black (http://www.dcs.qmw.ac.uk/~bob/goth/dye.html).

--more-->

Turlington, Christy Brinkley, and Jerry Hall. Once you're finished with these girls, click on "home" and you'll get more dirt on fashion, grafiti and media at a site called Total New York (http://totalny.com/main2.html). It's jammed with all sots of gritty glam, some of which you can catch on QuickTime videos.

PIT'S PAGE OF BEAUTIFUL WOMEN
http://www.cen.uiuc.edu/~morrise/girls.html
This is a guy who collects photos of women he considers beautiful and tacks pics onto his site for anyone to gawk at. He's got thirty-seven so far, which are broken down into the Calvin Klein Collection (any Kate Moss fans out there?), the Guess Collection, and a bunch of miscellaneous glam shots, including a pretty one of Madonna. A totally aesthetic site—no facts about anyone. Pit also has links to other model sites.

Models . . . .

YAHOO: SUPERMODEL IMAGES

http://www.yahoo.com/yahoo/Computers/
Multimedia/Pictures/Supermodel_Images
If you didn't get enough images with Pit, here's a huge
list of links to models and other handsome celebrities
for more star-gazing. You'll find babes like Sherilyn
Fenn, Christina Applegate, Marilyn Monroe, Linda
Evangelista, Paulina, Sharon Stone, Claudia Schiffer,
Stephanie Seymour, and too many others to name them
all here.

THE SITES PAGE

http://rulj287.leidenuniv.nl/robert/sites.html#models
Sheesh! You're still reading for more? Okay, here's one
last page of links that will take you to even *more* gorgeous celebs not mentioned above. Here you can stare
at Madonna, Meg Ryan, Pamela Anderson, Tori Amos,
Helen Hunt (she went to my high school, by the way!),
Uma Thurman, Michelle Pfeiffer, and *mucho más*. I like
this list better than Yahoo's, because a lot of the links
to these celebs take you to "unofficial" Home Pages,
which give you more than just photos (I mean, enough
is enough already). Bios, filmographies, and that sort
of stuff can be found as well. •

CLEAR PLASTIC FASHIONS

http://clearplastic.com/
An innovative fellow named Mark
Allyn will teach you how to make
your own clear plastic raincoat. (Hint:
you'll need two shower curtains, a
good pair of scissors, and strips of vel-
cro.) It looks pretty easy! Allyn wore
his own see-through slicker through
the streets of rainy Seattle and was
stopped by so many strangers inquiring about his garment that he decided
to share his creation with us Net-
goers. In fact, if he gets enough interest from his site, he says he'll start his
own plastic-wear business.

FASHION YELLOW PAGES

http://www.fashion.net
Want to be more dapper but don't
know where to start? Let your fingers
do the walking on your keyboard and
you'll find snail-mail addresses and
Net sites to très chic spots all over
the world. In other words, if you need
a fashion designer, hair stylist, makeup artist, modeling agency, photographer, modeling school, fashion rags,
accessories, or anything else in this
realm, you may want to start your
search here. And yes, these pages are
actually yellow. •

H◉T SITES:
Jewels

Smart girls can't be categorized in terms of the jewelry they wear. Like clothes, trinkets and jewels are a matter of personal taste. Some like earrings made of computer chips, while others are proud to drape pearls around their necks. It's a good thing such online diversity of jewelry sites exists!

BOB'S GUIDE TO CHEAP CLIP-ON EARRINGS

http://www.dcs.qmw.ac.uk/~bob/stuff/clipon.html

This guy Bob seems so cute. He's got all sorts of fun girlie sites and links (which are scattered throughout this book), and they're all very hip and handy. This one teaches you how to make funky hoop earrings without spending any moola. All you need is a spiral notebook, wire cutters, and a file (optional). His bright cartoony illustrations and recipe-style instructions remind me of a project that would be in a Brownie's Handbook.

VIKTOR VIKTORIA

http://www.vktr.com/

What a find—I want to order one of everything! Here's a cyber store where you can pick up stuff that you can't find easily in ordinary real-life jewelry stores—like these adorable belly charms or sterling silver studs shaped as a bug, frog, sun, moon, or butterfly, and a bunch of other body-piercing jewelry. The best part is that everything is dirt cheap. But jewels are just the beginning. You also have to eyeball their big assortment of bright colorful hair dyes (accompanied by instructions), overalls, hats, posters, and T-shirts (Hole, Nine Inch Nails, Beastie Boys, etc.).

--more-->

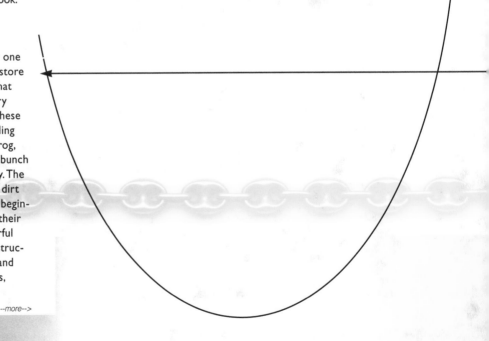

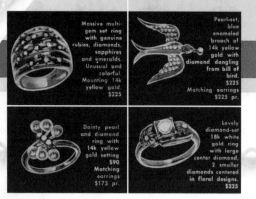

Massive multi-gem set ring with genuine rubies, diamonds, sapphires and emeralds. Unusual and colorful. Mounting 14k yellow gold. $225

Pearl-set, blue enameled brooch of 14k yellow gold with diamond dangling from bill of bird. $225 Matching earrings $225 pr.

Dainty pearl and diamond ring with 14k yellow gold setting $90 Matching earrings $175 pr.

Lovely diamond-set 18k white gold ring with large center diamond, 2 smaller diamonds centered in floral designs. $225

BODY JEWELRY BY JUDY
http://www.sexy-jewelry.com/
Those "Should be 21 or over" warnings get me every time. I fervidly raced past Judy's "Sensitive Material" notice, only to find the most gaudy body jewelry I've ever seen. These very long, dangling, plastic-looking pieces with names like Titti Twinkler and Bum Bauble are just some of what's on display—and they're not even piercing jewels, mind you, but clip-ons. Ouch!

God, now that I think about it, maybe it's not meant to be taken seriously, although you could order this stuff online. Hmm. In any case, the pictures are full of scary camp, and if you're of age (heh) you've gotta take a gander.

AUTHENTIC TREASURE COIN JEWELRY
http://www.cts.com/~khobbs/
"Antique" doesn't even begin to describe the jewelry sold here. Historical Interaction is the name of the company, which sells pendants, rings, cuff links, and rings that feature unrestored ancient coins dating as far back as 400 B.C. Many come from the eras of Alexander the Great (356–323 B.C.), Marcus Aurelius, and Christopher Columbus. These jewelers say they guarantee the fully certified authenticity of each coin. Obviously, each piece they list on their site is original, so once someone buys it, it's gone. Prices start at $350. •

H⊙T SITES:
Body Art

Piercing, tattooing, branding, scarring, and plastic surgery are just some of the ways to alter your bod, and info on all of this stuff can be found on the Web. The body makes a nice canvas on which all sorts of decorating projects can be performed. Check it out.

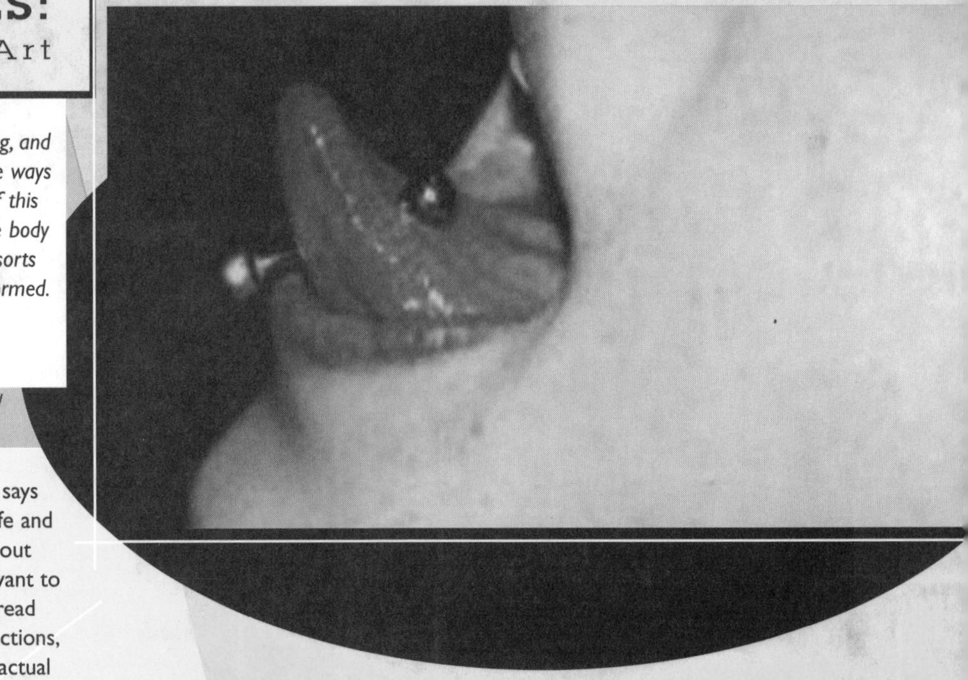

BOB'S GUIDE TO EAR PIERCING

http://www.dcs.qmw.ac.uk/~bob/stuff/pierces.html

Here's a do-it-yourself guide to piercing your ears. Friendly Bob says his advice makes self-piercing safe and fun. (Fun?? I remember blacking out when I tried this stunt!) If you want to try it, it would behoove you to read this comprehensive set of instructions, which includes preparation, the actual piercing, and maintenance. And don't forget to breathe!

Note: The Body Modification Ezine reviewed below warns us not to take friendly Bob's piercing advice! *My* advice is to read everything you can and then use your best judgment.

BODY MODIFICATION EZINE

http://www.io.org/~bme/

This is kind of embarrassing, but I actually gasped out loud at one of the photos in this completely thorough body mod Ezine. The pix of piercings, tattoos, scars, brands, and cuttings were interesting variations of stuff I've seen before, no sweat. But it was the lip sewing that got to me. Jeez! This close-up photo shows a guy with his lips stitched together, not very even stitches, mind you, with blood still oozing from under the thread. Fascinating, but a shocker for my virginal eyes.

It's not just your typical tribal modifications covered in this zine. They also have pictures and information on stuff that does alter the body but that's not

--more-->

Joshua Burgin

usually put in this category: plastic surgery, body-building, and foreskin restoration, for instance. Besides graphics and basic information, the zine also talks about the history, rituals, and culture of the different forms of body art, and gives you a piercing guide with care tips. There is so much here, I couldn't even get through it all. For those even mildly interested in mutating their bodies, this is a great place to start.

THE BODY SPACE
http://www.surgery.com/body/topics/body.html

Let's not forget plastic surgery as a means of reinventing the body. It's odd how people who revamp their bodies through modern surgery usually try to keep it a secret, while most who practice ancient methods like piercing and tattooing openly exhibit their modification. What gives?

Anyway, here's a site for people who are thinking about plastic. First you click on the body part you'd like to alter: face, arms, boobs, stomach, tuchis, thighs, or calves. Then you click on the type of alteration you want (do you want your butt to be firmer, bigger, etc). Finally, you can see before-and-after photos of someone who has already done the deed, find out the average costs, read a detailed article about the operation, and find out about doctors in your area who can give you more info and sculpture your body if you still want it.

SABINA'S BODY ART PAGE(S)
http://128.122.132.159:9999/~thebin/bodyart.html

Still not finding what you need? Try Sabina's growing list of links, images, newsgroups, FAQs, and articles on various types of body modifications. •

Being the shopoholic that I am, I made sure my purse was out of computer range before browsing through online Web shops, and girl, am I glad I did. It's amazing how much stuff is out there! All types of clothing, accessories, computer gadgets, books, records, flowers, and even condoms can be had via your modem. The following are some of my favorites.

Clothing:
NICOLE MILLER ONLINE
http://www.interactive.line.com/nicole
.cover_nicole.html

Ms. Miller makes online shopping for accessories easy. You get an image map that displays her always adorable merchandise, like the umbrellas with the cosmetics design, the ties made from old dress patterns, or the fancy cuff links. Just click on the item you want, and you'll get a larger photo to admire, a price list, and an order form. Voila! Four to six weeks later you'll be stylin'.

**NINE LIVES WOMEN'S CLOTHING
CONSIGNMENT STORE**
http://www.los-gatos.scruznet.com/
index.html

If you like popular designers like DKNY and Ann Taylor but don't have the bucks, you may want to check out this used and vintage clothing store. By typing in your size, price range, and the designer you prefer, you can see if they have something you want. You can even get a personal shopping assistant, free of charge, to watch for new arrivals and email you if they get something you've requested. Sound too good to be true? Maybe it is. One problem with this E-boutique is that there aren't any graphics to show you what the clothes look like. The major

--more-->

Safe Shopping

It's great to have the option of ordering stuff online with your credit card—especially when you're ultra busy or can't find the goods in your own town. But, as in the real world, you must watch out for crooks in Cyberland. When you send your credit card number over the Internet, the info usually has to make some pitstops along the way to its ultimate destiny. With every stop, the number is vulnerable to snoops who may jot it down and buy expensive toys with it later. So be smart—there are ways to encode your number before you send it so that only the receiver will be able to read the number. First you have to find out which security plan the virtual shop uses (they usually specify this loudly on their Home Page) and then encrypt your info with the same system. Here are the most common protection schemes:

Netscape: If you use Netscape to access the Web and the merchant is protected under their plan, click on the "Handbook" button on Netscape's menu bar, and then go to "Graphical Elements." From there you'll find "Security Information," which will give you the lowdown on their safe shopping procedure.

First Virtual Holdings Incorporated: First you register with this company by phone (for $2) and receive an account number. Then every time you buy from someone who uses this company, you just give them your account number. First Virtual will email you before they process the credit card number to confirm that *you* actually made the transaction. (So your Visa/MasterCard number is never exposed on the Internet.) For more info, log into:
http://www.fv.com/info/intro.html.

PGP (Pretty Good Privacy): This software is the coolest! It was created by Cypherpunk Phil Zimmerman not just for shoppers' sake but to protect *everyone's* freedom of speech and privacy from the slimy Big Brothers. It's public domain (no cost!) and can be used to encrypt not only numbers, but any kind of message you want. To find out more, tap into:
http://draco.centerline.com:8080/~franl/pgp/pgp.html.

Look what I found in one of my back issues of bOING bOING! Can you imagine downloading a real pair of jeans from your computer? It may not be so farfetched, at least not to one of bOING's writers, David Borcherding. He talks about using nanotechnology—the science of building robots and computers so small they're invisible to the human eye—to create and maintain your wardrobe. Although nanotechnology is only a theoretical science at the moment, it won't be just a theory for long, and when those little robots actually do learn how to stitch, I'm going to be the first on my block to luxuriate with nanofashion. Check it out!

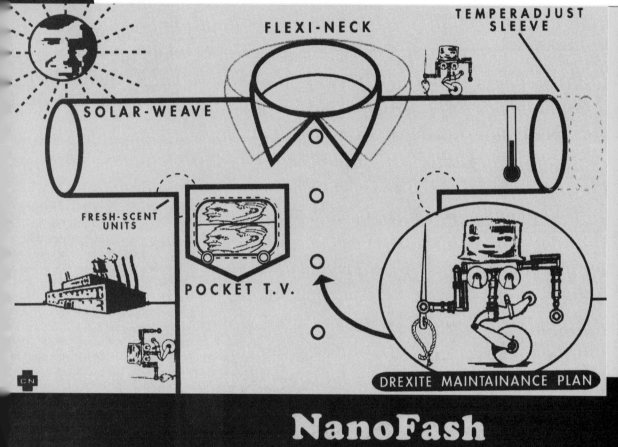

FLEXI-NECK
TEMPERADJUST SLEEVE
SOLAR-WEAVE
FRESH-SCENT UNITS
POCKET T.V.
DREXITE MAINTAINANCE PLAN

NanoFash
by David Borcherding
(reprinted from *bOING bOING #9*)

You sit outside on your lunch break, enjoying the warmth of the sun and munching a mustard-and-ketchup-drowned soydog. Lunch hour is nearing its end, and you still have half the dog to down. Taking a large bite, you squirt condiments down the front of your white shirt. No napkin? No worry! You're wearing the latest Betsey Johnson with Drexite controls. Even as you watch, the microscopic robots that inhabit your shirt detect the stain and begin to remove it. Atom by atom, they break down the stain and convert it to extra starch to be spread out evenly across your garment, or maybe shipped directly to the collar for a little added sharpness.

We are nearing the age of programmable clothing. Tomorrow we will get out of bed and, instead of staring at a closet full of clothes, we'll sit down at a terminal and bring up our selection of outfits on the screen. Once we decide on the basic design, we can work with the colors, type in our measurements (or perhaps just bring up the macro that has all of these already recorded), then hit the "Create" key. While we shower and eat breakfast, the microscopic robots in our CyberCloset will be creating our selected outfit. We finish our scrambled eggs, jog back to

problem, however, is that it only allows you to window, er, screen shop. You can't order online. If you like something, they'll hold it for you, but you've got to get to the little town of Los Gatos in twenty-four hours to claim it as yours. In other words, if you're not from or on your way to Northern California, forget it.

UJAMAA FASHIONS

http://shops.net/shops/Ujamaa_ Fashions/

Not a huge variety offered here, but the selection of African clothing that is on the racks looks exotic and fun. You can order things like the purple Grand Buba, an elegant dress perfect for girls who wear sizes 10–26, or clothes with colorful batik prints for women and men. This site is updated frequently, so if you don't find something the first time around, try again.

SHOPPING IN—"WOMEN'S APPAREL"

http://www.onramp.net/~shopping/ category/speedshp/wmnsaprl/ wmnsapr2.html

Lots of loose comfy-looking clothing here, including stuff from the Blue Fish label. Everything is 100 percent cotton, and prices range from around $11 for tank tops to over $100 for certain shirts and dresses. Nice crisp photos help you examine the goods. This online shop seems to have a friendlier, more authentic personality than most of the others I've been to.

Fetish Wear:
STAGE CLOTHES, USA

http://www.w2.com/stageclothes.html

If you like to romp hard, you should check out this twenty-two-year-old showroom full of leather, chains, and devilishly delightful toys. Their catalog has pages of leather corselettes, bustiers, chain chokers, restraints, master/submissive wristbands, garter belts, and even leather jeans. You can get sporting goods like paddles, whips,

--more-->

585L Create a eye-catching view in our PATENT Lace-Up MINI SKIRT. Black Only. Sizes: S-M-L.

NanoFash *continued*

the bedroom and get dressed for the day. No need for undershirts or deodorants; the Drexites (named for nanotechnology's creator, K. Eric Drexler) will keep us dry and odor-free. Or, as our suit is being finished, we can program in whatever scent we wish to wear that day. Select Escada, for example, and the Drexites will continue to exude that scent at whatever level we choose, never fading or becoming too strong as the day wears on.

Imagine, clothes that never smell of our co-workers' cigarette smoke at the day's end. Dark suits that don't show dandruff. Silky blouses that won't need armpit shields to keep away sweat stains. And we won't sweat, for the same technology that keeps us scented and clean will also keep us comfortable. A bit chilly in the office? The Drexites automatically adjust the weave of the cloth to be a bit thicker. And when those goose bumps go away and our skin temperature goes up, they will loosen the weave until maximum comfort is reached.

Our clothes will fit better, too. Program our blouse to be tight in the morning, and it will stay tight with no stretching, no matter how sheer the fabric, from the moment we put it on until the moment we take it off. No more choking collars or binding underarms. Comfort will be constantly monitored and maintained.

How much would you pay for a pair of shoes that always kept your feet cool and comfortable, perhaps even massaging them throughout the day? What if that same pair never wore out, polished its own scuffs, changed color to match your outfit? What if all your clothes acted this way? Ties that are never too tight or too loose, pants and skirts that adjust at the waist to accommodate that extra burger at lunchtime.

Stylin'. Newsgroups

For riotous dressers, spiffed-up chicks, and geek grrrls who need some pointers, nothing compares to Plumage, the ultra-fresh fashion conference that takes place on the WELL (see Magdalen's interview in this chapter). But for those not connected to that West coast virtual salon, here's a list of

fashionable newsgroups for anyone jacked into the Net.

alt.binaries.pictures.supermodels
A place to get pictures of chicks like Teri Hatcher, Pamela Anderson, and Kathy Ireland. In most cases you'll need special software to convert the pix, so is it even worth it?

alt.clothing.lingerie
Pretty basic lingerie prattle, but some interesting riffs on stuff like girdles and

what to wear under biking shorts.

alt.clothing.sneakers
Doesn't grab me, since sneakers aren't my bag, but if you're into rapping about high-tops vs. low-tops, shoe laces (with or without?), or smelly sneakers, maybe you'll dig this group.

alt.fashion

The attitude here is fun, trivial, young, and fashion-conscious, of course. The most popular question seems to be "What are you wearing today?" And people seem to take the question quite seriously, making sure to give details on their shorts, belts, and T-shirts. Other topics include what to do with curly hair, favorite jeans, and knee-length skirts vs. the mini.

alt.lifestyle.barefoot

I didn't realize that going barefoot was such a lifestyle for some people, but it certainly is. They're into being shoeless for the freedom, style, feel on the feet, and probably lots of other reasons I missed. A very interesting topic.

alt.lycra

Lots of Lycra fanatics here asking where to get certain items made from the form-fitting material and describing why they love the way it feels. I was surprised to find so many men who are into wearing lycra shorts to show off their package.

alt.models

Typical of what one would expect a models newsgroup to be. Info on modeling agencies, ads for models needed (I'd be extremely skeptical of those!), and modeling FAQs.

alt.society.underwear

Captivating discussion angles on undies I never would have thought to talk about, such as "Should a male model's penis be arranged up or down in a photo shoot?" If you're into trading underwear, this is the place to do it.

alt.supermodels

Again, typical for a models newsgroup. Questions, facts, and gossip about supermodels. Some pictures, too.

alt.tv.models-inc

Wasn't this show canceled? Dedicated fans of the weak Spelling series gather here for serious discussion.

rec.arts.bodyart

Nothing too outrageous here, just chatter about anything that has to do with tattooing and piercing, with a few threads on body painting as well. Topic examples: "Body Modification for Weddings," "Tattoo Artist Supplies," and "Pain."

rec.crafts.jewelry

Lots of shop talk for the professional (or wanna-be) jewelry makers. Everything from advice on repairing Native American jewelry to how to assemble puzzle rings.

NanoFash *continued*

Once the practical end of it all is mastered, nanotechnology will turn to style. Whole new fields will be created in fashion programming. Want *Casablanca* to play silently across the back of your leather jacket? Or how about having that jogging suit flash red at the shoulders? Not a problem for tomorrow's fashion wizards. Ties will be created that cycle through a variety of patterns during the day, from paisleys to fractals, perhaps, redefining the term "power tie." Blouses and accessories will be able to gradually change colors, working slowly through all the hues that match the rest of our outfit. Or they can flash through the colors, changing every few seconds for the ultimate party eye-catcher.

Our nanofashions will be better for the environment. No more will we need to have our clothes cleaned in toxic chemicals, stored in plastic bags and mothballs. And as we save the planet, we'll save money on cleaning bills, justifying the extra initial expense. We'll save time, too, since we'll never have to wait for our clothes to come back from the laundry or out of the dryer.

If the environment continues to deteriorate, our NanoFash will protect us. In the same way it rids us of our ketchup stains, it will convert toxins in the rain and dew into harmless elements. Walk out into the ultraviolet rays and our Drexite-enhanced shirt will shield us, storing up energy for its little robots and reflecting the excess.

Yes, our clothes will be powered by light. Nanotechnology requires only nanoenergy. Sunlight, neon light, and perhaps even moonlight will keep our NanoFash running smoothly, without the need for batteries. And in lieu of light, it will run easily off of our own body heat.

This is the future of fashion with nanotechnology: NanoFash. Programmable clothing that's easy to use, fun to wear, good for us and for the planet. Never again will we have to face a closet full of outdated styles or wonder where we will store the winter clothes for the summer. Our closets will be our disk drives, full of outfits that fit us perfectly, every time. Waste will be cut down, not only in cloth, but in fashion catalogs. No need for stores to have racks of clothes—no need for stores at all! We will be able to buy our fashions online and download them, or create our own. The future of NanoFash is as varied as our imaginations. •

and handcuffs, as well as edible undies, pasties, and condoms. But Stage Clothes sells even more than just bedroom gear. Take a look at their nice collection of Dr. Marten's, leather jackets, mini-skirts, and swimwear. You can buy everything online.

Jewelry:
SHOPPING IN—"JEWELRY & ACCESSORIES"
http://www.onramp.net/~shopping/category/speedshp/jewelry/jewelry2.html
This is a place that sells Native American sterling silver jewelry. Very beautiful looking stuff, mostly bracelets, with traditional meaning behind many of the pieces. Bright crisp photos accompany the descriptions.

Virtual Malls:
SHOPS.NET A.K.A. INTERNET SHOPKEEPER
http://www.ip.net/shops.html
"A place in cyberspace where people from all over the world can set up and manage their own shops." And for a minimal monthly fee, you too can set up your very own electric store, which they explain how to do with some easy instructions. With as much versatility and as many shops as the Supermall in your neighborhood, this cybermall is bustling with vendors selling computers, condoms, Tupperware, videos, books, CD-ROMs, screen savers, clothes, jewelry, condoms, gifts, beauty products, stuff, stuff, and more stuff.

SHOPPING 2000
http://shopping2000.com/
If you have to get a present for your granny or Aunt Myrtle, this is the place to do it. More than forty-five very mainstream stores like 800-Flowers, Pet Warehouse, Sears, Hanes, L'Eggs, and Nordic Track abound. The place is also loaded with gift stores. Barnes & Noble, Tower Records, and 800-Trekker are about the hippest things here, but it's a nice predictable mall that can be useful in a pinch. •

Before personal computers became a national phenomenon in the mid-eighties, self-expression wasn't a freedom easily exercised by way of the media. Most commonly, you'd either have to: be employed by a television, radio, or publishing kahuna (and then, is it really your voice being heard?); run a pirate radio or television channel (exciting but cumbersome and, of course, illegal in most cases); own your own press (expensive, difficult to keep up, and a space hogger); or you could painstakingly use a typewriter, stapler, and Xerox machine to get your words across, and then figure out ways

to entice others to read your none-too-pretty newsletter or zine.

But PCs changed all that. Because desktop publishing (writing and designing pages with a computer) allows one simply and affordably to create graphical pages that can look as sharp as the mainstream glossies, the surge of home computers has revolutionized the world of the alternative press. Now anyone with a computer can be her own publisher. Last I heard, the estimated number of different zines (homemade publications) floating around is 25,000!

So what does all this mean? It means we've entered an age when everyone's voice can be heard, not just those in control of the media's corporate purse strings. It means we can now be exposed to ideas and art from the whole gang, not just from the out-of-touch top of the media's hierarchy. It means more communication! (Anyone with the gift of gab will especially appreciate this.)

As the wordy uncorporate star-wanna-be Net Chick that I am, the concept of creating my own publication was golden. I couldn't stand the thought of seeing others bask in the liberating glory of zinedom without tossing in my three cents. Thus *bOING bOING* was born in 1988 (I cocreated it with Mark, my genius man). The beauty of doing *bb* is that its writers and I can say whatever the hell we think worthy, whether it's edgy news that the mainstream is oblivious to or frightened of, something personal we want to get off our chests and pontificate to the world, or contributing our notion of camp that we deem entertaining. And the fact that our circulation has snowballed from 100 to 20,000 proves that zines do have a place in the world of communications.

The two biggest problems most zinesters encountered (notice past tense) with their do-it-yourself endeavors were distribution and the cost of printing. Anyone who's had experience with zines will vouch that collecting money from small distributors is a major drag. Although a few wonderfully honorable distributors do exist, most hold off on paying you until you pull out the threats. Some never pay. As far as printing expenses go, even those who Xerox their copies will have to deal with the recent increase in paper prices. It's ghastly! Enough to turn any mild-mannered zinemaker into a raging bitch.

With yet another revolution taking place—namely, online publishing—the above problems no longer exist for the alternative (and commercial, if they so desire!) press. Those who would be turned off to the awesome title of Zinemaker because of the paper and distribution obstacles now have another avenue where they can strut their stuff. New zines are popping up every day on the World Wide Web. The advantages of publishing through this medium are many: It's astronomically cheaper than publishing on paper; distributors become obsolete; the potential audience goes into the millions; and, although I doubt many think of this, it's environmentally smarter.

I think the boundaries of what constitutes a zine have become more blurred with the WWW than ever before. While some artists formally refer to their Web pages as a zine, what about all of the other noncommercial creations that don't put themselves into that category? Like the countless autobiographical Home Pages in which the site's landlord talks all about her/himself, with photos, diaries, audio files, etc. Wouldn't their projects be considered zines if they were manifested on paper?

In "Media Freak" you'll meet lots of digital grrrls who have put up their own Personal Home Pages to share with us. If you feel left out after visiting their keen sites (I sure did! I wasn't satisfied until I built my own Home), you can read my tips on how to create your own hip Web pad. You'll find out where some of the edgiest grrrly Webzines are, including *geekgirl*, whose editor, Rosie Cross, gives us her take on chicks and tech ("Geekgirls like swimming in ether, they like dippin', divin', and dunkin', they like the goop melange of the Internet"). You'll also hear from author babe St. Jude, who's intent on hacking the future. ("Every generation that grows up normal is a loss to the planet. Ah, but with each new generation we have the hope of corrupting them into something cooler than what was and is.")

What I adore most about zines on the Internet is the anarchistic spirit that shapes them; there are no rules in cyberspace. So if you've got the urge to spew out your artistic or intellectual rays, do what the rest of us grrrls and boyz do: beam them at the Net.

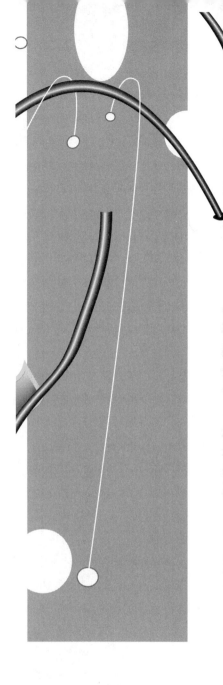

/HTML

The Personal Pages of Webgrrrls

One day while cruising the Net, minding my own business, I stumbled across something that looked pretty personal: Carolyn's Diary (http://www.io.org:80/~clburke/). Of course I was intrigued. My fingers timidly clicked over to her site, ignoring the involuntary guilt reflex shooting through my insides. The diary wouldn't be floating around in cyberspace if she didn't want us to read it, but still, I couldn't help feeling a little sneaky—and excited.

Along with chat rooms, personal Home Pages are one of the most voyeuristic facets of the Net. People with personal sites go out of their way to spoon-feed you slices of their life stories, and many even include photos and video clips. Thousands of these intimate Websites are out there, with new ones popping up every day. For avid people watchers, what better way to get the scoop on a random stranger than from the comfort of your own computer?

Net Chicks have some of the most engaging home pages, with lots of personal anecdotes, family photos, funky graphics, hotlists, blacklists, gossip, cool links, and tons of personality. Many of them are so jam-packed with goodies that it can take hours to get through one site. Two great places to start searching for these cyberchicks are Aliza Sherman's (see facing page) "Webgrrls! – Women on the Net" (http://www.cybergrrl.com/), or "Voxxen Worx" (http://www.phantom.com/~barton/ voxxen.html), both of which give you long lists of sassy URLs to rummage through.

Carolyn's Diary was all that I could have hoped for, by the way. It was fat, candid, insightful, and even rambled in some parts, as any authentic diary would. Unlike most Home Pages but just like most diaries, she doesn't include any graphics, just pure text. If anyone's got the gift of gab, it's Carolyn! A fun read.

The following are some of my other favorite grrrl sites, which I've hand-picked based on a high level of creativity, weirdness, frankness, sex appeal, or plain old charm. Of course many other peachy Webgrrls are out there, but you'll have to scout them out yourself. Most Home Pages include a personal email address, so if someone turns you on, drop her a line!

NAME: LAURA GIACOPPO

Website: "There's No Place Like Homepage"

http://www.getnet.com/~gia/

Her Gig: Gives us tons of cool links to weird kitchy offbeat sites like *Geekwear, Nerdity Test, Ted Kennedy Homepage,* and *How to Make Jumping Frog Origami.* Unfortunately, there's not enough about *her.* Give us some dirt, Laura!

Quote: "This could be a scary ride. Please remain seated and keep your hands inside the car at all times."

NAME: ALIZA SHERMAN A.K.A. CYBERGRRL (TM)

Website: "This is Cybergrrl!"

http://www.cybergrrl.com/

Her Gig: Likes sushi, Ayn Rand, *Ms. Magazine*, *Women's Wire*, *The Body Shop*, and her personal trainer. She's written *Everything You Need to Know About Surrendering Your Baby for Adoption* (Rosen Publishing) and hosts *Safety Net* on *Women's Wire* and *AOL's Women's List*.

Quote: "Ramble ramble ramble. Puff up my chest with self-importance. Pose. (Giving you my best side). Yahdah yahdah yahdah. Brag, boast. Blah blah blah. Now that I've gotten that off my chest, let's just say I love my computer, I love the WWW (surf the wave)."

NAME: CATHERINE "EPPIE" REBECCA SKIDMORE

Website: "Jesus in Trunk"

http://www.interport.net/~eppie/

Her Gig: Proudly displays her "tank" ('72 Dodge Dart), enjoys classical music, theater, reading, and her favorite color is deep raspberry red. The self-touted "HTML Goddess" has a fun WWW Hotlist and points us to "WHAT NOT TO DO with your home page."

Quote: "A Mac weenie by choice and a Windows and VAX fetishist by paycheck, I really hate computers and use them only to tie up the high-speed modem lines and to flirt with handsome Digital consultants at work."

NAME: BRIGITTE JELLINEK

Website: http://www.cosy.sbg.ac.at/~bjelli/bjelli.html

Her Gig: Getting her Master's degree in Math and Science in Salzburg; Has her own *Star Trek* Web page (see review on pg 123); Plans to make a career out of her Web work.

Quote: "It's almost one and a half years now that I've spent on the Web, and I consider myself quite a wizard. See my guestbook for an example of the magic I can do ;-)."

NAME: JAN HANFORD

Website: http://www.shelby.com/pub/wsg/html/jan/home.html

Her Gig: A Web page designer who's obsessed with creating beautiful music. Her first CD, *Vespers*, was just released by AD Music. Some of her favorite tunes come from Bach, Bjork, Walter Carlos, Front 242, Mozart, and Antonio Vivaldi. Lots and lots of stuff about music in her Home Page.

Quote: "I'm really busy preparing my first CD. This isn't work, it's heaven!"

NAME: SOREL HUSBANDS

**Website: "Just Sorel"
http://www.interport.net:80/~sorel/**

Her Gig: This mad girl will take you to her "Planet Known as Too Offbeat to Mention" where you'll find the Cafe-Queer Rest Stop, Sexy Matilda, Leathermom, and other luscious delights that will surely give you a noradrenaline headrush. Also the producer of "Stoli Central" (http://www.stoli.com/), where you'll experience vodka like you never have before.

Quote: "One very strange place where water glasses come when they are called ... and no one knows who's supposed to be on top or on the bottom, with very unusual inhabitants and secret fetishes."

NAME: SHELLY HOLUBEK

**Website: "Shellie's Ego Indulgence Page"
http://www.qrc.com/~sholubek/start.htm**

Her Gig: Devotes pages and pages of her site to scrumptious chocolate. Also has a cool online "Around DC This Week" column. Works as HTML coder and Website maintainer for Quantum Research Corporation. Hobbies include sleeping, reading, and 'blading.

Quote: "I need my chocolate!"

NAME: STEPHANIE BRAIL

Website: http://www2.primenet.com/~pax/

Her Gig: Hosts Spiderwoman Mailing List to support female Web developers and consultants. Also hosts forums on the WELL, *Mindvox*, and *Women's Wire*. Favorites on the tube include *Lois & Clark*, *Earth 2*, and *Forever Knight*.

Quote: "Finally updated after three months! I seem to have more fun creating new pages than updating existing ones, but I'm getting over it."

NAME: JESSICA GRACE WING

Website: "Jigsaw Cigar Scene"
http://www.end.com:80/~jessica/

Her Gig: She ought to be a model, but instead sings in her band, Weird Blinking Lights (you should hear her real-life musical answering machine!). She's also the music editor of *bOING bOING* and is fond of corsets. You can listen to her songs and read some of her writing from here.

Quote: "Welcome, my nosy little things! . . . I never wear underwear. Do you?"

NAME: BERDENIA WALKER

Website: http://www.gatech.edu/bgsa/people/
berdenia.walker/home.html

Her Gig: Studying to get her Ph.D. in Electrical and Computer Engineering. Digs traveling, plants, and skiing, and her latest passion is doll houses. An avid spectator of most sports.

Quote: "I really enjoy life and try to live each day to the fullest."

NAME: LAURIE MANN

Website: http://worcester.lm.com/lmann/index.html

Her Gig: A Net veteran for more than seven years, Laurie will create a Home Page for you for only twenty bucks. Her site has an organized list of 100 hot links. When she's unplugged, she sings for the Bach Choir of Pittsburgh, collects books, and is involved with sci-fi conventions.

Quote: "I'm not claiming to have an exhaustive index. I can only promise you'll never find a link to any of the following on these pages: OJ, New Age, trucks, football, n(N)ewts, chili peppers."

NAME: WENDI DUNLAP

Website: "Slumberland" http://www.seanet.com/litlnemo/

Her Gig: Works for seanet as a WWW page developer and is sysop of the Slumberland BBS (up since 1991). She also sings in the band Wink and is into skating and Gaelic culture. Her site has a bunch of musical and campy links.

Quote: "I don't really look as yellow in real life as I do in the picture on this page, but it's an ID picture—what can I say?"

NAME: CYNSA BONORRIS

Website: "cynsa beans" http://www.well.com/user/cynsa/

Her Gig: Hosts the GenX topic on the WELL. Also a computer consultant, HTML designer, teacher, writer, and singer in an a capella group called Mary Schmary. Get a load of her close-up nose at this site!

Quote: "I was born in 1965 and remember the moon landing but not the assassination of President Kennedy. As a result, I'm a closet optimist, and my pathetic dreams of a peaceful and fruitful future for the planet and the human race should be excused."

NAME: BONNIE BURTON

Website: "Bonnie Burton's Shameless Self-Promotion Page"
http://uesu.Colorado.EDU/~burtonb/Home.html

Her Gig: Into Betty Page, platforms, and the *X Files*. She's a Web designer, and she created the Unofficial MTV Real World Home Page (http://128.138.144.71/Burton/real.html). She also uses her Home as a place to strut her resume and cover letter (hint: She needs a job! Hire her!).

Quote: "Cyberspace is a wonderful place to exploit, and I sure do abuse it!"

NAME: CARLA SINCLAIR (Me!)

Website: "The Net Chick Clubhouse"
http://www.cyborganic.com/People/carla/

Her Gig: Oh goody! Another chance to toot my own horn! Visit my awesome clubhouse, where you can play with my toys, like the Magic 8 Bra, and can even win a key to my secret diary. Once you're done with your romp, feel free to primp in my beauty parlor, and then crash in my office or entertainment lounge. See ya!

Quote: "Stop being such a priss! If you want it, you've gotta stomp a little harder."

Burns

Aliza Sherman's Webgrrl(TM)

IT'S CYBERGRRL!

Q : *What do Webgrrls, Cybersisters, and Digital Women all have in common?*

A : They're all related to Cybergrrl!

Jaunty, benevolent, omnipresent . . . Cybergrrl is the cartoon version of Aliza Sherman, whose "whole mission in life is to get more women online." With every working hour, Ms. Sherman ingeniously intertwines her philanthropic nature with her sharp business sense to help get chicks on the Net. She does whatever it takes to achieve her mission.

I was first wowed by Cybergrrl when I stumbled across her Webgrrls site (see page 75), a sizzling hotlist of women's Home Pages that she compiled and maintains. I feel fortunate to have experienced Webgrrls' super estrogen-charge when I was still new to the Web;

CONTINUED ON PAGE 83 • FOLLOW THE YELLOW

<CENTER> A HOME OF YOUR OWN </CENTER>

<FONT SIZE="+6"></FONT>

T<FONT SIZE="+6"></FONT>here's nothing wrong with slumming around the streets of the Web, taking shelter in Bianca's Shack (http://bianca.com) or prolonging your stay at one of the hospitable Homes lining the Webgrrl neighborhood (see pages 74-79). We've all been there. But the day comes when you want a place of your own, a place you can call Home. When that moment arrives, don't let intimidation hold you back. Building a Personal Home Page is much simpler than you may think.

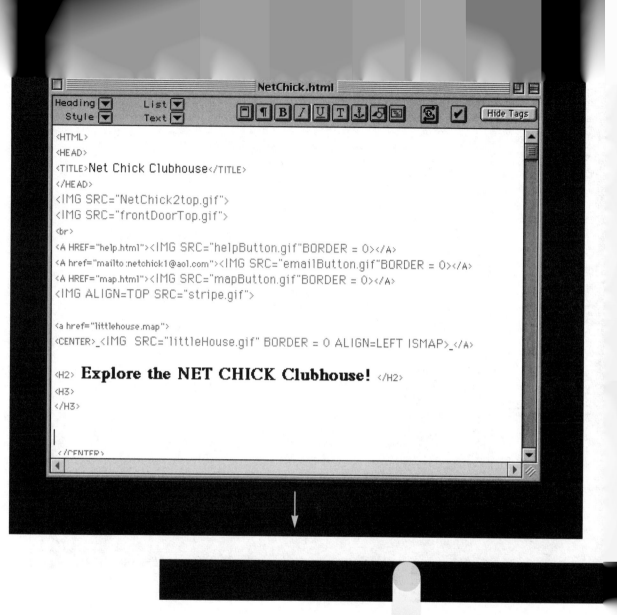

```
NetChick.html

Heading ▼    List ▼         □ ¶ B I U T ⤓ ◪ ▣    🅢  ☑   Hide Tags
Style ▼      Text ▼

<HTML>
<HEAD>
<TITLE>Net Chick Clubhouse</TITLE>
</HEAD>
<IMG SRC="NetChick2top.gif">
<IMG SRC="frontDoorTop.gif">
<br>
<A HREF="help.html"><IMG SRC="helpButton.gif"BORDER = 0></A>
<A href="mailto:netchick1@aol.com"><IMG SRC="emailButton.gif"BORDER = 0></A>
<A HREF="map.html"><IMG SRC="mapButton.gif"BORDER = 0></A>
<IMG ALIGN=TOP SRC="stripe.gif">

<a href="littlehouse.map">
<CENTER>_<IMG  SRC="littleHouse.gif" BORDER = 0 ALIGN=LEFT ISMAP>_</A>


<H2> Explore the NET CHICK Clubhouse! </H2>
<H3>
</H3>


</CENTER>
```

<UL> Programming, designing, finding a carrier, and schmoozing are the four components to getting your Home Page up and running.</UL>

<P>

<B>**Wait!**</B> Don't let the programming aspect turn you away. It's *easy*. Either find somebody to program your Web pages for you (it's the newest hot employment trend at the moment, so finding a Home builder is easy; getting her to do it for free is the tricky part), *or* teach yourself how to program HTML (hypertext mark-up language—the formatting codes used to script your page), which is truly a cinch. It only takes

approximately $19.95 to buy one of the many HTML programming books and about an hour of your time to learn how elementary it is.

Designing, or interior decorating, is where the creative fun begins. Visually you can do just about anything. Here are a few basic aesthetic ideas:

● **Wallpaper** your pad with a "background" so that the backdrop of each Web page is pink, a psychedelic swirl, tiger stripes, or whatever. (Go to Backgrounds at http://www.yahoo.com/Computers/Internet/World_Wide_Web/Programming/Backgrounds/ for inspiration.) Each room can be a different color or pattern, so mix, match, and experiment. But don't overdo it—make sure you can still read the text on top of the background.

the feminine current of the Net ran through me right from the get-go.

But Webgrrls is more than just a digital site. Sherman holds frequent face-to-face Webgrrl meetings in New York for women who are programmers and designers for the Internet. (Other Webgrrl groups have formed in Washington, D.C., and San Francisco.) Why is it necessary to hold meetings that cater specifically to women? "It gives women a voice and opportunity. In NYC there's the New York New Media Association, which is a great new association, but you go to one of their gatherings and it's 90 percent men. The 10 percent women are these fantastically talented, dynamic, powerful women who stand in this room and can't even see each other. Then I bring them to the Webgrrl meetings, and it's a whole different world. We sit in a circle, it's not super crowded, it's not hot and sweaty with people talking about things other than business. We just sit in a circle and talk about what we're doing."

Then there is Cybersisters, another group that Sherman hosts—but this one meets only in cyberspace. Rather than focusing on business, this charitable forum is for women artists and writers who are involved with the Web, and it offers these sisters free exhibition and publishing Net space. Way to go Cybergrrl! To subscribe to the mailing list, just send email to majordomo@pmedia.com. Leave the subject blank (except AOL members, who must type a "." in the subject line), and write "subscribe cyber-sisters" in the body of the message. Make sure it's spelled exactly like that or it won't go through.

Ms. Sherman's most involved undertaking at the

CONTINUED ON PAGE 84 • FOLLOW THE YELLOW

- Add photos and graphics, especially personal ones. It's always gratifying to see who's running the joint and what her friends and belongings look like. After all, you're appealing to the voyeurs of the Net! Keep in mind, however, that too many images will hinder the downloading process (and visitors will want to flee!), so don't go overboard.

- After exploring other Homes, use the best design ideas you've seen and drum up some original concepts of your own. Some of the finest sites are the freshest, most original ones. (If you don't feel you have much of an artistic flare, then get really intimate with us. Tell us your secrets. We'll be so drawn in we won't notice the crummy furnishings.)

CYBERGRRL'S TIP
to Commercial Page Creators

"Something I always say in my classes is 'Your Web page is not an island.' The whole purpose of the Web is to be interconnected, interlinked, to be reaching out to others, and to have others reach out to you. To have your site isolated is a complete disservice to every single thing that this medium is supposed to do. The most important thing about creating something on the Internet, even if it's advertising your business or service, is to create value. Don't just get up there and put up information about your company. Give something back to the community at large."

To add value, Cybergrrl suggests adding links to other spots, sponsoring a charitable site by putting them on your Page, or including a database of women's resources. ... Get the picture?

moment is her self-started company, CG Internet Media (yep, CG stands for Cybergrrl). CGIM has a two-part agenda: 1) to develop online communication and marketing strategies for corporations and nonprofit organizations, and 2) to develop interactive multimedia products.

The first part basically means that CGIM shows clients how to set up a presence on the Internet or the Web. It teaches them how to take advantage of all available resources to promote their business, organization, services, or the fact that they have a Website. You can compare CGIM to a PR marketing firm, but one which exclusively uses online resources. The beautiful part of Sherman's enterprise is that although she enthusiastically embraces capitalism (which is great, don't get me wrong), she transcends its ultimate goal of making a profit. CGIM is geared toward working with large corporations, but it also does pro bono work for charities, women's issues, and women-owned businesses. Some of

CONTINUED ON PAGE 86 • FOLLOW THE YELLOW

Other tips for creating an alluring Home (not necessarily aesthetic but just as important) are:

- Have a section that talks about YOU. Getting confidential is one thing that differentiates a Personal Home Page from product- or corporate-based sites.

- Let US interact with each other by incorporating: a bulletin board or chat area, games, polls or surveys that will later have the answers posted, a Q & A center, etc.

- Include an email center where we can send comments. This will help you determine what's working and what ain't.

Think of your Home Page as a party house. People are constantly coming and going, and whole reason for visiting is to mingle with others and to be either entertained or intellectually charge want to kick ass, be a mutator. Listen to comments, and constantly evolve and redefine your Home. stagnant sites suck!

Once your pages are set up and programmed, you need to find someone wit server—a special computer that will store your files and allow Web surfers to access them. If you are using a service provider like AOL, Prodigy, or the WELL, they will put your pages up for free. Otherwi cost you a small monthly fee (unless you have the right kind of friends or bartering chips). I'm using

H⊙T·SITES:
Grrrl E-zines

from GEEKGIRL

Zines pulse to the rhythm of the street, bringing you closer to now-culture than any other type of publication. And the remarkable thing about E-zines is that anyone with a modem can access them. It doesn't matter if you live in Pigsknuckle or some remote island off of Rarotonga—you can get your hands on the same stuff the city-slicking cool girls are reading. My favorites are of course the grrrly zines, which are by far the smartest and sassiest pages out there. I only wish there were more. Here are the few that I've found online:

Electric ANIMA
http://www.io.com/~ixora/

"Technological fun with a feminine twist . . . not for the vaginally-feared!" I love it! Co-editors Ixora and Effluvia are so damn cool. (I talk about one of these women in my Webgrrls section, but she's in disguise here, so mum's

--more-->

her pro bono clients include: Avon Breast Cancer Crusade (http://www.PMedia.COM/Avon/avon.html); MidMarch Press (http://www.cybergrrl.com/info/midmarch/); and PrePARE (self-defense for women) (http://www.cybergrrl.com/health/prepare/).

As for CGIM's second agenda, "In terms of product, I want to create places and resources for women in cyberspace. As long as they feel they have a place to go or things that they can find that pertain to them, then they have a reason to be online."

Sherman has created two products, or services, through CGIM so far. Her first one is SafetyNet, a valuable Website of resources dealing with domestic violence (see page 207). The second one is Women.Org (http:www.women.org), a searchable database of women-related resources on the Internet that helps chicks map out their cybertrips. And this is where you'll find Digital Women, a nonprofit organization that helps hook up women and girls with organizations that can offer them cheap or free technology training and equipment. Now there is no excuse for women to remain unplugged!

Sherman describes Net women as creative, innovative, and adventurous, and says in a flabbergasted tone,

Cyborganic (http://www.cyborganic.com/), which may be a good starting point for your search.

Finally, schmooze, schmooze, schmooze. No one will visit you if they don't know where you are. Become chummy with other Home owners so that you can swap links. Contact Cool Site of the Day (http://cool.infi.net), Yahoo (http://www.yahoo.com/), and other search engines, and see if they'll add you to their database. Find zines, mailing lists, and appropriate Usenet groups to promote your site. Market yourself properly, and your hit-odometer will spin itself out of orbit (that's a good thing!). ▪

"The fact that lots of women are still not getting online is just flooring me! When women just look at me with this blank look, I'm like, 'Wait a minute, what is keeping you from this?' It's such an amazing resource and wealth of information and way of connecting and networking and organizing and reaching out."

Although I think it's a little farfetched, Sherman blames the media for women's reluctance to get online. "Not to get all huffy about it, but I really think that the media, which is obviously male dominated, is setting out to dispel this Internet thing to keep women off."

And so, as Sherman wrote in *Ms. Magazine*, if we're going to see more Net Chicks, we need to squash the five myths which are now keeping women away from modems: 1) It's too hard; 2) It's too expensive; 3) It's too dangerous; 4) There's nothing in it for me personally; 5) There's nothing in it for me professionally.

"I want to tell women, hey, open your eyes, stop buying into all this dreck. Get online and have completely equal footing with men around the world."

Cybergrrl is always finding new ways to get her message across. If you keep your eyes peeled, you'll soon see her and Aliza's new character, Webgrrl (modeled after Aliza's sister, Leah), in the comic book and CD-ROM she is currently working on. Does this grrrl ever sleep?!? •

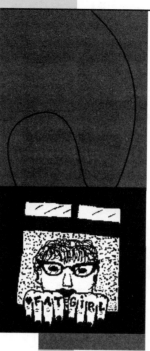

the word). Every article in this chick zine kept me rapt from beginning to end. In their first issue, Effluvia writes about her titillating experience meandering through Fredrick's of Hollywood, Sophie explains how boxing is a great workout for girls and tells us how to get started, and Carla gives us the lowdown on biking in Death Valley. All sorts of other interesting tidbits and links to other women's Websites. If you like the zine you can submit stuff to them online.

FAT GIRL—"THE ZINE FOR FAT DYKES AND THE WOMEN WHO WANT THEM"
http://www.icsi.berkeley.edu/ ~polack/fg/
A fatter version of this San Francisco based zine exists in hardcopy form, but you can get a peek at *Fat Girl* here. It includes articles on (big) corsets, the propaganda-spewing diet industries, and growing up as a fat kid, as well as comic reviews, a list of recommended books, mags, zines, clothing catalogs, movies, etc., and samples of back issues. *FG* also gives you links to other fat-related sites. Editor Max Airborne and her "eclectic collective of Fat Dykes" encourage online readers to submit their fat experiences and photos to this enticingly forthright E-zine.

GEEKGIRL
http://www.next.com.au/spyfood/ geekgirl/002manga/index.html
Interviews with Kathy Acker (titled "Pussy and the Art of Motorcycle Maintenance") and St. Jude (about women and modems) are just some of the tough girls you'll read about in this Aussie rag. Other goodies include a must-have hotlist, and articles on "Electronic Witches," cryptography, alien Schwa stuff, and Noam Chomsky. Editress Rosie Cross does a great job of blending chicks, tech, and pop culture into a smooth swirl, and had me printing most of the articles so that I could give them further attention later. •

(About the *geekgirl* Webzine:) "Molding an archetype for the online woman warrior."—June Cohen, *HotWired*

INTERVIEW

ROSIE (X) CROSS

Physically based in Australia, Rosie Cross is the geekgirl, queen of "the world's first cyberfeminist zine, to go where no grrrl zine has gone before." She's played all over the media spectrum, producing radio shows (on stuff like cryptography and dance-rave culture), producing and writing for TV (her latest gig was for ABC about cyberpunks and hackers), and constantly showing up in print. I was especially impressed with "Modem Grrrl," a fun Q&A she did with former Mondo 2000 editor St. Jude (Rosie was the Q, Jude the A) that originally appeared in Wired *magazine. But all of the above has been put aside, since* geekgirl, *her Webzine (she quickly corrected me when I called it an E-zine), is now demanding her full attention.*

I'm not sure which is sassier, geekgirl *or Ms. Cross. She's wickedly sharp, mischievous, animated, and never lets a word pass unchecked, twisting and tossing it back at you with a whole new meaning. You've gotta wake up pretty early (Australian time) to sneak anything by this madam of electronic zinedom. Being eighteen hours ahead of me for starters, I knew telephoning her would be futile. So we opted for the email interview instead.*

What is a geekgirl?

> Just like when Ricki Lake said in that movie (*Crybaby*), "Our buzzoooms are our weapons," geekgirls say, "Our machines are ours." Geekgirls like machines, 'specially computers. They like the feel of keyboards blasting the unexpected and unpredictable. They wanna get history straight, they wanna subvert the mainstream. Boring ol' mainstream. Geekgirls like swimming in

ether, they like dippin', divin', & dunkin', they like the goop melange of the Internet. They investigate the murky and sometimes mean worlds of post-modernity and the obsession with technology. They like to understand these worlds as much as they wanna create new ones. Fun ones, fanciful, individual stars.

> **Why did you decide to do geekgirl as a Webzine?**

> Well, it kinda made sense, didn't it? Geekgirls' motto is that ol' St. Jude line, "Grrrls need modems." So, have modem—use it, grrrl! We wanted to get that zine on the Web and get the girls to follow! Sure, though, we've still got our hard copy for the gals and boys who don't have their modems yet, and that's important, too. But we mostly like the immediacy, the color, the cool, the experimentation of the Web version. Heh, it's a cool place to be, and an important place for grrrls to grab onto, get a foothold and help others to come on up.

> **How big is the Net scene in Australia? Especially with the girls.**

> Australia is the hub of a lot of radicalism and creativity. We've got lots of girls breaking loose right now. Really, it's just like jailhouse rock 'cept the chorus has a little more shape. Girls in Oz are tuff just like you American chicks, 'cos we got a lot of open space. They say that countries like Australia and America capture the psyche of adventurers, and did you know supposedly even serial killers? Some correlation with driving through them expansive motor ways and obsessing about machines. Well, there ain't no bigger stretch than the Internet, so us gals and I guess the occasional serial killer are having a ball. Warning: Don't pick hitchhikers up on the Net! Natural Born Geekgirls! *geekgirl* features lots of Australian women who wanna mix it up in cyberspace.

> **Tell me about yourself and how you got involved with the digital culture.**

> RosieX blurb . . . culture, aww, I thought it was a subcul-ture. Looks like I've got to find something else to do now. ;-) Hmmm, well I had a crush on someone about five years ago

and found out they ran a bulletin board. I thought, "Heh, an electronic space for text talkers and exhibitionists; that'll suit me." So, like most geekgirls/journos/broadcasters/video makers/radio producers, I thought to myself, hmmm sounds good. Bought a reliable secondhand 2,400 from a legal firm, which didn't know what to do with an over-order of 500 tools of the revolution, and I was away! Like a big bowed beauty with a magnum of champagne slapped on her backside at a christening and a bon voyage "may you never be the same again," I chugged off.

There I was the first day thinking, "Ooops, damn, shit, you know, this is hard, what have I got myself into?" But I persevered. After a couple of months the sysop found me annoying, and I found myself enamored no longer by them but the technology. Crushing as it was to find out not everyone got my sense of humor and didn't understand my motto "Speak now and forever more shoot yourself in the foot," and getting really sick of the company of really boring conservative righteous sexist bloody men who really needed to get a life, I found myself wanting wanting wanting to develop the skills of independence. I also discovered that it had dawned on me in the process that as a little grrrl, how come no one ever taught me, or showed me, or encouraged me with machines? I always liked 'em, always, so I also decided to digitally make up for lost time. Rules, blerk! What did anyone ever do without digital?

> **Where are geekgirls headed?**

> Well, it's so popular, it's taken over my life. I quit my bread-and-butter job to devote all my energy to *geekgirl*. I really enjoy knowing it's a worthwhile thing to do, and some of the designs and images are so fabulous. I now spend a lot of time designing stickers, T-shirts, etc., 'cos everyone keeps asking me to do them and they are really cool pressies for people just getting on board. There's no stopping a geekgirl with the tenacity of a Taurean. I am out there doing it. Lisa Pears and I will continue to work on the hard copy version, 'cos we believe in distributing information for people who can't access it any other way, and for those people who are teeter-tottering on the edge of taking the plunge, *geekgirl* is a crucial element in the process of demystifying computers and being online, especially for women. The Website will be changed more often, the look and feel of the project will definitely keep changing depending on new software and authoring capabilities. The content or focus will remain similar and we might even start up a *geekboy* for all those guys who feel left out. <smile>.

> **Um, I'm glad you answered that, but actually, I was asking where the actual geek girls are headed. Do you have the gumption to answer that?**

> Gumption is a brand of floor polish and we don't have any about at the mo'! Back to housecleaning those files.

> **Rosie! You're a brat! >;-)**

> Why thank you, Carla, you say the nicest things. •

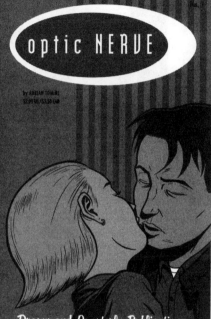

HOT SITES:
Comix vs. Comics

r e v i e w s

When I was younger I was a devout comics reader, never missing an issue of Archies, Broom Hilda, or Richie Rich. I didn't even know alternative stuff—or comix—existed until college, when I got my hands on Love and Rockets #10 (and thereupon obsessively collected every back issue AND some original art from the first L&R). Raunchy, fresh, real, sexy, grotesque . . . comix are definitely my bag.

UNDERGROUND COMICS
http://www.hooked.net:80/buzznet/
pulp/comics/index.html

Comix connoisseur Michelle Anderson (she's been hanging in the zine scene for a long time now) reviews some of my faves, including Dame Darcy's *Meatcake*, Ariel Bordeax's *Deep Girl*, Adrian Tomine's *Optic Nerve*, and Shannon Wheeler's *Too Much Coffee Man*. From each review you can jump to the artist's sample page.

TANK GIRL
http://www.dcs.qmw.ac.uk/
~bob/stuff/tg/

This "unofficial" site created by a man named Bob is *Tank Girl* intensive! The best page (and the longest to download) is the *TG* picture gallery, which exhibits a bunch of this punk fighter-girl's portraits—as a cartoon from her comic strip, in the flesh from her movie, as a kid, and counterfeited by a couple of *Tank Girl* clones. Besides reading everything you've ever wanted to know about *Tank Girl*, you can also check out the comic magazine *Deadline* that introduced her to the world, find out about her easy and hard-to-get merchandise, or jump to barely TG-related links (like how to

—more→

make homemade jewelry, or the Home Pages of the bands who strummed to her movie). While you're at it, click on Bob's name and visit his Home Page, which will give you tons of other chick-like links. This is almost as action-packed as the Girl herself!

**WONDER WOMAN
WWW PAGE**
http://www.io.org/~arhythm/
phpl.cgi?ww/ww.htm

The cheese factor is high and oh-so-yummy! I spent way too much time reliving the '70s television series *Wonder Woman* by reading each episode's summary, taking in photos of Lynda Carter in her patriotic garb, and the very best part—downloading the audio file of the theme song which comes with written lyrics so you can sing along. I was really jammin'! After I got over the nostalgic rush of my adolescent TV days, I got a kick out of the old reprints of the *Wonder Woman* comic book covers. It's interesting to see how her costume has progressed from a flouncy skirt in the '40s to the sparkly bicentennial leotard to the black bicycle shorts and combat boots of today. For more trivia and amusing observations on Her, try: Wonder Woman Home Page http://www.knowsys-sw.com/ Mike/WonderWoman/.

--more-->

TiPS

on Doing Your Own Webzine

"I think like with anything in the online world you have to work out a few factors. A reliable, friendly, and supportive service provider is the most important thing to organize. Then you've got to sort out hardware (fast modems, enough gig, ram, etc.) to put the whole thing together. And as is the case with everything, enjoy what you do or it's not worthwhile and it shows. Try to be different, and be yourself—it'll make it unique and popular!"   —RosieX, *geekgirl*

"Tips? Gosh…that's hard. When I started doing *Anonymous* I had no clue there was this big huge zine underground. The only zines I had ever seen were Milwaukee (where I am from) rave zines and the zine of the month in *Sassy* magazine. What I'm saying is that I do not consider myself a zine 'pro,' so the tips I will give are just things that work for me, and I'm still experimenting myself…

1) Don't worry about what others will think about your articles...just write. People don't have to read it if they aren't interested.

2) Pictures! Pictures! Pictures! I like lots of pictures. I think photos of people and random silly drawings and such within the text keeps the reader more interested. I need to do more of that myself on the *Anonymous* site.

3) Change and add things as often as you can. Write more articles, put up more pictures, keep it as interesting as possible so people will visit your site often and not get bored with it.

4) If you have files readers can download make sure you put how big the file is...People may want to know how long it will take to download that .gif of your brother sticking straws up his nose. (I still haven't even done this myself but I plan on it real soon!!)"

— Miss Wiggles, *Anonymous*

ALTERNATIVE COMICS: REVIEWS

http://bronze.ucs.indiana.edu/~mfragass/myrev.html

Some random guy, Mike, reviews the very comix I read: Megan Kelso's *Girl Hero*, The Hernandez Bros' *Love and Rockets*, Mack White's *Mutant Book of the Dead*, *Deep Girl*, and more. Gotta love it!

DONNA BARR

http://www.tooluser.com/comics/barr/

Check out Donna Barr's pages and admire her pen-and-ink drawings that illustrate elaborate tales. Her titles include *The Desert Peach*, *Stinz*, and *Hader and the Colonel*, which have unconventional plots. Wander through her art gallery and flip through her catalog to see what goods are available.

KATHLEEN BENNETT'S COMIX REVIEWS

http://weber.u.washington.edu/~keb/comix.rev.html

The thing I don't like about Kathleen's reviews is that there are no graphics. Shameful! But I do like her taste— more of the above, plus Chris Ware's *Acme Novelty Company*, *Prick* Comics, and other delightful gems.

YAHOO—COMIC BOOKS

http://www.yahoo.com/Entertainment/Comics/Comic_Books/

This index doesn't cover everything, but it's got more than a hundred comic links that'll keep you busy for days. •

St. Jude

Irresistible Future Hacker

Jude Milhon, "the patron saint of systems programming," was hacking comput-ers before the word "hacker" was even around. By the time she became manag-ing editor and the "Irresponsible Journalism" columnist for Mondo 2000, *programming, online systems, and cryptography (encrypting messages to keep them private from lookie-loos) were ancient knowledge for the Saint. A member of the privacy-protecting group Cypherpunks (a name which she coined), Jude plays with encoded words while she works on decoding the next millennium—she calls herself a future hacker.*

Since she left Mondo 2000 *a couple of issues ago, she's been a writing machine. She just finished* The Cyberpunk Handbook—The Real Cyberpunk Fakebook *(Random House) and* How to Mutate and Take Over the World *(Ballantine), both co-written with R.U. Sirius. Although I've run into St. Jude a number of times at parties in San Francisco, we've never really conversed. Being so much more sophisticated than me in the area of technology, and being so cute in her tough leathers and with handcuffs dangling from her belt buckle, I was a little too timid to make small talk with her. So when I emailed her to ask for this inter-view, she said she'd be happy to do it (and ended up being totally cool and friendly), but for a moment she rekindled my timidity with this response:*

i'm very very o god

sob

agggghh

very very busy right now...

snrrrfff

sorry

Bart Nagel

>**Oh dear! I hope I'm not the one who makes you snap! What's been keeping you so BUSY, to the point of tears?**

>No tears. I'm writing two, three, maybe four books, and I'm happy for the first time in my life. It's my fifth decade—and the first four were agonizing. Books and Zoloft have made me a happy woman.

Heh, that >snivel< and all, those were smileys. I've spent my life around people who used smileys even in their spoken conversations—you know, finishing a sentence with a monotone "sob," or "whimp," or "shudder." Nerds, we're talking nerdz-rootz.

>**What was it like being not only one of the first hackers but one of the first hacker chicks?**

>Truthfully—glorious. We had the best of everything at Community Memory Project, aside from being in a collective which synergized the worst features of marriage, slavery, and living in a very small town.

>**Ooo, that sounds kind of weird. Explain the Community. Was it a commune? And what town was it in?**

>Community Memory Project was a political technical project. Steve Levy's *Hackers* had a fair bit of detail on it, much of it wrong, because we couldn't be honest about some of the financing, or some of the internal dynamics, which were often brutal. That was the marriage aspect—we couldn't talk about the dodgy or abusive stuff to outsiders. The small town aspect was that we were all living together for too much of our time, that we had almost no lives outside the project, and that we lived and worked in a slurry of gossip and factionalism, ugh, both of which I fucking hate. (I wanted it to be a HAPPY marriage…) And slavery, and little town.

The slavery aspect was that we were so certain that we were doing the good work—and the ONLY good work at that time—that we couldn't leave the project, however intolerable the human situation became. Because we were IT. We were the only people trying to create a humane technology to bend the future into something more humane. We were future hacking, for real. Our immediate present, however, was ironically inhumane. Horrible, at times. We were all getting the same pay—the secretary (Chris Carlsson of *Processed World*), the programmers, designers, everybody, all fifteen or so of us—and we ran by consensus in our good weeks and majority rule in the worst.

Aside from that, we knew we were doing tech for the right reasons, we were on the leading edge of design, the future was ours.

I've always loved the feeling of being on the leading edge of anything. Like being a bowsprit, leaning into the wind and feeling the future stream over you!!!!! And for a mostly het girl person, it's certainly where the boys are. As a female, I was a man among men.

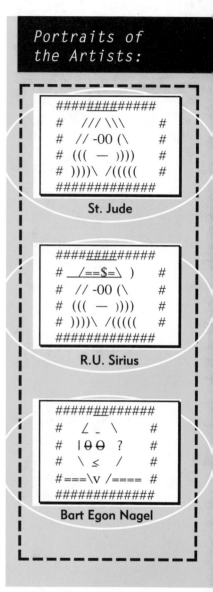

Portraits of the Artists:

St. Jude

R.U. Sirius

Bart Egon Nagel

>**What was this humane technology you were creating?? I'm still unclear as to what this project was about.**

>Back in the seventies we were operating on the mistaken idea that computer power was going to stay unaffordable for ordinary people. We originally got a castoff huge mainframe and the idea was to put it at the disposal of "the community," by providing the technology that would allow an online local community to create itself. Community Memory was supposed to be storefront computer setups where you could enter a virtual town-meeting hall and get into all aspects of that online community—bulletin boards and Usenet-type discussion groups, all reachable by a search on keywords. We got bogged down in endless database and front-end development, and hardware upgrades, and trying to sell commercial software to support the political project, and on and on.

>**Wow, sounds like you were ten years ahead of the times! How did the boys treat you (and you them)?**

>When I first started programming, in the late sixties, it was in the real world—Horn & Hardart in Manhattan. Our Catholic boss went out of his way to grind me, as the only woman programmer and a non-trad sort at that. He'd snidely make me fetch coffee at meetings, etc.—"women's work" stuff. I made horrid coffee, spilled it, "SORry, not used to this, really, not my field, heh." Sort of reverse camp-acting like a male in the situation. Embarrassed the fuck out of most of the guys. When I'd learned enough to get a real job, I left. In those days programmers changed jobs every six months, always trading up.

I got hired by a high-level software design company, and in the tech community the situation was reversed. The males usually treated me like a blue rose, you know, a precious freak.

As for my treatment of them, I really like intelligent males. And sexually, you know, we've all gotten lucky, here in Nerdland. Intelligence seems to drive libido here—just think of all those juicy, throbbing, oversized thinking-organs…o god o god. And it's statistically favorable to women. Other female mathematicians and programmers say the same. Maybe nobody knew what to do with us in high school, but from college on we were belles of the ball. And because we were operating with different models, we girl-nerds tended to be bisexual.

>**I don't get it. What do you mean by different models? And why did you girls tend to be bisexual?**

>Me, personally? Just lucky, I guess. I get hypnotized by male AND female pheromones. And it's about operating on alternative models. …See, when I was in the third grade in Virginia, and our teacher told us about Tibetan polyandry, I said (to myself) YESSsss! Why in hell would a pre-pube react like

that? It wasn't a sexual reaction—I didn't even know what sex was—it was a sort of cultural kensho, a breakthrough into weirdness. Then later I started reading science fiction in junior high, and when I came across Olaf Stapledon's *Odd John*, I had the same reaction: YES! *Odd John* was about mutant Homo sapiens sapiens sapiens, the next species, who didn't form couples. They lived in polymorphous perversity; they all had it off with one another just as it occurred to them. Odd John is like reading Nietzsche—it makes you want to prove yourself by loving the future and repudiating what is currently all–too–human…

And later, *Stranger in a Strange Land* was just icing on that same cake. Heinlein showed humans being intellectually and sexually polymorphous—not by physical but by cultural mutation. Notice that I was bent by books, by ideas, not by experiences or people. The utopian ideas came first, and the personnel sign up later, maybe, if you're lucky.

People of all sexes in the nerd community brought themselves up this way, via the same books. Notice I keep saying nerd community. I feel there is such a thing, and it's the only community I've got.

> **Is the nerd community as fun as it used to be now that being a nerd is a hip thing for the mainstream to emulate?**

> Egad, outsiders still don't make it IN, do they? The nerd community is as it always was— polymorphous yet cliquish. Strange, but true. And I feel the same closeness as always to that strange subset of humanity. I love people who live for the future, who live to reconstruct what human being is. I identify with and cherish future hackers…I LOVE NERDS.

> **What were you interested in, growing up, and how did you get into computers?**

> Science fiction, to both questions. My father was a free-lance writer, and we were dirt poor in everything but books. I read Freud when I was around ten, which is not a great idea. You get bent in ways that are magical but conventional— the worst. Kraft-Ebbing, the Encyclopedia Brittanica. And since my male relatives were reading science fiction, in junior high, I got into that. From that point I was divided—I wanted to write, I wanted to paint, but because of

Heinlein and Asimov, tech was more glamorous than the arts. Later, programming seemed the ideal synthesis. Programming was like composing sonnets—better— you can't proof-test a sonnet.

> **How did you get into programming?**

> I got into that when I was at a low spot in my life. I was in recovery from politics and the Civil Rights movement, hiding out in Richmond, VA with my little kid. I was burnt out on politics and out of hope. Efrem Lipkin, my eighteen-year-old nerd boyfriend, was writing me from Antioch, and gave me a Turing machine problem. And I couldn't get it out of my head until I solved it. Another breakthrough: Eureka! AHA! I can DO this shit! And moreover, I LOVE thinking about this stuff.

So I went to the Richmond library and got the green book that people used to start with, *Teach Yourself Fortran*, and that was that. Efrem talked me into looking for a job in Manhattan. $85 a week, Jr. Programmer. There I was. I loved it. It was terrifying, but I loved it.

> **I loved your column Irresponsible Journalism. Tell me about your experience as a writer for *Mondo 2000*.**

> Heh. As a writer? As an editor it was sheer hell. I didn't have much time or confidence for writing, anyway. I could put out a column every three months, fine, but even that scared me. In the beginning I was always writing about self-experimentation with smart drugs and creativity extenders. Getting the facts exactly right but making it funny. When I extrapolated from fact I said so, but I got apprenticed in the Emergency Rooms of a couple of hospitals. You get used to seeing medical protocols as chord changes that you riff off of. I took it from there, and branched out to cryptography and sex and other tech. But the early stuff set my method and my motive— I just want to tell people the possible truth, in ways that they won't necessarily believe. Bahaha.

> **Tell me about your work with cryptography, and how did you come up with the term "Cypherpunks"?**

> I don't do any work with cryptography. I do play with it. …I use PGP (Pretty Good Privacy), which is good fun, and I hang out with the more local Cypherpunks. Some of us meet at a Thai brunch at a Berkeley Buddhist temple every Sunday—home Thai cooking under awnings in a little courtyard behind a Queen Anne monk house. Great fun. And there's the Cypherpunks' physical meeting in Silicon Valley the second Saturday of the month. Sometimes they crank up the M-bone (super high-speed Internet network) so that the Cypherpunks' meeting in Boston or DC or wherever can participate via the world's most expensive conference call.

I came up with the name one morning while I was ruminating on the group. We'd just had our first meeting and it was boggling my mind unceasingly.

I was editing something for *Mondo* about cyberpunk and the name hit me like a meteorite—Cypherpunk!! (with a Y, of course!) I was literally staggered, then I was staggering around laughing. (I write like that, too. I think up stuff and laugh at it through five or six edits.) I suggested the name at the second physical meeting and everybody PHREEKED...that is, they liked it. Adopted instantly. At intervals, some of the guys on the list have complained— Cypherpunks is a silly, degrading name, and the World will not take us seriously. These people always get shouted down. Cypherpunks IS a silly, degrading name, and the World fails to take us seriously at its own peril.

> **It's a great name! And so are the names of your books. Tell me about them.**

> The spirit of Cypherpunks inspired me while I was writing *How to Mutate and Take Over the World*. Dada revolution, virtual revolution, instant Underground! *The Cypherpunks' Virtual Underground* is one of the heroes of *Mutate*. (R.U. Sirius and I co-authored it along with our posse on the Net.)

The other book is *The Cyberpunk Handbook—The Real Cyberpunk Fakebook*. It is so funny...I still crack up thinking about some of the stuff. My boyfiend [sic] is on the cover—Eric Hughes, real Cypherpunk—with Tiffany Lee Brown, real cybergrrl. The book's a satire, but they're very real. Actually, the book is real too. It's a peek into the nerd/hack/phreak scene that I've been living in and around all my life. And the book is a piece of agitprop. It's a DIY, how-to sort of Anarchist Cookbook for hacker-mind, exploratory intelligence. I hope thousands of twelve-year-olds become corrupted by it and take up lives of discreet and highly intelligent outlawry. I even told them how to corrupt their younger siblings and couslings— make hackers out of THEM...heheheheh.

With both books we're operating on this premise: Every generation that grows up normal is a loss to the planet. Ah, but with each new generation we have the hope of corrupting them into something cooler than what was and is. Cultural mutation is our whole purpose, our imperative. That is— well, yes, I might as well say it—mutate now! •

Cypherpunks IS a silly, degrading name, and the World fails to take us seriously at its own peril.

JILL ATKINSON:
WIRED WITH
A SMUT SHACK

W hen Jill Atkinson created "Electronic
Publishing" as her major at the Rochester
Institute of Technology in New York, her
colleagues thought she was nuts. "Everybody
laughed at me. They thought it was such a crazy

major. They were all guys whose fathers owned printing companies, and they were like, 'Publishing without paper? That's so ridiculous!'"

But this chick knew that something was brewing in cyberspace, and after turning her back on the more obvious options of signing on with CD-ROM companies or pre-production houses, *HotWired* (see sidebar) reared its galvanizing head and snapped Ms. Atkinson up as soon as she contacted them.

Jillo, as she's known to her electronic peers, is now production manager of *HotWired*'s Renaissance section, which covers all types of global artists. Ms. Atkinson says the advantage of a multimedia publication over a paper one is that it brings you closer to the featured artists. For example, instead of just reading about a choreographer, you also get a chance to see the dancer's work through QuickTime video clips and audio files.

And *HotWired* makes sure to represent both commercial art and the work of edgier street-level maestros. "We have the chance to cover all these crazy artists that no one's ever heard of, and then right next to them we'll put up something more famous like the photographs of John Waters. It breaks down the barriers of who's famous and who's not. Everyone becomes famous."

Atkinson prefers working for a Web rag over a paper publication, saying that the biggest advantage is

BUSTER KEATON: THE MAN WHO FELL TO EARTH

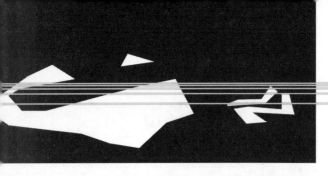

HOT SITE:
biancaTroll
Productions

JILL ATKINSON: WIRED WITH A SMUT SHACK *continued*

"not having a press date to blow." With traditional print magazines, she says it can cost $20,000 for every day over deadline, since foregoing a scheduled day is costly to the printer. Of course there is no printer to contend with when you're publishing online.

Yes, *Hot Wired* is definitely hip and happening, but it's Bianca's Smut Shack (see sidebar) that first turned me on to Atkinson. She created her voluptuous street-culture site with friends Dave Thau and Chris Miller before all three of them became employed by *Hot Wired* (which has since generously put the Shack on their T1 connected server). They formed a company five or six years ago called biancaTroll Productions after "this really wild night. We were up in a cabin, drinking a lot, and who knows what else, and we were running all around, acting really crazy. Then we woke up the next morning with Post-it notes all over the house that said biancaTroll, biancaTroll, biancaTroll. ...We're not sure how we started that, but it grew into the Smut Shack."

She says the Shack was their "fun" project before they got "real jobs," and that it now pretty much runs itself. When I speculated with some disappointment that there probably wasn't a real Bianca (I had built her up in my head to be this sexy slutty tough femme fatale), Atkinson set me straight. "We had this vision of Bianca, and then we met a woman named Bianca and asked her to be our muse. So it's more of a spiritual Bianca with this physical person we found later." A prime example of life imitating art! What Atkinson loves about her work with the Shack as well as at *Hot Wired* is that no one stands over her shoulder—she's able to "print" just about anything that fires her up. "The cool thing about the Web is that you can totally self-publish, and I think *Hot Wired* is really into pushing the edges of the Net, and testing the boundaries of what's okay." She thinks *Hot Wired* wants to be a

continued on page 104

Just because I adore my grrrly zines doesn't mean I can't groove to the slicker world of magazines. While I love E-zines for their street-level sensibilities, financially supported or company-owned E-mags make me happy because they come out regularly, and the good ones have high-end graphics. If you don't believe me, check these out!

BUZZ ONLINE

http://www.buzzmag.com/
This review would've been in my Stylin' chapter over a year ago. But that was before *LA Style* became *Buzz*, which now covers pop culture, enter-tainment, media, and politics. Better known in its paper form on the news-stands, this rag is also online. It is bright, hip, and innovative. My favorite section is their "literary salon," held live from LA's famous/notorious hotel Chateau Marmont, where they invite authors to interact with online partici-pants. They're the first Website to use a "CU-SeeMe" video to bring this and other major events to the Net.

URBAN DESIRES

"An Interactive Magazine of Metropolitan Passions"
http://desires.com
I just read issue 1.2, and I'm impressed! The design of *UD* is deli-cious, with lots of pinks and reds, fancy handwriting, and a clean, sharp layout. Everything I read tickled my brain, from a wonderfully long interview with Camille Paglia ("Sex, Prostitution and Pornography") to "Vera's Flirting Tips for Boys Who Want to Be Girls" to "Understanding Barbie-Phobia." There are also lots of fun tidbits on food, fashion, books, music, and toys. But it's not just a passive read. An interactive

---more--->

piece I really enjoyed had you "Poke an Eye, See an Outfit, Read a Resolution." Just like they suggest, you click on one of around fifteen eyes that are collaged together, which then brings you to the owner of the eye (a full-body shot) with her/his name, occupation, and resolution. Simple but engaging.

BUZZNET

http://www.hooked.net:80/buzznet/

Buzznet makes me happy. It's so much fun to look at! The table of contents consists of an image map of retro clip art with a '50s muted color scheme. Click on the cute icon that says "beats" and get a slice of the music scene; click on "pulp" and read about comics, underground magazines, and poetry; "gallery" will take you to some interesting photojournalistic pieces, etc. I was told by one of the founders—Lior, who's now at *FAD* (below)—that *Buzznet* was "given to a bunch of kids." Whoever these kids are, I really dig their street sensibility and nose for what's up.

FAD

"Spinning the World Wide Web"

http://www.hooked.net:80/
buzznet/fad/

Stories are told with few words in this beautifully photo-intensive mag. Lots about fashion, women, and the arts, all poetic and visual. I haven't paid much attention to the paper version of this magazine before, but I'm eager to get myself a copy now. •

JILL ATKINSON: WIRED WITH A SMUT SHACK *continued*

" 'lighthouse home,' so if you have this really great site that people like, and for some reason either your machine is too slow or your service provider is rude, or for some reason you can't keep your site up, just let them know and maybe they can help you." But don't mark Atkinson's words in stone! So far the Shack is the only Website squatting on *HotWired*'s T1 line.

So what do the Rochester dorks think of her now? "They're so jealous. And I just love to rub it in their faces!" •

hitch your wagon to the net

FAD photo

HOT SITES:
Look at Books

ATOMIC BOOKS

Literary Finds
for Mutated Minds

While I wouldn't want to read a novel on my computer (it's much cozier to turn pages on my couch or under a tree), I love the fact that you can read about books and even order them online. It's especially convenient during foul weather. The only drawback with book-browsing via your modem is that you don't get that exciting fresh pulpy smell found in physical bookstores and libraries. Shucks.

NANCY DREW: GIRL SLEUTH, GIRL WONDER

http://sunsite.unc.edu/cheryb/nancy.drew/ktitle.html

I haven't given Ms. Drew much thought since I was a young teen, but visiting her site has sparked a new interest in her that I've never had before. All sorts of questions are looked at here, such as, "Is Nancy a feminist or merely a keeper of the social order?" "How does evil have sexual undertones in the Nancy stories?" and "What do settings and objects used reveal about how Keene views women and society?" Drew stories are examined to answer some of these questions. I enjoyed reading this, since it brought me back to my happy-go-lucky days of junior high. What's particularly intriguing is the dispute surrounding author Carolyn Keene, a pen name for Harriet Stratemeyer . . . or was it Mildred Benson? Apparently these two women both wrote at least some of the Drew volumes, and both claim to have been the primary voice behind Keene. Sounds like a good mystery for Nancy to tackle! You can't order Drew books from this site, but it sure was cool to see her again.

ATOMIC BOOKS GIRLIE STUFF

http://www.clark.net/pub/atomicbk/catalog/wimmens.html

Shelves and shelves full of reading material here, including fiction by Kathy Acker and Lydia Lunch, magazines and zines such as *Bust*, *Cup Size*, and *Femme Flicke*, comix by Donna Barr, Lynda Barry, and Dame Darcy, and audacious book titles like *At Your Fingertips: The Care and Maintenance of a Vagina*—"A Humorous Collection from Hysteria Magazine." These pro-chick book sellers also carry grrrl music, have frequent contests, and sell all of their titles online.

CONARI PRESS CATALOG

http://www.organic.com/Books/Conari/Catalog/index.html

A catalog of books for and/or by women, Conari carries a long list of titles, such as *Sister* by Elizabeth Fishel, *Opposite Sides of the Bed* by Cris Evatt, and *Wild Women* by Autumn Stephens. If you want to get the details on a specific book, just click on the title and an image of the cover will pop up along with a description of its contents. Although you can't actually order these books online, you can call their 800 number (given at the site) and order over the phone. This company will even gift wrap your books for you.

CIRCLET PRESS WWW

http://www.apocalypse.org/circlet/home.html

Devoted solely to erotic science fiction and fantasy publications, Circlet sells erotic horror, S/M erotic classics, sexy nonfiction, erotic SF/fantasy from other publishers (like *Love Bites* by Amarantha Knight and *Equinox* by Samuel R. Delaney), and other miscellaneous sex books. They also sell magazines such as *Latex*, *On Our Backs*, and *Blue Blood*. You can print out their order form from the Website, but unfortunately you can't order online, since they don't take credit cards. Have a good erotic story you want to write? If so, check out their writers' guidelines. •

ENTERT

AIN ME!

If the phone and cable companies have their way, you'll soon be able to log onto the Net and call up a video of your choice to view on your computer screen. And as cable companies continue to get more involved in the Internet access business, your computer and TV will start morphing into each other. Which one will you use to surf the Net? Which one will you use to watch movies? The big corporations are jumping up and down with excitement over this so-called convergence. And yet, my only reaction to these technological "advances" is, *so what*?

What's so great about watching a movie or the nightly news on your computer? I sure as hell don't want to spend my precious few hours of free time sitting in my computer chair next to some file cabinets in my cluttered office, doing the exact same thing I could be doing in front of the fire-place in my cozy living room, or better yet, in a movie theater. It's silly to think that the Internet will replace entertainment as we know it.

Don't get me wrong—I'm not saying that cyberspace isn't going to be a source of good entertainment. Its potential for delivering captivating amusement is great. But the wrong way to create online content is to take existing media—novels, movies, and comics—and "repurpose" (another buzzword used by clueless executives) them for the Net. The right way to create fresh entertainment for cyber-space is to recognize the Net's unique qualities—interactivity, immediacy, and multimedia—and incorporate them into entertainment that works only on the Net.

And indeed someone already has. I'm talking about the unprecedented episodic series called *The Spot* that's now running on the Web. A cross between *The Real World* and *Melrose Place*. *The Spot* features five twentysomething Hollywood wanna-bes who live in a Los Angeles beach house. The story is told through each character's daily journal that the audience can read by clicking on an icon. At first browse you might wonder what the difference is between this Website and a TV nighttime soap. But the fantastic distinction is that the ongoing storyline of *The Spot* is shaped by its more than 1.5 million international "viewers" per week. The audience can send private email to their favorite—or most hated—character, give advice to the characters in live chat rooms, and talk among them-selves on *The Spot's* bulletin board. Even though the characters aren't supposed to know what the others are writing about in their secret diaries, the audience spills the beans all the time by gossiping to their favorite character about what the others are doing. *The Spot* is the type of interactive fiction that could only happen in cyberspace, and for something as engaging and gossipy and melodramatic as this, I am more than enthused to sit in front of my computer.

I'm sure *The Spot* (which uses real actors, by the by) is only the first of many Web series like it to come. Besides the Net's phenomenal potential to weave the input of the characters and the audience together to create a plot, the real beauty of cyber-entertainment is that anyone with a creative streak can be a star. In Hollywood you have to have talent, luck, and a connection to the movers and shakers to make it. But on the Net you can reach the top of the charts on sheer talent (a little luck wouldn't hurt, though). No one controls the strings in cyberspace.

In addition to being fertile soil for such interactive projects, the Net is also revolutionizing the politics of the music industry. Just a couple of years ago a new band faced the grueling task of enticing a music company to sign them in order to get their music distributed. And even then, signing didn't guarantee big exposure. Now musicians are turning to the Internet as an alternative way to be heard. This shift to the Net began in 1993, when IUMA (Internet Underground Music Archive) was formed to distribute independent bands and artists in cyberspace, free of charge. By offering either samples or complete music cuts, along with photos and biographies of the musicians, IUMA connected these artists with an audience who otherwise may have never had the opportunity to access the music.

"Entertain Me" is a tour through Hollywired, where the audience helps sculpt and influence their entertainment. You'll hear more about *The Spot* from my Wired Hollywood friend, Katrina Holden ("The coolest thing to me about *The Spot* is creative control. . . . You don't have to wait for a seventy-year-old male TV executive with script approval to make decisions about female characters in their twenties"). I'll also give you the details on IUMA's Web page, along with hot sites that will make you drool over grrrl music, art projects, TV trash, and movie starlets.

And cyber entertainment extends past the Net, as you'll see with D'Cückoo, an interactive all-chick techno-pagan band whose tribe member, Linda Jacobson, gives me the scoop ("Technology has been viewed as a dehumanizing force, and the whole goal behind D'Cückoo is to humanize technology").

On the Net, the line between artist and audience member may soon become as fuzzy as that between online journalist and news receiver. I mean, every time you post an online message, aren't you reporting news to a potential audience of millions? In the same light, while you're contributing to online fiction—such as *The Spot*—as an entertainee, you unwittingly affect potentially millions of spectators, and therefore become an entertainer as well. In this new age of cyberspace, we all perform with—and for—each other.

With some exceptions, I've found that the music sites that call themselves "official" are usually the straighter, slicker, less personable spots, while the funkier "unofficial" sites are usually created by zealous fans whose enthusiasm permeates every one of their pages. From Riot to Ambient, these girls conquer the air waves, and now they're thrashing the Net lines as well!

LIZ PHAIR WEB SITE
http://www.armory.com/~fisheye/lpml.html
Gives you the lowdown on Liz Phair: her history, lyrics, tour dates, photos, and articles about her. You can also join her mailing list. Pretty straight, but Phair fans will find it worth their while.

BUZZNET'S MUSIC REVIEW—AMBIENT
http://www.hooked.net:80/buzznet/02/beats/ambient/
Issue two of the online magazine *Buzznet* gives a rave review of Alaura's debut solo album, *Sacred Dreams*. This ambient chick used to be in Psychic TV, and has worked with psychedelic Kahuna Timothy Leary. There's background info and a photo of her for you to gawk at. Buzznet is also wowed by the ambient-trance compilation of *Amatoria* by Art. Indust, which is reviewed here as well. Get a load of the beautiful graphics for both albums. They're gorgeous! This E-rag knows how to deliver great-looking visuals.

---more--->

JAMMIN'.NEWSGROUPS

Besides gossip and amusing rows about musical artists, music-focused newsgroups can be really handy for groupies looking for tickets and inquiring about nationwide—or international—tour dates. There's always someone with an answer!

alt.fan.madonna
Passionate Madonna fans battle with those who dis the material girl in gossipy topics like "Madonna Plastic Surgery." I was glued. You can also catch the latest on tour info and other performance updates.

alt.music
Oh my, I've never seen so much variety in one newsgroup, with confused ones asking who Nine Inch Nails are, debates like alternative versus rap music, notices for keyboard players, questions about Megadeth, etc. A little too chaotic for my liking.

alt.music.a-cappella
Although there's some junk mail cluttering this group (Make Money Fast schemes), a cappella aficionados may find this spot—with audition notices, club queries, and concert info—a good place to connect with others in the scene.

alt.music.alternative
Yay, more focused than alt.music. Much better!

alt.music.alternative.female
Elastica, Veruca Salt, Courtney Love, and the like are the topic of conversation in this grrrl-zone.

alt.music.bjork
Lyrics, Web pages, tour dates, and other media and music-related stuff on Bjork here. Not too chatty, just informative.

alt.music.enya
If you're into Enya, make sure you visit this group, and not alt.fan.enya, which royally sucks.

alt.music.indigo-girls
The usual fannish talk about tours, records, and lyrics.

alt.music.shonen-knife
Aw, how disappointing. No one's around except creepy con-artists trying to trick you with more Get-Rich-Quick angles. Doesn't anyone normal like this cute bunch?

alt.rave
Raves and rants on drugs, clubs (including the international scoop), music (with a funny riff on Traci Lords), DJs, etc. Fun people here.

Brandee Selck and David Beach

IUMA
(Internet Underground Music Archive)
http://www.iuma.com/IUMA/index_graphic.html
Packed to the brim with sounds and surprisingly cool art, IUMA is a blast to both your visual and audio senses. I don't even know how many bands are listed—I couldn't find an end to this joint—but it seems like hundreds, and you can listen to music samples of each group. From rock to opera to folk to undefinable, it's all here. You can also choose from a long list of record labels, each offering contact info and audio samples of some of there bands. And as if this weren't enough, they also have publications and merchandise for you to lap up.

HOLE
http://geffen.com/hole.html
VERUCA SALT
http://geffen.com/veruca.html
Both of these sites were created by Geffen Records, and both sites look the same. They are decorated with the bands' CD covers and offer sound samples. Hole's page is a little lengthier, however, with a bio of the band. And, of course, you can order their records online. Good sites for starters, but homemade Home Pages created by fans or enemies are where it's at.

BJORK MAINPAGE
http://math-www.uio.no/bjork/index.html
Way to go, Bjork! Lots of stuff here about this Icelandic music queen: "The Secret History of Bjork," which is a nice lengthy bio, a discography, lyrics, interviews from *Face* magazine, an article from *Details*, and some interesting black-and-white photos of the former Sugarcube that I hadn't seen before. You can also learn how to get on her mailing list.

BELLY
http://www.evo.org/html/group/belly.html
This is kind of a strange site for a band. Very skimpy with graphics, no personal bios, but heavy with information relating to the band's discography and the resumes of lead singer Tanya Donelly and the rest of the Belly clan. You can also get the same type of information for the Throwing Muses here.

10,000 MANIACS
http://www.indirect.com/www/mecheves/misc/1000.html
A pretty straightforward music site, complete with the usual discography, lyrics, and album covers. You can also listen to some of their songs and admire photos of everyone in the band, with extra shots of Natalie.

---more--->-

D'CÜCKOO

Organically Techno

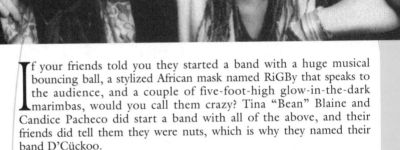

Hot Sites: Music Grrrls *continued*

THE OFFICIAL BREEDERS WEB PAGE

http://www.nando.net/music/gm/Breeders/

A Dutch boy named Patrick put this site together.

Along with lyrics, pictures, and audio samples of their music, you can experience the Interview Disk that "combines both verbal and musical secrets into the history of the Breeders." You can either read the Disk's fully transcribed interview, which is long and quite interesting, or preview audio excerpts from the interview.

ENYA

http://www.bath.ac.uk/~ccsdra/enya/home.html

Everything is color-coded in fluorescence to indicate whether something is new, updated, unchanged, or an external link. Very bright and pretty! Coolest stuff here: "The Enya Papers"—a stack of magazine articles and radio and TV interviews that were originally posted on Usenet. I also like the lyrics that have been translated into English, and the photos.

THE OFFICIAL UNOFFICIAL CRANBERRIES HOME PAGE

http://www.nada.kth.se/~dao-fgi/Cranberries/index.html

Pretty spiffy for an "Unofficial" Home Page. Everything is very organized and shiny here, and I mean that in a good way. These pages are loaded with Cranberry juice, including tons of information, pictures, audio files, and

---more--->

If your friends told you they started a band with a huge musical bouncing ball, a stylized African mask named RiGBy that speaks to the audience, and a couple of five-foot-high glow-in-the-dark marimbas, would you call them crazy? Tina "Bean" Blaine and Candice Pacheco did start a band with all of the above, and their friends did tell them they were nuts, which is why they named their band D'Cückoo.

The five-member all-woman tribe is "the world's only post-industrial neo-classical techno-tribal world funk ensemble," according to Linda Jacobson, the band's public speaker, schmoozer, ideas person, "virtrilliquist," and former manager. Ms. Jacobson is the voice behind their 3-D digital mascot, RiGBy, which is projected on a screen above the stage. When their shows first open and in between songs, RiGBy picks out people in the audience (with the help of Ms. Jacobson, hiding behind a screen), and interacts with them. "The audience eats it up," grins Ms. Jacobson.

I've only been able to catch the band on television and on a video tape, but even through a two-dimensional screen my temperature shot up from their pounding music, rhythmic movement, wild dancing and visual aesthetics. Bean was inspired to create synthesized soul music after living and traveling through Africa for two years, where she performed with the Senegalese national ballet. With the added worldly experiences of the rest of the band, D'Cückoo is a radically vibrant heart-racing blend of African, Latin, Japanese, and various other cultural rhythms, which are combined with smart-girl digital know-how, techno-sounds, and interactivity. Merely watching them is only one piece of the experience, since audience participation with their electric gadgets runs rampant during a D'Cückoo performance. (I could kick myself for not yet having played with them live!)

"The first of what we call 'digital show toys' is the MIDI (Musical Instrument Digital Interface) ball, which is this giant five-foot floating sphere that has transmitters in it," Jacobson explains. "We toss it out to the audience, and when audience members bat the ball, they trigger sound effects or music or images on the computer screen." The band also hands out various six-foot MIDI bamboo "trigger sticks" and keyboards so that the audience can jam with the band and affect the visuals.

So where in the world do these chicks get tall glowing marimbas, interactive musical spheres, and MIDI trigger sticks? After looking around in stores and coming up empty-handed, they decided the best way to get what they wanted was to make it themselves. Ms. Pacheco used her software engineering and sound-design background to invent their original digital instruments, and all five band members—Pacheco, Blaine, Terrie Wright, Luanne Warner, and Susan Jette—know how to use a soldering iron.

When I ask Jacobson if technology ever gets in the way of music, she says absolutely not. "Technology can sound very natural and organic when executed properly." On the other hand, she says dealing with so much digital equipment in a show can be trying. "The D'Cückoo performance is really a mother to put on. It's a big, big production and requires a crew, a lot of time to set up, and a lot of testing. They have to worry about clean power, worry about what circuit they're on, make sure their instruments aren't on the same circuits as the lights, and then there's programming . . ."

When they're beating on their instruments, vibrating with an audience, you'd never guess that worry was even in their vocabulary. The band has opened for the Grateful Dead (they programmed Dead riffs into their MIDI ball), played at too-numerous-to-list digital conventions, jammed at Reggae on the River, and recorded with Brian Eno and the Neville Brothers, among a ton of other credits.

It's hard to believe that synthesized instruments could unleash such a throbbing, sweaty pulsation. Obviously it's not the instruments, but the spirit and knowledge of D'Cückoo's plugged-in riot grrrls that make it happen. Jacobson sums it up when she says, "Technology has been viewed as a dehumanizing force, and the whole goal behind D'Cückoo is to humanize technology."

For info on D'Cückoo CDs or catching them live, make sure to check out their Website (see sidebar). •

HOT SITE: D'Cückoo
http://www.well.com/user
/tcircus/ Dcuckoo/index.html

Groove to D'Cückoo's sound clips from their first CD, D'Cückoo, as well as from their latest release, UMOJA (which means "unity" in Swahili). Or browse through their funky photo album, and go "backstage" where you can order their goods and hear the praiseful gossip people offer about these grrrls.

links. You can also order CDs online, which makes me wonder how unofficial this site really is. Hmmm.

MAZZY STAR
http://www.unc.edu/~hondo/
mazzy.html
The highlight of this site is the ever-growing photo page, where you can see Hope Sandoval in lots of black-and-white photos. She's so fetching! You can jump to a Mazzy Star newsgroup (alt.music.mazzy-star) from here too. The rest of this site has the typical offerings of lyrics, discography, etc.

MADONNA
http://www.mit.edu:8001/people/jwb/
Madonna.html
I couldn't leave out Madonna. This is one of the more packed pages I've found of her, with a Madonna FAQ, songlist, lyrics, and the beginnings of a transcription of her *Truth or Dare* movie. Although the gigantic collection of photos comprises mostly album and poster shots, there are some gorgeous portraits I haven't seen before titled "Versace" (did she model for the designer?). If your Madonna fix hasn't been fulfilled after visiting this spot, check out her other links offered here. •

Not only can modems transport ideas, sounds, and financial transactions, they can also bring beauty to your screen. Visual artists from all over the planet can now converge to share delicious eye candy with each other and with us. Look!

LIESBET'S ATELIER
http://www.xs4all.nl/~ziklies/

Take a tour through Liesbet's virtual art house, situated in Amsterdam (text is written in English *and* Dutch), where every room has a secret waiting to be discovered. You can wander through her hall, living room, bathroom (don't forget to pull the chain and hear the flush of the toilet!), stairs, kitchen, art studio, bedroom, and visitor's lounge. Most rooms are filled with muted, slightly abstract hanging art, the bathroom has a graffiti-covered wall that you can scribble on, and the kitchen has a cookbook with a secret recipe (in Dutch only). If you need a breath of fresh air, step out into her garden or meander down to the alley. If you speak Dutch and want to meet a neighbor, visit Christine, who has her own Home Page. I gleefully lost myself exploring this mysterious and fanciful abode.

FRIDA KAHLO
http://www.cascade.net/kahlo.html

Take delight in the powerful self-portraits of Frida Kahlo as they narrate parts of her tumultuous life. Through a large collection of her paintings accompanied with few words, the artist's childhood, bus accident, polio illness, and rocky marriage to Mexican muralist Diego Rivera are depicted here. Although phone lines could never do her work justice, the digital images

---more--->

Artistic.Newsgroups

Art talk isn't as rampant as I would have thought when it comes to Usenet, so I've only got a stubby list for you to investigate. If you want more, start your own newsgroup.

alt.art.colleges
A very small group, but if you're looking for an art school, poke around. These artistic academics seem to know about colleges from all over the world.

alt.art.scene
More of a vocational scene, actually, with artists looking for jobs, asking about schools, and selling/buying art. Also, festival and art event dates are posted here.

alt.artcom
Ew, I was so grossed out by some of the mean elitists barking in this forum. But if you can ignore or joyfully snicker at them, you'll probably find the political and creative issues regarding art quite interesting. Some help wanted ads are stirred into the mix as well.

alt.ascii-art
I never realized people were so into ASCII-art—including myself! I was amazed to see some of the complex drawings artists can make with just the characters on their keyboard. In one visit I saw a monkey, armadillos, a birthday cake, a map of Mexico, and someone's "Fluffy the Cat." There were also requests from less talented folks challenging ASCII-artists to make a baby, a cockatiel, and even Bruce Lee. I can't wait to go back and see what they came up with.

Images on this page by Julia L. Kay, photo entitled "Binghamton Light"

of her art are pretty crisp and still reveal the depth and intensity of her work.

ART ON THE NET
http://www.art.net/
Amble through these art studios that offer bios and tours of international painters, sculptors, poets, performance artists, and musicians. Or visit the Gallery, which has several different halls, each containing three-to-four exhibits. Besides receiving visual gratification, you can also listen to sound bytes (some are amusing, and some will make you want to throw something at your computer for wasting so much of your time). So far more than sixty-five artists are involved with this project.

From here, jump to
LINK TO OTHER RELATED SITES
(http://www.egallery.com/egallery/ homepage.html), and you'll be in touch with over 100 other art studios and exhibits with titles like "Art Crimes: The Writing on the Wall" (graffiti art from cities worldwide), The Electric Gallery, and The World's Women Online which features more than 750 female artists.

YAHOO—ART: EXHIBITS
http://www. yahoo.com/ Art/Exhibits/
For hundreds of other artsy sites, make sure to go to Yahoo and click away! •

SIZZLING HOT SITE: THE SPOT

http://www.thespot.com

I would have given you the details of The Spot *myself, but I have a friend, Katrina Holden, who's even more of a fan of the online soap than I am! I think this is due to her Hollywood background. Besides being a writer for* Wired *magazine and getting an acting part in an upcoming independent feature film called* The Find, *she's also conjured up a television series idea that she's currently in the middle of negotiating with the man himself—Aaron Spelling!* The Spot *is totally Katrina's bag, so here's her take:*

A dd me to the list of *Melrose Place* addicts. I'm proud to say my girlfriends and I have spent many Monday nights yelling futile directions to the tube screen: "Jo, maybe it's time to think about Prozac." Or "Jane, get a clue, will you? Don't be such a victim." So, you can imagine my delight at encountering *The Spot*, the Net's first interactive soap! *The Spot* is not just any old *Days of Our Lives*–type soap. It's campy, clever, and hip. *The Spot* calls itself an "Episodic Website." It covers, in intimate detail, the lives of five Southern California twentysomethings. Each of the Spotmates, Tara, Lon, Carrie, Michelle, and Jeff, have their own distinct icons on the Home Page. Click on them and you can read their private journals.

Because I have a tiny bit of experience in writing for TV, the coolest thing to me about *The Spot* is creative control. Watch the credits of most prime time sitcoms and you'll notice too few women on the creative teams. But with *The Spot*, through email, you're able to communicate and participate with the actors on the show. *The Spot* receives about 300 emails a day from thirty countries. You can actually have a significant influence on the plot lines. You don't have to wait for a seventy-year-old male TV executive with script approval to make decisions about female characters in their twenties. I hate to think what Aaron Spelling would do to Michelle, the spunkiest Spotmate. When I last tuned in to *The Spot*, Michelle was in jail for drunk-and-disorderly conduct; of course she didn't remember it because of a blackout. Through Tara's icon I found out this was pretty normal behavior for Michelle. Tara was deciding whether to bail out Michelle again or let her learn a lesson. Now at this point, I bet Spelling executives would have Michelle hop hop lickety split to a quaint Alcoholics Anonymous meeting, and for the next twelve episodes we viewers would be forced to hear all the horrible things that happened in her childhood that led her to drunken blackouts and consequently to blissful sobriety via AA. I decided this would be the perfect place to participate, so I emailed:

> *Tara should let Michelle's ass rot in Jail for the night. [That's another thing I like about* The Spot—*you don't have to watch your language.] She should wake up with a massive hangover to discover her cellmate is none other than Courtney Love. Courtney is impressed by Michelle's extensive knowledge of Hole. Michelle convinces Courtney to ditch her guitar player—Erik what's-his-name—citing the only reason he's famous is because he's Drew Barrymore's boyfriend. Michelle confesses she was really a child prodigy on the guitar. They have a serious lesbian affair and the big cliff-hanger is, will Michelle leave the Spotmates to tour with Hole?? Ha, take that Fox TV!*

The story lines unfold with daily graphics, video, and text entries. Here's an excerpt from Lonnie, who seems to be most like Jane on Melrose; she's always taken advantage of:

> *"Any place else," I said to Gak. But he insisted we meet*

HOT SITES:
Chicks and Flicks

Whether you're just a moviegoer or are actually into creating films, the Web will suck you in. Once I started searching for these grrrlish film sites, I couldn't stop! I'm way off-schedule now. Gotta go!

GIRLS ON FILM

http://www.itp.tsoa.nyu.edu/~student/GirlsOnFilm/Girls.html

Wanna see a movie but can't decide between *Die Hard 7* or the latest Tarantino flick? Students Lise and Sibyl will set you straight—they review everything from fluff to the heavies. First they let you know where they're coming from: Lise loves *Dazed and Confused*, grooves on *Barbarella*, and hates Eric Stoltz. Sibyl adores *Point Break* and Tim Roth, but loathes Kevin Costner. Besides movie reviews, these women have a monthly "Bad Hair" citation, which they gave to Mel Gibson in May for his 'do in *Braveheart*. They also have a beer campaign going in hopes of getting six-packs behind cinema confection counters. There are other fun tidbits to savor here, including a "link-o-rama" page. Siskel and Ebert, move over!

A SANDRA BULLOCK WEB PAGE

http://weber.u.washington.edu/~louie/sandra.html#film

Gary, a true-blue Bullock worshiper, has put this online fanzine together, with cute photos and a fat table of contents containing Sandra's Excellent Adventure (her bio), In Print, Incredibly Trivial Trivia, FAQs, On Television.... With such a sharp, clean-cut layout, you'd think this site was created by her professional "handlers," but Gary says he's an ordinary dude.

---more--->

THE ALICIA SILVERSTONE SHRINE

http://www.engr.unl.edu/~tory/alicia.html

A student and Alicia-adorer is constantly updating this temple, so you'll forever get fresh facts and photos of the *Clueless* goddess. Lots of other Silverstone pages to jump to from here.

THE MARILYN PAGES

http://www.ionet.net/~jellenc/marilyn.html

I couldn't leave out Norma Jean! Some chick named Ellen is in charge of this spot, which includes Monroe's bio (with some of Her quotes), her filmography, glam images (some that I've actually never seen before), and a "memorabilia" area with links to more Marilyn sites as well as to pages of her stamps, phone cards, and other fannish merchandise.

CYBER FILM SCHOOL

http://www.io.org/~cincan/cfs.htm

If you don't think there's enough chick flick action on the Web, then make a film of your own! The Cyber Film School will hook you up with the tricks of the trade. From here you'll take field trips to lighting sites, camera departments, online movie reviews, access to screenwriting tools and tips, pages of movie studios and TV networks, and all sorts of other places that'll get you up to speed in the world of filmmaking.

---more--->

SIZZLING HOT SITE: THE SPOT *continued*

again at the Beanery. He said he wanted to reminisce some more and felt at ease there. He was quiet and moody. He just wanted to play pool. He didn't want to talk. The silence went on until our burgers came. Then he suddenly started crying. I was stunned. In between sobs, he talked about how hellish his marriage was. He said he didn't think he could stay faithful to Susan—how he didn't want to hurt her, but he was miserable. I reached out to comfort him, when he popped his head up smiling.

"What?" I said, startled.

"Lonnie, you're such a sensitive friend," he said mockingly.

"So the tears were just a joke, you sick bastard?"

"Uh huh," he laughed.

"So your marriage is good then."

"No, I just told you . . . I'm miserable with Susan." He then chugged his beer down in one gulp and laughed.

The man is a maniac.

I find *The Spot* to be a place of equality on the Web. It's a fun forum for grrrls to let loose, to participate, and most importantly, to see results! •

The Classroom

Hollywood.Newsgroups

I was surprised that not even one newsgroup is dedicated to a specific actress (contrary to music groups, where female singers are in many cases the main focus). But starlets are worshipped as well as snickered at within some of these forums, which also engage in the glitz, commercialism, artistic edge, and kitsch of Hollywood.

alt.cult-movies

Seen a movie more than three times? If so, your obsession may be appreciated in this crowded nook, where you can participate in conferences like Worst Movie Ever, Best Shaving Scenes, Russ Meyer Movies, Vampire Films, etc. Camp-o-rama!

more on page 121---->

FILM REVIEWS

http://www.inform.umd.edu:8080/EdRes/Topic/WomensStudies/FilmReviews

Hankering to see a grrrly film but don't know which one? More than 100 films by, about, or starring women are reviewed here. The only thing I don't like is that the reviews aren't accompanied by pictures. Star-gazing is half the fun!

LILLIAN GISH AT BOWLING GREEN

http://www.bgsu.edu/~pcharle/gish/

First let me warn you that this heavy-duty graphical memorial should only be viewed by owners of Netscape with a respectable modem. Otherwise, you'll sit for an excruciatingly long time. If you're still reading, and you're a Gish fan, you should definitely visit this silent star, see her old theater, look at her family photos, and get a whole historical tour of her life.

For more heavenly silence, dial into **SILENT MOVIES** at: http://www.cs.monash.edu.au/~pringle/silent/.

MANDY'S FILM AND TELEVISION DIRECTORY

http://www.mandy.com/

Oh my, this Home is so loaded with film resources (a place to scout out worldwide film schools, trade shows, festivals, facilities, producers, technicians ... you name it) that I was drowsy after scrolling through it all. For serious film chicks!

---more--->

Here are some other movie starlets that I like:

DREW BARRYMORE HOME PAGE
http://www.primenet.com/~rwilli/drew.html

WINONA RYDER
http://www.sch.bme.hu/~joker/winona.html

JODI FOSTER
http://www.tcp.com/~mary/foster.html

HALLE BERRY
http://www.wmin.ac.uk/~srcec/index.html

HELENA BONHAM CARTER HOME PAGE
http://www.nada.kth.se/~nv91-gta/www/HBC/welcome.html

AUDREY HEPBURN
http://grove.ufl.edu/~flask/Hepburn.html

THE BRIDGET FONDA HOME PAGE
http://www.cs.utexas.edu/users/ddk/bridgetfonda/bridgetfonda.html

And there are some sexyboy actors too!

KEVIN BACON
"The Kevin Bacon Game"
http://www.sic.com/other/kbacon/
Yes! It's actually a game!

THE UNOFFICIAL BRAD PITT WEB SITE
http://www.sils.umich.edu/~mortal/bradpitt/bradpitt.html

CHRISTOPHER WALKEN
http://www.ma.man.ac.uk/~traslers/movies/christopher-walken.html

alt.film

If you're part of **ECHO**, New York's savvy online service, keep on the lookout for its new film series, "alt.film." Once a month the Echoids do a live chat with an independent filmmaker, and in turn the filmmaker will participate in their Movie and TV conference. Then ECHO will have a movie screening along with a party, and will create a Web page for each director or producer. The best part is that ECHO builds up a great library of cool artsy Web pages, and its virtual community also becomes a face-to-face community. Don't be jealous, just call and find out how you can join! (212/292-0900)

alt.cult-movies.rocky-horror
Rocky Horror groupies unite on the Net, reciting songs, asking for the details about nationwide Rocky casts and costumes, and swooning over Magenta et al.

alt.fan.actors
If you don't have an *Enquirer* lying around, just pop into this gossipy group. Scattered around the piles of dirt you'll also run into star-struck fans looking for celebrity sites and memorabilia.

alt.fan.tank-girl
Way to go Tank Girl! She's the only female film character (I know, she's *really* a comic book celeb) who has her own newsgroup.

alt.movies.independent
Movies made by smaller, independent production houses make it into the conversations of this group. Don't even think of prattling about this year's biggest blockbuster here.

alt.movies.indian
A place to rap about every aspect of Hindi or Indian films.

alt.movies.silent
Devotees of silent movies enthusiastically discuss the genre's films, celebrities, directors, and general history.

rec.arts.movies.people
Less sensational and more fannish than alt.fan.actors. Lots of "What ever happened to ..." threads.

rec.arts.movies.movie-going
Chatty and humorous movie-going anecdotes, like how people have handled view-blocking big hair, and the drag of small screens that chop off the edges of a film. Also lots of griping about sticky floors, ear-blasting sound, etc.

rec.video.releases
For those of you who gotta know when a movie will be going to video or how to get your hands on a rare film, these video junkies will tell you.

reviews

Why would you want to run from your TV set to your computer just to see more of the same? Beats me. But I know how tasty processed tele-programs can be, and everyone's entitled to lounge as a mouse potato when the urge hits. Your friends don't need to know. Just lock the door, toss up your feet, and click away!

MELROSE PLACE UPDATE

http://www.speakeasy.org/~dbrick/Melrose/melrose.html

Okay, I admit it. I'm a *Melrose* junkie! So shoot me!

The Website title's a little misleading, since the *Melrose* babble is a bit behind in episodes, but you can't beat a place that gives you photos of Amanda, Sydney, Jane, and chipmunk-cheeked Alison. You can also study the detailed synopses for most of the earlier episodes and enlighten yourself with poignant quotes such as the *9½ Weeks* exchange between Jake and a random temptress: "I've always liked you in red." "You've always liked me in bed."

Unfortunately the guy who started this is now really hectic, and rumor has it he may not continue. Oh well, it'll still be a good place for newcomers who need to catch up, or for plain old *Melrose* maniacs.

---more--->

TEEVEE.NEWSGROUPS

One of the better Seinfeld episodes I've seen was when Jerry wouldn't admit to a prospective date that he watched Melrose Place, and thus was subjected to a lie detector test (which he failed). If you're a closet potato, these newsgroups might be just the place to rave and vent about your programs. You can even sign on anonymously!

alt.mtv-sucks

Apparently most channel grazers don't agree with this title, since there's not much noise here. If you happen to have some pent up MTV hostility, however, you know where to go. For more action from both MTV groovers and dissers, you may prefer alt.tv.mtv.

alt.tv.90210

Oh goody, tons of dirt to be had in this Beverly Hills neighborhood. But I don't want to be the one to ruin the upcoming plot for you. . . .

alt.tv.brady-bunch

Just when you think you've heard all the Brady babble there is to know, this group finds more! My favorite topics are the ones about real-life encounters with the Bunch (I didn't realize Jan was such a bitch! . . . I met Greg once, by the by, and he was soooo nice!). The BB fans also let us in on upcoming appearances by the actors, Brady Bloopers, favorite lines, etc.

alt.tv.commercials

I had a great time reading about commercial lingo, rules, plots, and props for tampon and condom ads. All sorts of other commercials are scoffed at, dissected, and picked apart as well.

alt.tv.friends

An arena where Friendly worshipers swoon over the cast, exchange Web page and fan club info, and recapitulate episodes.

SOAP LINKS

http://www.cts.com/~jeffmj/soaps.html

If you're surfing for your favorite soaps, you've hit the mother lode! You'll first run into a *Hollywood Squares* type of image map that will transfer you to the virtual zones of: *All My Children, Another World, As the World Turns, The Bold and the Beautiful, Days of Our Lives, General Hospital, Guiding Light, The Young and the Restless, Beverly Hills 90210,* or *Melrose Place.* Below the map is a list of links to sudsy newsgroups, chat rooms, and non-U.S. soaps.

DAYS OF OUR LIVES PAGE

http://weber.u.washington.edu/~pfloyd/days/index.html

Devoted fans of this twenty-year-old soap will be in hog heaven here. You'll be bombarded with photos, video and audio clips, info, episode summaries, upcoming teasers, links to even more glittery Days pages, and even (I can't believe this) *DOOL* addresses and phone/hotline numbers.

STAR TREK

http://www.cosy.sbg.ac.at/rec/startrek/index.html

Brigitte from my Webgrrls section puts together this extensive collection of *Star Trek* info. Look up anything you've ever wanted to know about these space explorers by tapping into her lists of resources and newsgroups.

---more--->

She's also got a bunch of episode guides from various fans that contain *Star Trek* quotes, plots, special guests, and even dates when each episode first aired. If you want to speak Klingonese, read about the Klingon Language Institute or look through their dictionary. For a nostalgic rush, download pictures from the Trekker scrapbook. Log on and prosper!

J'S X FILES HOME PAGE
http://www.interpath.net/~cybervox/x.html

A glowing green site with audio files, Q&As, and lots of links to other worldwide *X Files* sites.

FX
http://www.fxnetworks.com/fx/

Fresh layout and design! Besides admiring their look, you can read about FX's NYC apartment, jot down their airtime schedules, and jump to their Usenet groups to chat about favorite TV oldies. And make sure to investigate their "downloadable goodies and surprises"!

---more--->

alt.tv.infomercials
Of course it's mostly sarcasm over the weird world of infomercials. Even weirder, though, are the handful of posts from viewers who take this stuff seriously!

alt.tv.liquid-tv
For excited watchers of MTV's *Liquid TV*. "Aeon Flux" is especially admired.

alt.tv.mad-about-you
Would having children ruin the show? Has Helen surgically enhanced her bod? Where can one find photos of her on the Net? This is the kind of stuff these Mad fans gab about.

alt.tv.melrose-place
This group is about as gossip-laden as the soapy series itself! What more could you ask for?

alt.tv.party-of-five
Not a lot going on at the time that I scoped out this nook, but with the renewal of the show (yay!) I bet the chatter has picked up.

alt.tv.real-world

All seasons of the *Real World* (especially the third and fourth) are discussed. When I was lurking around these parts, somebody claimed to be Puck. It was probably an impostor, but you never know....

alt.tv.ren-n-stimpy

Joy joy, *Ren and Stimpy* are still a source of entertainment for newsgroupies.

alt.tv.seinfeld

Seinfeld buffs love to relive storylines (I don't blame them!). Typical topics include "Best Elaine/Jerry scene," "bro or manzierre," and "Smelly Car: Best Episode."

alt.tv.simpsons

The most crowded group focused on a particular TV program that I've seen. Go, Marge, go!

alt.tv.x-files

Lots of *X Files* talk, not only revolving around the series but the supposed upcoming movie as well.

rec.arts.tv.soaps-misc

Although all soaps are open for discussion, it's almost all *Days of Our Lives*. Didn't realize *DOOL* was such a hit! (But by all means, feel free to veer from the main threads and talk about your favorite soap.)

SLEAZE
http://metaverse.com/vibe/sleaze/
Started by former MTV-er Adam Curry as an online newsletter, Sleaze gives you the dirtiest on Hollywood's scene.

MENTOS
http://www3.gse.ucla.edu/~cjones/mentos-faq.html
The only thing sleazier than Sleaze is Mentos commercials, especially after you've read the detailed synopsis of each "episode." What is a Mento, anyway? Read the trivia and details about the mints themselves (ingredients, packaging, etc.) and find out, if you dare. •

PLAYTIME

Life's waking hours used to be simply divided into two clear-cut categories: work and play. It was black and white, nine to five. With personal computers, the Internet, and telecommuting, however, these areas have blurred together for many unsuspecting souls into a murky concoction of three

amorphous groups: work, play, and being online. I know, because it happened to me.

Last spring, before I finally set up solid boundaries to recreate the definitive separation between career time and downtime, I was "playing" with CD-ROMs in order to write about them later, using my Sundays to complete my freelance articles (justifying that it was okay to write on a play day, since freelancing was just a "temporary" gig), answering email seven days a week (since part of it was from friends), I rationalized, and I found myself only going to parties to "network." Suddenly, it dawned on me: I had no life. I felt trapped, modem-hooked, and out of control—that same feeling as the sickening phenomenon of Tetris or Nintendo addiction. My modem and work had both sneaked into part of every waking hour, and I had become a miserable geek. I realized that the flexible schedule and freedom from corporate politics that this work-at-home-with-a-modem kind of lifestyle was supposed to be granting me was backfiring. My lifestyle was so elastic that I had unwittingly crammed too much into my limited timetable (there are, after all, only so many hours in a week!). I also realized that only I could transform this girdling situation into a liberating one.

Being a Net Chick doesn't mean that all of your time should be spent online or that the rest of your life is going to disappear once you've gone digital. Obviously, overuse of the Internet defeats the whole reason for having access to it. The Net's purpose should be to enrich your life with new, easy-to-grab information, to open up alternative ways of communicating with one to millions of people at once, to connect you with people from around the globe who have similar interests as you, and to give you more free time. The key to this end is to take charge: schedule specific times into your week to do your email and surf the Net and, for those of you who work at home, map out your work hours beforehand. Be strict about keeping to your schedule! And of course, leave lots of hours free to play offline, away from your computer.

One thing I really like to do when Web browsing is to visit sites that will enhance the time I spend out of my office. For instance, traveling is one of my big (and expensive!) hobbies. So I love to search for travel sites, which can give me insight to unseen regions (I never like to go to the same place twice). They can also inform me about different cultures and info about how to get to my next destination. So I use the Net to enrich my "real" life, and in the meantime I get a rush when I'm online.

I also like to snoop through Personal Home Pages to see what others are doing, since I'm always game for new diversions. While I was cruising through various sport and hobby sites for this chapter, I became fascinated with the number of Barbie mutators out there! I'm not sure when this hobby—or is it an art?—erupted, but you've gotta get a load of the way these artisans convert Barbie (see page 144). With new props, body positions, and outfits, the blonde mall queen is metamorphosed into a bondage, rocker, or hacker babe. With pages like this, Barbie (and my time away from the computer) takes on a whole new meaning.

The point of this chapter, "Playtime," is to give you a taste of sporty, recreational, metaphysical, or hobby-related Websites and newsgroups. Whether you're into cooking, basketball, fortune telling, quilting, or hanging at raves, you should find pages that will motivate or inspirit your idle hours. This section also features underground comic artist, girly CD-ROM maker, and self-appointed "paper doll queen of San Francisco," Trina Robbins. ("There's this weird theory going around.

They say that girls will watch stuff with male leads, but boys won't watch stuff with female leads. Well that's just bullshit!") See what she's doing to keep girls playfully engaged.

Don't be unnerved. Playing is all that it's cracked up to be, both online and offline. You just have to learn the jig!

Sporty. Newsgroups

With hundreds of sports groups, it was tough for me to choose which ones to review, since I don't know what all of you are into. I avoided all the fannish talk on football and baseball teams, only because it bores me to death, and decided to just visit the areas that interest me the most. Sorry if I left out your sport of choice.

alt.sport.racquetball

Read what players have to say about court etiquette, lists of tournaments and Websites, players looking for partners, and even gripes about playing with the opposite sex.

rec.sport.basketball.women

Basically just stuff like college and high school women's teams looking for players, searches for girls' sport camps, and female basketball schedules. Important for basketball buffs, I'm sure, but I was hoping for more down-and-dirty discussion.

alt.sport.jetski

A little too macho for my taste, but if you're a JetSkiier you may find the talk on equipment, happening ski spots, and gory details on JetSki accidents interesting.

rec.sport.rowing

Mostly recruiters looking for team rowers, with other various row talk like "Help for Blisters" and "Varying Techniques."

rec.sport.skating.ice.figure

The gabbiest sports group I've seen, with chatter about skate couples, Michelle Kwan, skater fan clubs, the sexiest skaters, and much more. Oh, and some expected stuff, too, like competition dates.

rec.sport.skating.inline

Everything from skate and kneepad brands to how to skate downhill. Action-packed!

rec.sport.swimming

All sorts of swim topics here, including professional info, tips on swimming strokes (like the butterfly), water in the ear, and maternity swimsuits.

rec.sport.tennis

Very crowded, with much more said about pro tennis players than tennis playing.

rec.sport.waterski

Lots of equipment babble, ski trick how-tos, and various want ads.

Even though I force myself to sweat once in a while, I'd personally rather play Scrabble or eat popcorn in a cool movie theater. I just don't find pleasure in pumping my arms and legs in a hyper fashion just to lose my breath. But I know that lots of humans are excited by this type of irrational behavior, so I spent a lot of time in a reclined position looking for some spots for the sporty woman.

WOMBATS
http://www.wombats.org/

The cutest sports page I've found is WOMBATS, the **Wo**men's **M**ountain **B**ike **a**nd **T**ea **S**ociety. Wombats (the furry animal) appear all over the Home Page, and clicking on one allows you to read about this adventurous pack of bicycling women founded by biking pro Jacquie Phelan. Find out about WOMBAT chapters across the country, get links to other Websites for bicyclists, or amble through their very cool and extensive art gallery. They even have a page of WOMBAT news, updated regularly. Phelan describes WOMBATS as: "Half furry animal, half refined Victorian rebel, we're unique."

THE TENNIS SERVER
http://www.tennisserver.com/

For the tennis connoisseur who's stuck indoors, this Net spot is as close as you can get to a virtual tennis club. Read the *Daily Tennis News*, browse through the photos of champs like Graf, Novotna, Sabatini, and Seles, and study the rules and codes of tennis. You can leaf through the long FAQ list which covers info on tournaments, rankings, players, equipment, and the media. And every month a different tennis pro offers their tips. If your

---more--->

S K A T E
G I R L S

by Sorel Husbands

tennis wardrobe is looking tired, jump over to the Tennis Warehouse (http://www.callamer.com/tw/), where you can buy racquets (of course), shoes and socks, court clothes, and accessories like tennis bags, towels, and elbow supports.

FIGURE SKATING HOME PAGE
http://www.cs.yale.edu/homes/sjl/skate.html

It was fun rummaging through the tall stack of photos of Harding, Kerrigan, Yamaguchi, and other skate pros accessible here. Student Sandra Loosemore has put a lot of work into this project, which also includes skate humor, info on rinks and clubs, and links to other skate sites. She also answers FAQs about competitive figure skating, rules and regulations, technical elements, events, and professional skaters. Interesting even for a wobbly-ankled skater like me!

WWW WOMEN'S SPORTS PAGE
http://fiat.gslis.utexas.edu/~lewisa/womsprt.html

If you haven't had your fill of sports sites, check out the long list of articles and links offered here. Pages on women's basketball, gymnastics, weight lifting, rowing, volleyball, handball, waterskiing, and tons of other sweat-producing activities are waiting to be explored. •

Skategirls soar down city streets.

Skategirls leap railroad tracks
and endure gravel paths
as they seek mysteries
behind darkened
warehouses.

S K A T E

Skategirls strap
PowerBooks
to their backs.

Skategirls are refreshed
by the
perfectly chilled
Schweppes seltzer
from the perfect vending
machine
on the side of the road.

Skategirls dodge floppy
disks and
fish heads on the streets.

Found on the Net as part of Sorel's Home Page.
http://www.interport.net:80/~sorel/skategirls.html

H◉T SITES:
Shake it!

I remember in junior high school I hid by the wall whenever we had a dance. What a dork! I just didn't get it. But now I love dancing, whether I'm watching or participating. Even visiting dance sites is a pleasure!

DISCOWEB
http://www.msci.memphis.edu/
~ryburnp/discoweb.html
All dressed up in your Spandex best with nowhere to go? Maybe this disco guide to clubs and clothes (nationwide) will help. But if you're stuck in a nostalgia-free town, no prob. Just download one of the many disco hits offered here (allow at least four minutes for each song), turn off your lights, and click on the strobe light sitting at the top of the Web page. Boogie down!

DANCE PAGES
http://www.ens-lyon.fr/
~esouche/danse/dance.html
Coming to you from France, a femme named Estelle is in charge here. She shows us some beautiful old photos of Parisian ballet troupes that accompany articles on historical dance theaters. She also writes about the Paris Opera

---more--->‌

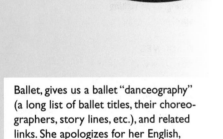

Ballet, gives us a ballet "danceography" (a long list of ballet titles, their choreographers, story lines, etc.), and related links. She apologizes for her English, although it seems perfect to me.

BELLY DANCE HOME PAGE
http://cie-2.uoregon.edu/bdance/
Nothing intoxicates me more than the snakelike writhing of a belly dancer. (I even took classes for a while, but never got past the wormlike stage.) Anyway, here's where you can learn the history and origins of Middle Eastern (or Oriental) dancing and read about its music. You can also jump to "Veil and Drum," a newsletter about costumes and classes, and to other belly dancers' Home Pages—including that of a woman who's a snake doctor!

Dancing.Newsgroups

Pro and recreational dancers will find Usenet helpful for scoping out what's happening on the dance front.

alt.arts.ballet
Girl and boy dancers talk about ballet schools, dance studios, stretching techniques, and costumes, and they ponder questions like, "Is weight training useful or not?"

alt.music.dance
You don't need to be a professional dancer to fit in with these gabby clubgoers. Also a place for DJs, wallflowers needing dance advice, and serious ravers looking for particular records.

ba.dance
Bay Area (San Francisco region) dance classes are posted here with their times and locations. This includes tango, salsa, swing, country, ballroom, etc.

rec.arts.dance
This newsgroup really ain't my bag, but if you're into "Leading Spins for Ladies," "Baton Twirling/Majorettes," and "Boogie-Woogie," then you've come to the right spot!

rec.folk-dancing
A chatty area for—you guessed it—folk dancers.

ANONYMOUS
http://www.anonymous.com/
Ms. Wiggles and Jewleeya put out this rave zine, which is so grrrly cute. They do this comic strip called "The Adventures of Smilee: The Superhero Raver Chick," and show us snapshots of adorable boys they know. Some articles I liked in issue #6 were "Reality Check" (about raver's rights vs. the Law), "What Bugs the Hell Out of Me" (a funny rant from a raver who's sick of seeing adults with pacifiers), and the Dunkin' Donut horoscope (pick a donut and read your future).

YAHOO: RAVE AND TECHNO
http://www.yahoo.com/Entertainment/
Music/Genres/Rave_and_Techno/
For more on the rave scene, scroll through this index of at least sixty-nine relevant sites. •

Ms. Wiggles and Jewleeya

If you saw the documentary Crumb, you'll remember comic book artist Trina Robbins as the person who opposed Robert Crumb's comix for their constant depiction of women as "mutilated and dismembered." Because of her objection to this kind of art, Robbins was "punished by the [underground comix] industry" from the very beginning, excluding her from the scene. But there's a bright side—it pushed her into the direction of creating hip girly playthings, a rare but needed market in the world of entertainment.

Ms. Robbins says she considers herself to be the paper doll queen of San Francisco, having done five paper doll books and the paper doll cover to a recent issue of the lesbian zine Girl Jock. She's also the creator of Hawaii High, an adorably smart CD ROM adventure game for young girls (see sidebar), which has earned her some awards. She's currently planning the CD ROM's sequel. Other than CD ROMs, she says she appreciates computers most for the comic-related forums, which she uses to research her books.

In 1970, after being shut out one too many times by the comix "boys' club," Ms. Robbins edited the first all-woman comic-book, It Ain't Me Babe, and then went on to found the Wimmen's Comix Collective. She later focused more of her energies into writing books, and has an impressive resume to show for it. Some of her books include Women and the Comics, A Century of Women Cartoonists, Catswalk, and Barbie's Garden. Recently she's also been a regular writer of The Little Mermaid comics.

Girls want girls!

When I interviewed her by phone, her soft, fluttery voice made me smile, bringing me to a comfortably familiar place. Later I realized she sounds exactly like Mia Farrow, with excited stammer and all. At the moment she is completely slack-free, busy writing/editing three books: Matchbook Cover Art, [a gothic novel that takes place in Scotland in 1902], and The Great Superheroines, which, "if there really is a goddess," will be out in 1996.

How did you first get involved with cartooning? What made you interested in that, especially since it was more of a boys' thing when you started?

>Well I didn't know it was a boys' thing. I've just always drawn and written. When I was a kid, in grade school, I remember all the girls saying, "When I grow up I'm going to be a nurse," or a secretary, or whatever the hell, and I used to

think, well, I want to write and I want to draw, what should I do? And then I'd think, I'll write stories and I'll illustrate them. And of course that's what comics and CD ROMS are.

> **What elements are important when creating a game or comic for girls?**

> First of all, girls are interested in girls. There's this weird theory going around and they use it to not do stuff for girls. They say that girls will watch stuff with male leads, but boys won't watch stuff with female leads. Well that's just bullshit! This is bullshit! If girls are watching stuff with a male lead, it's because they're watching it out of desperation, because there's nothing for them. The comic publishers and the TV networks, they go out of their way to make sure they're not hurting the feelings of boys, but they don't really give a damn about girls. The fact is that what girls like to watch is other girls.

> **It's true. I hate watching movies that are all boys.**

> It's boring! So give them girls, give them girl heroines. And for good-ness sake, give them action, too. But not violence. They don't like violence. That's horrid nasty stuff—that's boys' stuff—but action, action and adventure. You don't have to have blood and guts everywhere, but you can have action and adventure. Give them real strong girl characters.

> **Do you think it's hard to create games for girls without promoting stereotypes?**

> I don't find it hard at all.

> **Is there a particular type of girl your CD ROM is aimed at?**

> I think the ages were something like seven to thirteen. But I think women and younger girls can also enjoy it.

I got mostly really great reviews on it, which made me feel good, but I also got some really strange criticism, and one of them was that I was stereo-typing girls because I had a paper-doll game on it. A dress up game. And you know, I think you must not throw out the baby with the bathwater. Everything must not be this humorless, "Yes, we must all grow up to be brain surgeons." You know what I mean? I think we all do want to have fun, and I still like to play dress-up.

> **And there's nothing wrong with it! I hate it when people say it's wrong because it's a girl thing.**

> You're right! And what they're doing is saying girl things equal silly and frivolous, and boys' things equal important.

> **It's funny, but I also have a paper doll game on my Website for *Net Chick*. Out of seven or eight items of clothing, the player has to get the right combination of three items to win a key to my secret diary.**

> That's incredible! That's what I have in my—oh! you will love my CD ROM! It has a wardrobe full of clothes, and she's wearing a night shirt and fluffy slippers, and the Hawaiian girl says, "Come on, let's go out and have our adventure," and she says, "As soon as I decide what to wear." And until you click on the right outfit, you can't move to the next screen.

> **Oh Trina! This is so weird! I thought I was being original.**
(laughs, then gets serious)

> And then someone criticized me because one of my characters wears pink all the time. It's the blonde, the Jewish mall rat from New York. It's just who she is! She likes to wear a lot of pink! The other character wears very bright colors, reds and blues.

> **It frustrates me when people criticize stuff like that, because it takes power away from feminine qualities. There should be power in pink and in paper dolls.**

> You are absolutely right. When I researched *A Century of Women Cartoonists* one of the first things I discovered was that the early women cartoonists had specialized in the comics about cute little kids. And at first I was a little embarrassed that they did this trivial thing, just comics over and over again about little kids, and then I thought, "Wait a minute! If men had done comics about cute little kids and women had done comics about superheroes, then superheroes would be considered trivial and cute little kids would be considered a real major importance.

> **Yes, that's exactly right. It just infuriates me! The thing is, it depends on how you portray it. If you have a girl wearing pink and she's an idiot, well then she's an idiot. But if you have her wearing pink and she's tough and cool, then great!**

> What happens to my character is that she starts off as this New Yorker who knows nothing, and she becomes strong and brave and learns about Hawaii.

> **Do you think that comics and CD ROMs are mediums in which boys naturally gravitate toward more than girls, or do you think girls could be just as involved if…**

> Girls have been involved with comics in the past. This is one of the discoveries I'm going to put in my next book. There were many superheroines aimed at girls. So many girls read comics in the past. I have figures from a study made in the WWII years showing—I don't have them in front of me so I may be off a point or two—that with school-age children, 97 percent of the boys read comics, and 94 percent of the girls read comics! That's incredible. And then a 1994 study by DC Comics shows that 92 percent of their readers were boys, and 6 percent were girls. Look at the difference! It's because there were comics for girls in those days. So of course it's total bullshit to say that girls don't read comics. Girls read comics when there are comics for girls to read.

> **So what caused the change?**

> A number of things happened. First of all, we had the WWII years, which were fantastic for women. I mean, obviously they weren't fantastic years—hundreds of thousands of people died—but on the home front it was a real woman's world. Women were doing everything. They weren't just working in factories, they were the street-car conductors and the mechanics, they were doing everything.

> **Even baseball players.**

> Exactly! So in a way they really were superheroines. The home front was a woman's world, and it's reflected in the comics. There was nothing women couldn't do, and it was the same in the comics. There were all these strong heroines, and there was nothing they couldn't do. Now it didn't all go away right after the war, you have to understand, it kind of died down slowly. For instance, 1948 was a fantastic time for superheroines. From '46 through '48, Marvel Comics put out four superheroines—each had their own book—and they were obviously meant for girls. They advertised in Marvel's girl magazine which was called *Miss America*, and in each other's comic books as well. One of them lasted til '49, another til '52. It was kind of like a six-year superheroine slumber party.

But very slowly, through the '50s, what happened was that action comics in general—both superhero and superheroine comics—went downhill. There were less and less of them. I think it was a result of two things. One was the war, people had really had enough of violence. And then also, a book called *Seduction of the Innocent*, written by a psychologist named Dr. Frederic Wertham, was published in 1954, and it kind of was the death nell for action comics, because it was all about how comics caused juvenile delinquence. There were even Senate Subcommittee meetings on this. They even had mass burnings of action comics, and he [Wertham] called everything a crime comic, even *Wonder Woman*. He just lumped them all together.

Hawaii High:
The Mystery of the Tiki

The tiki-pop surf music immediately drew me in and had me going throughout my mission of returning the stolen ancient tiki. Being a game freak, I'm not sure which was more fun, solving the puzzles in order to continue on with my adventure or the adventure itself. What I do know is that I thoroughly enjoyed playing—and solving—the tiki mystery with Hawaii High's Jennifer and Maleah. It was great to finally be part of a strong girl team in a digital game. It is a little young, though. If only someone would make similar games for grrrls. Hurry, Ms. Robbins, and give us more!

(Written and illustrated by Trina Robbins, produced by Sanctuary Woods: 415/578-6340.)

So there was this period where superheroes and superheroines just kind of died, and then when they came back, superheroes came back in full force, but the superheroine was literally weakened. In my book I say that in 1961, when the superheroine returned to Marvel Comics, she was literally invisible, and that was Sue Storm, The Invisible Girl [from Fantastic Four], who is such a wimp! I mean all she ever does is faint and have to get rescued. And after all these fabulous strong women. The superheroine really never recovered, because the guys took over.

> **Name one or two of your favorite superheroines of the past. I'm not too familiar with that era.**

> One of them was Mary Marvel. She was just great! Mary Marvel, in real life, was Mary Batson, the twin sister of Billy Batson, who became Captain Marvel. Both of them just had to say the magic word "Shazam!" and they became these great superhero and superheroine characters. And the thing about her is that she was a girl, she wasn't a woman, she didn't have breasts, she was maybe twelve or thirteen, and she was invincible. This twelve or thirteen-year-old flat-chested girl! She could fly, bullets bounced off her, she could do anything.

> **Now this wasn't related to Isis, was it?**

> No no no. O Mighty Isis was a great character, but she was really a TV character from the '70s. You know, in the '70s there was this very very brief resurrection because of feminism. Suddenly there were these neat superheroine characters on TV and in the comics again—very very briefly. They didn't last, because there was such a backlash against feminism.

They also brought Wonder Woman back to TV...

> **And the Bionic Woman...**

> That's right. But if you look now, you won't find anything like that. There's nothing. It's pathetic.

> **Your new book, *History of Super Heroines*, sounds inspiring.**

> Well it's going to tell people a lot that they didn't know before, because, you know, in every field men have written the history, and they've always left out the women. Even contemporary men who've written books about comics talk about superheroes, and they totally neglect the superheroines. Or if they talk about them at all, it's one of two things: It's either very negative, like it's just a bunch of lesbians who want to beat up men, or it's this whole nudge-nudge, wink-wink thing, which is even worse.

> **What I admire about you is that you're always this pioneer breaking new grounds in a so-called "man's field."**

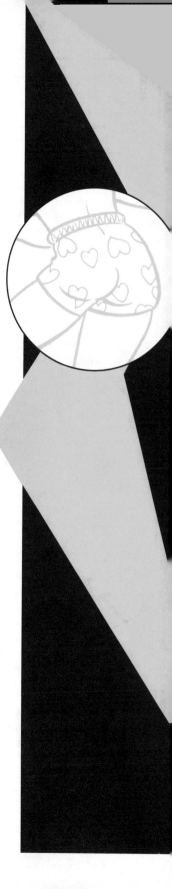

> Well I don't set out to be a pioneer, I just set out to do things I like, but then I discover I'm being left out because I'm a woman, and I get mad.

> **How did you start off in the underground comic scene?**

> There's a classic example [of being left out]. My first comic was printed in 1966 in the *East Village Other*, which was this underground newspaper in New York. And I was just this hippie who very seriously and sincerely believed in peace and love—and I still do—and it didn't occur to me that anybody would leave me out. But within two years I discovered that these guys [comic artists] were asking each other to be in each other's books, and they were just completely ignoring me. Or like Ed Sanders—a writer and poet who was in the Fugs, a major figure from the hippie days—had an exhibit of underground comics in the Lower East Side in 1968 and asked all the guys to be in it and just completely ignored me. And here I was, appearing in the *East Village Other*, in *Gothic Blimpworks*, which was this other underground newspaper, and he just didn't ask me. Some other guys in Chicago put together a benefit book for the Chicago Eight, and again asked all the guys and didn't ask me. I slowly started realizing I was being left out, that it was a boys' club.

> **So what did you do about it?**

> By 1970 I put together the first—the very first in the universe—all-woman comic. I had moved by then to San Francisco, and I joined what I believe is the first feminist underground newspaper on the West Coast. It was called *It Ain't Me Babe*, and I put out a comic also called *It Ain't Me Babe* in conjunction with the paper. It was the first all-woman book in the world.

> **Have you enjoyed your career as an artist, despite the boys' club?**

> Well, I'm drawing less and less and writing more and more for that reason. You really can't continue to hit your head against the wall....

> **But don't you find that changing? I see lots of women comic artists now.**

> What I see is women drawing for the independents and the black-and-whites, and that's all very nice, but I don't think there's anything wrong with asking to make as much money as the guys...

> **So is that why you don't do underground comix anymore? Because of poor pay and the way you were treated?**

> Well yeah. I'm better than that. I'm better than twenty-five dollars a page. I really want to do stuff for girls these days, and there's nowhere in the under-ground.... The underground has gotten very typified, stereotyped, with lots of angst-ridden strips, semi-autobiographical or just stone autobiographical. And that's not what I do. I want to put my energy into positive things, like the books that I'm writing. I also want to stories, and I want to do stories for girls. •

Aren't hobbies the best? There are so many ways to be diverted! Unfortunately, I couldn't even begin to cover them all here, so bear with me. I chose some random leisure sites of distractions I'd like to try some day (stuff I think I'd be good at!), and hopefully at least one of them will catch your interest too. Oh, and excuse the Barbie explosion—I was just going to sneak in one of her pages for fun and got a little carried away!

INTERNATIONAL PEN PAL PAGE
http://www.magic.mb.ca/~lampi/penpal.html

An avid letter-writer and pen-pal collector named Jill runs this site. Preferring paper and pen over electronic correspondence, she focuses on how to find snail-mail pals (but mentions e-pals as well), giving lots of addresses to get you started. In case you've already got some faraway friends, she also has worldly links to places like Hotel Guide Taiwan, Welcome to Saudi Arabia, A Gateway to Suriname, and Virtual Vacations.

WORLD WIDE QUILTING PAGE
http://ttsw.com/MainQuiltingPage.html

Quilting has always seemed to be an old-granny's kind of sport to me, but looking at the intricate how-to diagrams and pretty designs shed a whole new light on the matter. Quilters should find this site useful. It has online catalogs so people can modem in for supplies, a bulletin board, a FAQ, info on shows and fabrics, a page on the history of quilts, and links to other textile Webspots.

--more-->

Leisurely.
newsgroups

Got a geeky pastime your friends aren't interested in? Have no one to share that fine moment when you've scored big in your field of hobbyism? (Mine is Scrabble—problem is, I can never find anyone to play it with.) Who cares? Just pop into a group of like-minded leisurely nerds and you'll be able to brag and gab to your heart's content!

alt.books.anne-rice
A place where Lestat and Louis worshipers run rampant. Being a sucker for vampire culture myself, I was highly entertained by so much Rice character and plot analysis, as well as the random goth talk.

alt.books.reviews
I love this opinionated literary salon—it's refreshing to hear what unpretentious nonjournalists have to say about a book for a change. All genres are open for discussion.

alt.sewing
I'm not used to seeing so many chicks in one group! (There were a few boys braving it out.) Anyway, sewers of all genders should like this group, which manages to make subjects like patterns, fabric stores, special projects, and dyeing material actually seem interesting.

alt.smokers
I was hoping for more cultural conversation on the art of smoking: favorite brands, smoking accessories, etc. Instead I was surrounded mostly by political rants about smokers' rights, with only a dash of lighter tobacco chat. But smokers may enjoy the anti-smoker bashing.

rec.antiques

Lots of action in this nook, with buyers and sellers of antiques or vintage items trying to connect with each other, novice collectors wanting to know how to repair particular pieces or asking about which books they should read, etc.

rec.antiques.radio+phone

Almost as busy as rec.antiques, but with much more of a focus. I was quite a fascinated lurker reading about all of the old communication gadgets.

rec.crafts.brewing

Enthusiastic brewers exchange their ideas and beer-making techniques.

rec.crafts.textiles.quilting

Quilting fabrics, kits, classes, projects, Web pages . . . if it's quilting-related, you'll find it here.

rec.crafts.textiles.sewing

Read the above review, but replace "quilting" with "sewing."

ANTIQUES
http://www.ic.mankato.mn.us/antiques/Antiques.html
This is a good place for the novice antique collector, with an index explaining what to look for when determining the value of items such as magazine ads, dolls, furniture, Disney memorabilia, and African masks. You also get guidelines for choosing and negotiating with dealers. I only wish there were more photos here, especially of the kitschier items.

THE ROBOT GROUP HOME PAGE
http://198.6.201.224/robotg/robo.html
Some innovative artists and engineers got together in 1989 to start the Robot Group—an excuse to explore ways of merging technology and junk to create art. Based in Texas, these 'botheads have regular meetings and annual shows to strut their creations, which you've got to see to fully appreciate. All interested artists and nerds should check this out.

PHOTON
"The Art and Science of Light"
http://www.scotborders.co.uk/photon/index.html
Photon, whose UK roots are in paper, is for the more serious photographer who wants to sharpen her skills in the areas of lighting and film processing. Examples of what you'd be reading include "The Simplest Developer of All," "Sterling Premium and Lith Papers," and "Electronic Imaging News." You can access back issues and browse through their index of photo sites, which is updated regularly. Don't let the ads bum you out—they allow this sharp vivid rag to stay online.

YAHOO: GARDENING
http://www.yahoo.com/Entertainment/
Home_and_Garden/Gardening/
It's all here! Pages on bonsai, flowers, agriculture, trees, and gardening books, terms, products, photos, mailing lists… This huge arboreal database will point you to the foliage of your choice.

THE BEER PAGE
http://www.umich.edu/~spencer/beer/.
I must admit I can't stand the taste of beer, preferring crass tropical drinks myself. But I still found this online brewery to be quite interesting. They give you a bunch of different beer recipes, some home brewers' reports on their (sometimes botched) experiments, downloadable beer labels, cans and bottles from around the world, and so much more. If only beer mugs and paper umbrellas mixed!

HACKER BARBE DREAM BASEMENT APARTMENT
http://www.catalog.com/mrm/
barbe/barbe.html
Get the scoop on Barbie and Ken's creators, find out how they were named, and then make a beeline to the down and dirty hack-jobs on Barbie, er, I mean Barbe (I'm not sure why these site masters insist on hacking the "i" out of her name). It's always fun to see ol' Barb in nontraditional clothing and poses.

--more-->

Leisurely.
newsgroups

rec.crafts.winemaking
There's more to this craft than I realized, with topics like preparing corks, to stir or not to stir, and making piña colada and mandarin wines. Yum!

rec.gardens
Having such a general newsgroup name, the spectrum of topics here is huge. You'll find discussions ranging from Jamaican Mint Bushes to pesticides to Japanese Beetles to growing tomatoes.

rec.photo.advanced
You don't need to be a professional, but you ought to know a little more than how to snap a photo to get along with these camera junkies.

rec.photo.darkroom

I couldn't understand most of the dialogue, but I'm pretty sure this group is hip enough for you know-it-all film developers.

rec.photo.help

Ah, finally a photo newsgroup I could jive with. The ABCs of photography are spelled out simply in this forum.

rec.photo.marketplace

Selling or shopping for a camera, developing equipment, or lenses? Look no further!

Collector's Groups:

alt.collecting.8-track-tapes
alt.collecting.autographs
alt.collecting.teddy-bears
alt.disney.collecting
rec.collecting.coins
rec.collecting.phonecards
rec.collecting.stamps
rec.collecting.barbie

THE BARBIE PAGE

http://silver.ucs.indiana.edu/~jwarf/barbie.html

Oh my. A seriously obsessed Barbie collector indeed. But it's her (random chick) sincere enthusiasm over the plastic beast that makes this site a joy-read. She shares her personal collection with us, including her "special awesome Barbies," and gives lots of literature and tips for other Barbie zealots. Of course her pages are adorned with pictures galore.

THE BEACH CITIES BARBIE DOLL COLLECTORS CLUB

http://www.primenet.com/~gambit/barbie.html

Into trading and selling Her, this club puts its newsletter online and posts Barbie personal ads (including prices).

PETITE PRINCESS PAGE

http://deepthought.armory.com/~zenugirl/barbie.html

"The Online Zine for Adult Fashion Doll Collectors"

At first my eyes did a big loopdy-loop when I saw yet another page for Barbie collectors, with the usual low-down on Barbie stats including info on doll shows, Barbie clubs, identifying and restoring dolls, etc. But then I scrolled down to The Plastic Princess Freak Circus and realized that these Barbie collectors/fans had some funk to them as well. In the Circus you can enjoy the Mattel creatures posed as Nicole and O.J., biker Barbies, and Babs as hacker-nerd, among other sideshows. Lite but entertaining. •

H⊙T SITES:
Hitting the Road

Whether you're skating around the block or getting a one-way ticket to Timbuktu, traveling can always be an adventure. The following will give you a peek at what's out there, as well as offer you some hot vacation tips and the low-down on the best travel buys around. Bon Voyage!

IN SARDINIA
http://www.crs4.it/~cirio/ISV/

Mamma mia! If you haven't yet booked a trip to Sardinia, you'll be itching to after reading this online magazine. Written in English as well as Italian, *In Sardinia* covers the island's popular traditions, tourism, and info on direct connections and flight timetables. It's loaded with engaging articles such as "Riding in Marmilla," a woman's account of her horseback riding excursion through Sardinia's wild surroundings. Gorgeous photos accompany most of the pieces. If you can't fit Europe into your budget, you can at least visit Sardinia vicariously via the Net.

HIGHLAND RANCH
http://www.gulker.com/hr/index.html

Two hours north of San Francisco lies this low-key ranch-style resort, which has horseback riding, tennis courts, wine tasting, a swimming pool, and a two-acre lake. You can make reservation inquiries here, as well as find out about the weather, get a detailed map, and look up other travel facts about the area. The downside of this site is that they're too skimpy with the photos. From what I can see it looks lush and serene, but I'd like to see more.

---more--->

Traveling.Newsgroups

Planning a journey of some sort? If your Fodor's isn't enough, I'll bet some of these professional tourists can help.

alt.travel.road-trip
Mapping out a road trip? You may want to start here. You'll run into drivers and passengers trying to hook up, travelers asking for the best route to take and what to see and do once they get to their destination, etc. Also lots of inquiries on motels, truck stops, etc.

alt.vacation.las-vegas
I love Vegas (and I'm a pretty good gambler, if I do say so myself!), so I had to stick this in. It's all about glitzy hotels, glitzier shows, gambling tips, sights to see, and more.

rec.travel.air
Airfare, plane food, favorite airlines, hijacks...anything you've ever wanted to know about air culture—and more!

rec.travel.asia
rec.travel.europe
rec.travel.latin-america
rec.travel.usa-canada
These four groups attract nice, savvy travelers who answer any questions on what to pack, hotel prices, trains, food, hiking, national parks, airlines, etc., that the newcomers throw at them.

rec.travel.cruises

Don't even get me started on the god-awful cruise I took. But that was Carnival. (I could've kicked Kathie Lee!) Maybe some exotic line going to Alaska or out of Singapore would be different. ...If you dare, check out the various cruiselines, prices and discounts, and harsh cruise rants.

rec.travel.marketplace

Kind of like the travel section in a newspaper, this crowded group puts up wanted and for sale notices on tickets, accommodations, and other random travel items.

rec.travel.misc

"African travel," "Where to find Monarch butterflies in Mexico," "Thailand shots needed" ...an interesting mix of miscellaneous travel talk.

HOT SITES continued

FLEET HOUSE: CANADA, THE CANADIAN TRAVEL MAGAZINE
http://www.fleethouse.com

This is a great resource for people traveling to Canada for business or pleasure. Read about Canada's hotels, attractions, entertainment, and local information. The best thing about this online magazine is that you can get special deals through its sponsors, such as the Hyatt Regency, just for being on the Net.

PLANET HAWAII
http://planet-hawaii.com/

The photos here are enough to make me want to pack up and head for the white beaches and mango trees of the Polynesian islands. If you're planning a trip to Hawaii, this site should come in handy, with descriptions and room rates for a variety of hotels and B&Bs. You can also get info on the many different airlines that fly there, and find out about the islands' rafting excursions and airplane and helicopter tours. I absolutely love Hawaii, so I was happy to find a Website that focuses not only on Hawaii's tourism but that also gives extensive info on the islands' culture, business, and history.

CARIBMOON
http://www.caribweb.com/caribweb/caribmoon/

Wanna get married on a warm, breezy, tropical island? If that's the plan, you should definitely find your way to this site, which lists various Caribbean spots (Virgin Islands, Anguilla, Antigua, Barbuda, etc.). It tells you about the marriage fees as well as what kind of documents, special licenses, and other paperwork you'll need in order to have a legal wedding on the island of your choice. You can also read about other couples' Caribbean weddings and honeymoon experiences (or share your own) here.

If you're not into getting married at the moment but want to go to the Caribbean anyway, just for pleasure's sake, check out http://www.caribweb.com/caribweb/ to access lots of photos, restaurants, maps, and hundreds of hotels that the islands have to offer.

ALL ADVENTURE TRAVEL
http://www.alladventure.com/

From Boulder, Colorado, this travel agency books any type of trip that caters to the adventurist, including "biking, hiking, walking, rafting, sea kayaking, wildlife tours, and expedition cruises all over the world." Check out their online vacation directory; if something sparks your interest, jot down its code number and then fill out their "worksheet" to get more detailed information on the trip.

All Adventure also has a great hotlist (http://www.netweb.com/danr/links.html) full of links to other travel pages, which contain info on ski tours, mountain biking, a collection of Websites about Europe, a travel magazine called *Outside On-Line,* and more. •

g

o

HOT SITES:
Tasty Bytes

I'm one of those people whose day can be ruined by a bad meal. If I wait too long to eat, I get extremely shaky and mean. Eating is a satisfying, sensual, gleeful experience. Even talking about food makes me happy. So of course I had to explore every food spot I could find on the Web. I realized I'm not the only one who's so fond of food—there are way too many delicious sites to cover here! So I picked the ones that interested me most, and have included a few that have enticing foodlinks so that you can discover a lot more on your own. For a list of more than eighty recipe sites for everything from candy to ethnic cuisine to soups, salads, and seafood, browse through Yahoo's Search Index at http://www.yahoo.com/ Entertainment/Food/Cooking/. If you find recipes that interest you, remember to print them out and file them in your kitchen.

Bon appétit!

CHOCOLATE LOVER'S PAGE
http://www.ios.com/~mb/chocolate/

Yum! Here's a list of more than twenty-five chocolate links; you can salivate over the goods from sweetshops like Godiva's, Hershey's, the Seattle Chocolate Company, Hawaii's Treasures, and Casa de Fruta. You can order your candy online at most of these sites, which also include lots of

---more on page 150--->

family digi dish

20,030 bytes
3 floppies (naked)
2 rotten apples

* fry above ingredients with large magnet
* mix in 1 mouse cord, 1 shredded graphics card
* serve steaming on a clean bernoulli!

bon bytin'!

— jorja

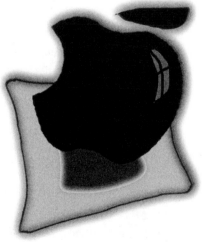

Eats.Newsgroups

The Usenet food titles that first caught my eye were ones I could personally relate to, like alt.college.food, alt.food.cocacola, and alt.fast-food. Unfortunately, these seemingly kitschier groups were actually pretty meek and dull (except for alt.cereal), whereas the more general, typical-sounding conferences were unexpectedly quite interesting and useful. Get ready to drool.

alt.cereal

Saturday morning cartoons, feet-pajamas, a hidden toy, and a big bowl of sugar-laden Quisp. Or Freakies. Or was it Booberry? Nostalgic cereal talk runs rampant in this nook.

alt.coffee

I didn't know so much could be said about coffee! When I last lurked around this group the buzz was about Starbucks, carrot coffee cake, home roasting, decafing techniques, and Jamaican Blue Mountain coffee. Coffee worshipers can find even more at rec.food.drink.coffee.

alt.food.fat-free

I usually shy away from fatless food, but *mmm*! These fat-watchers actually have some recipes that make me salivate.

alt.food.sushi

Raw fish enthusiasts rave about their favorite Japanese restaurants, show off their knowledge of sushi etiquette, and talk about their experience with the deliciously slimy delicacy.

rec.food.cooking

A bustling hangout where cooks swap their culinary tips and secrets, as well as share recipes (guacamole, gazpacho, onion rings, blackened anything, etc.). Humorous off-the-subject discussions sneak in here too, like debating whether eating around the corn cob instead of across it (typewriter style) is rude. This is the most crowded of the food newsgroups that I've seen.

delicious pictures, gift ideas, recipes, and chocolate trivia.

DON'T PANIC EAT ORGANIC

http://www.rain.org/~sals/my.html ● ● ●

Have you ever eaten—or even seen—a cherimoya? They're weird green hard-looking bumpy fruits, which is all I knew about them before finding this site.

This is the Home Page of Noah's Ark, one of the world's suppliers of organic cherimoyas. They give you a full report on the "sweet custard-like" fruit, which comes from Peru and Ecuador. Learn how to detect a ripe cherimoya and how to cut and eat the fruit. You can get recipes on how to prepare Cherimoya Bavaroise and Cherimoya Custard Pie. If you don't know what cherimoyas look like, get a load of all the pretty photos. Now I can't wait to have a cherimoya experience!

CHEESE RECIPES

http://www.vuw.ac.nz/who/Amy.Gale/ ● ● ●
recipes/cheese/cheese.html

Check out all the cheesy recipes Amy Gale shares with us and learn how to make beer cheese soups, cheese fondue, mozzarella cheese sticks, Greek cheese pie, and more. She also gives simple instructions on how to make your own cheese. These recipes are graphic-free, which makes them easy to print out. Gale is a student at the Victoria University of Wellington in New Zealand and has a cool Home Page, which you can get to from here.

HERBS AND SPICES

http://www.teleport.com/~ronl/ ● ● ●
herbs.html

Of course you get pointers on how to flavor your victuals with recipes for herb sour cream bread, tofu balls, anise biscotti, and other zesty delights. But what's far more interesting is the herb and spice "index," which gives you a brief history of each herb/spice

---more--->

rec.food.drink.tea

Tea punch, how to prepare tea leaves, Kombucha, Turkish tea glasses . . . Like alt.coffee, except it's all about tea.

rec.food.historic

Did Marco Polo introduce spaghetti to the West? Where did pizza originate? What is Neruda pudding? Food trivia is asked and sometimes answered here. Also a good place to find old-fashioned cooking techniques, like instructions on making historic sourdough starters.

rec.food.recipes

No chitchat, just a huge mound of single-post topics offering mouth-watering, mostly unusual recipes, like thumbprint cookies, curried orange roughy almondine, Thai iced tea, and French silk pie.

rec.food.veg.cooking

A meeting place for vegetarians.

and alternative ways to use these seasonings. For instance, if you click on ginger, you'll find out that the Greeks have been making gingerbread for 4,000 years and that ginger was used by the ancients as both a spice and a digestive aid. Ginger is also supposed to relieve motion sickness, help improve circulation, and make a good tingling bath (read how to prepare a ginger bath!). If you're left wanting more, check out the sizable list of spicy cookbooks.

THE CHILE-HEADS HOME PAGE

http://www.netimages.com/ ~chile/

If you want something hotter than herbs and spices, you'll definitely find it here. Besides getting peppery recipes, restaurants, and festival info, you can stroll through the chile gallery, which has more than fifty colorful pepper photos and more than twenty-five descriptions of the various species. You can also learn how to grow chile peppers (even in your apartment in cool climates!), as well as how to harvest, preserve, roast, and peel them. After you think you've mastered the pepper, quiz yourself with their trivia questions.

ROLLING YOUR OWN SUSHI

http://www.rain.org/~hutch/sushi.html

For you raw fish spurners, not all sushi includes uncooked seafood, so stop wrinkling your nose.

Once you have all the foodstuffs and equipment needed, I don't think it's as hard as it looks to make these exotic treats. At least it doesn't look hard, with the simple instructions and diagrams offered here. These Japanese chefs teach you how to make all sorts of sushi, including California rolls, hand rolls, and tamago (sushi omelets). They also teach you some essential vocabulary so you can act like a real pro when you serve your fancy dishes to your friends.

---more--->

THE BURRITO PAGE

"Worldwide Web Headquarters for Burrito & Burrito-Related Information"

http://www.infobahn.com/pages/rito.html

This is a fun one! Choose your favorite burrito and find out what it says about your character and personality. I ordered my usual: rice and beans, no cheese, tomatoes, lettuce, guacamole, sour cream, and mild salsa, and was told that I'm resourceful (because the burrito I ordered only costs $3.49) but that I have a great fear of risk (since I avoided all strong flavors). Of course the last part is totally false! If you're a real fan of this Mexican dish, peruse the burrito articles and other literature linked here.

HEALTHY GOURMET VEGETARIAN FOOD PAGE

http://www.dfw.net/~planedoc/food.html

The problem I find with a lot of vegetarian food is that it's either bland or it feels like something's missing from my meal. This site, however, features vegetarian recipes that look like they'd trick even the most critical carnivore into thinking she was eating a hearty and savory feast. The specialties I came across (they feature at least one new recipe a month) were Mexican Empanadas and Enchiladas, which I saved onto my desktop for future experimentation. If you can't find some of the ingredients or tools needed to make one of their entrees, you can order them from the site by emailing Teresa, the creator of this page.

HAWAII'S FAVORITE RECIPES

"Aunty Leilani's Cooking Show"

http://hisurf.aloha.com/Recipes.html

Aunty Leilani will teach you how to make all sorts of tropical dishes, like Internet Island Fruit Salad, Guava Delight, and Lolo's Ono Aku Poki. (I looked up "aku" in both my Webster and Scrabble dictionaries, but it's not listed in either. Sounds pretty exotic to me!) The recipes are very simple, and Aunty makes the place so quaint. •

Kirsten Wild

S I T E S S

Too impatient to wait for the future? Put away your crystal balls. Now you can catch a peek into your tomorrow without leaving your computers. But don't be sore if you get a bad forecast—enter these sites at your own risk!

ASTROLOGY: WEEKLY CYBER-STARS
http://www.realitycom.com/cybstars/stars.html

The position and dynamics of the planets and stars are explained as though they were part of a Hollywood plot. After reading the entertaining analysis of our solar system's demeanor, point to your sign and read your weekly horoscope. It will start to make sense like it never has before!

CHINESE ZODIAC
http://falcom.cc.ukans.edu/~mothball/mystik/Chinese%20Zodiac/

Are you a dog, tiger, snake…?
There are twelve astrological animals in the Chinese zodiac, each with different strengths and characteristics.
All you need to know is your birth year to find out what animal you are. This site will give you a brief description of your traits and will tell you which animals you get along with best. Don't be offended if you're a rat! It just means you're honest, ambitious, and clever.

MADAME ANANSI'S READINGS, FORTUNES AND HREFs
http://main.street.net/fortune/

Venture into the abyss of Madame Anansi's blue velvet curtains where the fortune teller awaits you. You must pay her before she reads you, but don't worry, she's a bit rickety and won't notice if you pass her some funny money. Seems like she took a few nips before I came in. First she offered me coffee or espresso, which I thought was a nice gesture, so I clicked on espresso.

--more-->

I-CHING
http://cad.ucla.edu/repository/useful/iching.html

It's easy to get an I-Ching reading. All you have to do is concentrate on a question or problem that's bugging you and then click to cast the coins. The hard part is understanding the results, since the oracle here uses lingo that only experienced I-Chingers would completely grasp. But after I read their brief lesson, I was able to make some sense of my current and projected forecasts, and I found the whole system of I-Ching to be intricately fascinating. If you want more intelligent information on this ancient method of fortune telling, you can jump to the article "Advanced I-Ching: The Structure of a Well-Ordered Family," by Terrence Payne. (http://cad.ucla.edu/repository/useful/iching-tpayne.html)

w.w.w.hoa

That shuttled me over to a cappuccino maker (http://www.cs.su.oz.au/~bob/coffee.html), but no one was there to serve me. I stared at the espresso machine for a few secs, and then went back to Madame, coffeeless, for my fortune. This is what the biddy came up with: "Learn all you can about a man, Howard Stern. He will slander you in the future." Let him try! I then clicked on Howard Stern and a HS Home Page popped up (http://krishna.cs.umd.edu/stern/). I think all of her fortunes take you to some strange new Website, which makes Madame all the more intriguing. As far as her tarot readings go, read the "Know the Future: TAROT" review in this section (that is where you'll jump to from here).

INTERNET HOROSCOPES

http://www.ws.pipex.com/tis/horoscop/horo5.htm

Astrological Angela is your "resident horoscope expert" at this neon ward from the UK. Just click on your zodiac sign and she'll predict what the upcoming week has in store for you. She'll also tell you what your sign means, and offer you links to other hot horoscope interpreters.

JONATHAN CAINER'S ZODIAC FORECASTS

http://194.70.238.1/webstars/index.html

This horoscope is from England's *Daily Mail Newspaper*. You have the option of either reading today's fortune or listening to it in real time audio. If you want a more in-depth reading, you can order a full-fledged personal horoscope by sending them your date, time and place of birth along with £17.99 (or the US equivalent).

KNOW THE FUTURE: TAROT

http://cad.ucla.edu:8001/tarot (short reading)

http://cad.ucla.edu/repository/useful/tarotceltic/tarotceltic.html

You get a choice with this tarot reader: If you're in a hurry, go to the first

--more-->

ANGELA

I've run into some cyberspots that kick my adrenal glands into unknown regions because of their super-high creativeness, outlandish subject matter, or flare for being weeeird. But I wasn't sure where to put them. I mean, where do you stick a site that startles you with a huge staring unblinking eyeball? Or that casually talks about ghosts who take over living bodies so that they can tell the future to eager fortune seekers? So, for lack of a distinct category, let's just mark these with an X.

SCHWA: YOU HAVE FOUND US
http://fringeware.com/SchwaRoot/Schwa.html
Warning: Enter at your own risk.

Alien Repellent Patch: The Plutonium™ coated patch at left will prevent abduction for up to 48 hours. Clip & tape on skin. Relax.
For more information on alien defense send a stamped, self-addressed envelope to Schwa, Box 6064 Reno NV 89513

WEIRDNESS
http://www.paranoia.com:80/~fraterk/weird.html
One of the weirder hotlists in the netsphere, where you can catch links to: an experiment involving a toaster, Pop-Tart, and blowtorch; a virtual Lite-Brite (it really works!); a lesson on how to fill a Pez dispenser; a place where you can type a message to a real cat who supposedly will hear your words; and even more weird stuff.

address, where you'll get a brief reading. You begin by concentrating on a question or problem that's bugging you. Then three cards pop up and give you the scoop on your past, present, and future. About as in-depth as the daily paper's horoscope.

At the second address you get a full-fledged Keltic reading. The invisible fortune teller first asks you to choose a card that you feel best represents you and then lays out a whole batch of cards that describes all aspects of your life. It takes a while to download all of the fanciful cards, but if you're curious enough, it's worth the wait.

REAL ASTROLOGY
http://www.butterfly.net:80/astro/
This is a syndicated weekly horoscope by one of my favorite astrologers, Bob Brezny, whose column I've faithfully read in *Details* for a long time. Even if you don't believe in the stars, he gives good simple advice that would enrich anyone's day, and does it with a sense of humor. His forecasts are updated every Wednesday.

WORLD WIDE WEB OUIJA
http://www.math.unh.edu/~black/cgi-bin/ouija.cgi
Ouija boards have always given me a rush—until I actually play with them. The idea and look of the game is so much more intriguing than its practicality. So of course I felt that old familiar surge when the electric version of the Ouija popped up on my screen. The foreboding letters and numbers look just like the cardboard version's, and the mouse is used as the plastic slider. After concentrating on a question, I closed my eyes and spun myself around the room, as was suggested, and then, with eyes still closed, clicked my mouse a few times. The computer kept track of the letters and numbers that I randomly pointed to, but none of it made sense. Deflated once again. I think you need to play this with friends so that at least someone can cheat. •

SPIRIT WWW
http://zeta.cs.adfa.oz.au/
Graphically lame, but this nonprofit cosmic connection has more info on matters of "spiritual conciousness" than any other site I've seen. Read about channeling, UFOs, out-of-body experiences, reincarnation, etc. Then, if you're still interested, check out their huge list of recommended books.

WELCOME TO SPATULA CITY!
http://www.wam.umd.edu/~twoflowr/
What a trip! If there's such a thing as virtual drugs, I think someone slipped me a dose. Wander into this surreal spatula-laden supermarket and take a stroll through one of its four aisles, each one braided with humor and the bizarre. I became involved with "the world's first virtual reality staring contest" (and lost), went through around ten pages of amusing "warning" signs to get to a nude photo (which, when I finally got to it, induced a bitter chortle out of me), flipped through a spatula catalog that could only exist in Wonderland, and stumbled upon many other peculiarities that can only be experienced firsthand.

COMMOTION STRANGE
http://ecosys.drdr.virginia.edu/~jsm8f/commotion.html
Welcome to Anne Rice's irregularly published newsletter, which is put onto this site by her fans. Rice keeps her readers updated on coven parties, shares her feelings on the *Interview with a Vampire* film, defends her decision to promote her new book on the *Vampire* video, and welcomes fans to call and leave a message on her answering machine (she gives us her phone number!). She says she sometimes returns calls to answer questions. These pages also sport a photo of Rice's house in New Orleans, offer transcripts of TV shows that have interviewed her, have the address to the *Vampire Lestat* Fan Club, and give you links to other Rice pages. I'm now a converted fan!

ILLUMINET PRESS
http://illuminet.com/~ron/inet.html
For further exploration into the X-zone, you may want to browse through Illuminet's books. They cover topics on conspiracy, UFOs, Magick, alternative science and energy, and more. Order their free catalog or splurge on some books via your modem.

web witches

No, you're not going to see any pictures of Elizabeth Montgomery here! Instead, this chart will point you to various branches of Witchcraft and Paganism, the most goddess-respecting religions around.

JOAN'S WITCH DIRECTORY

http://www.ucmb.ulb.ac.be:80/~joan/witches/index .html

Highlights: •A list and description of accused witches; Letters written by witches from the 1600s; •Joan's pondering notes on the history of witchy icons (brooms, moons, cats, Voodoo, etc.); •Witches in art and in excerpts from books; •List of upcoming pagan festivals.

Lesson I learned: "...witches were mostly mid-wives, knowledgeable in the use of herbs and medical procedures that weren't approved by the church. The witches were also the men and women who followed Pagan religions, which threatened the control by the Catholic church."

the covenant of the goddess

COVENANT OF THE GODDESS HOMEPAGE

http://www.crc.ricoh.com/~rowanf/COG/cog.html

Highlights: •A good explanation of what COG is about; •A witchcraft "press packet" with definitions, their basic philosophy, answers to FAQs, etc; •Guides to Wiccan and pagan publications, student groups, special herbs, and on/offline "witch" stores.

Lesson I learned: "The Covenant of the Goddess is one of the largest and oldest Wiccan religious organizations... Wicca, or Witchcraft is the most popular expression of the religious movement known as Neo-Paganism."

CIRCLE SANCTUARY

Circle Sanctuary

http://www.computel.com/~muralynd/Circle.html

Highlights: •A description of Circle Sanctuary and their raison d'etre; •A glossary of pagan-related terms; •Info on how to become part of Circle's community; •Links to related sites.

Lesson I learned: "Founded in 1974, Circle helps people from many spiritual orientations connect with each other as well as with the spiritual dimensions of Nature."

INTRODUCTION TO WICCA

http://faraday.clas.virginia.edu/~crf8a/wicca.html

Highlights: •Many very interesting sound clips from an NBC interview with Selena Fox and Laurie Cabot about Witch tools, rituals, spells and more.

Lesson I Learned: "A Witch seeks to control the forces within her/himself that make life possible in order to live wisely and well without harm to others and in harmony with nature.... We do not accept the concept of absolute evil, nor do we worship any entity know as 'Satan' or 'The Devil' as defined by the Christian tradition."

WICCA RESOURCES

http://prod1.satelnet.org/fuchsia/wicca.html

Highlights: •Description of Wicca; •A bunch of links to Wiccan, pagan and Magick FTP sites, newsgroups, and other Web pages.

Lesson I Learned: "Wicca is a nature-based religion and way of life.... Wiccans generally celebrate the presence of a divine entity, manifest in all things. This entity is polarized into feminine and masculine aspects—a Goddess and a God...."

MINERVA'S MYSTIC TEMPLE TO THE GODS

http://mithral.iit.edu:8080/~cousmel/mystic.html

Highlights: •Simply written for the beginner; •Good FAQ; •Explains the holy days of the sun, the elements, and auras and their meanings; •Recommended reading list.

Lesson I Learned: "For us, spells and rituals are a matter of arranging elements to encourage a frame of mind conducive to working Magic. This may involve burning candles and/or incense, making talismans of stone or wood or paper, chanting rhymed formulae, using herbs or essential oils, turning down the lights and playing some atmospheric music, or whatever the imagination of the Witch can devise."

The God	The Goddess
the Sun	the Moon
Active	Passive
White	Black
Light	Dark
Visible	Invisible
Fact	Fantasy
the World	the Otherworld
Gold	Silver
Male	Female
Knife	Cauldron
Day	Night

THE DARK SIDE OF THE WEB

http://www.cascade.net/darkweb.html

By far the lengthiest and most unique list of pagan/witch/ghoulish links. I can tell that the site mistress, Carrie, dedicates her soul to these pages!

HEALING ON THE INTERNET

I poked around the newsgroups, trying to find someone who actually attempted to cast spells over the Net (do witches find that hokey?) Instead I found a witch who does online healing. She either goes by her IRC nickname, TheGoddess, or Kari. I emailed Kari the Goddess a few questions about her practice, and here's what she said:

How do you go about "healing" on the Net?
My healing is mostly done by connecting, spiritually, with the other person. They may have said they needed help in something, and I would encourage them to do basic Candle Magick. After getting permission to help, I would send them energy, to help brighten their space. I would light an appropriate colored candle, just for them, empowering it with healing energy designed to help the one who needed it.

What kind of results have you seen?
Well, I haven't really seen results, but I have often gotten email, or a later chat in the IRC from the recipient. They'd be happy, thanking me for helping, as well as acknowledging that they had felt my energy, and that my magick had helped.

How does healing work via the Net—I mean, does the energy really pass through the phone lines?
This is a tough one to answer, Carlata. I wouldn't say it goes through the phone lines…. It is more a matter of intention and a wee bit of faith. My intense desire to help another is strong enough to reach them spiritually. I don't tell them anything they don't already know…. I just try to reinforce, support and/or encourage them to use their own powers, with my energy to back them up. And, not to sound egotistical, but I know I have a gift, and I don't doubt that I can help another, should they allow me to help. But, I guess it's a matter of agreement on both sides, and not a point to ridicule or scoff at. I mean, if they don't believe I can and will help, then they get nothing. Make sense?

The New Improved WELL Prayer

Oh, Lord God Who is All-Male, All-Knowing, All-Giving and All-RightMightyFine:

Bless now this WELL, that it may be a beakon unto the darkness. Bless it, we say, dear FatherNotMother God, and maketh it to lie down in green pastures with lambs and sheep and wooly creatures. We pray thee, oh RealGodsAreRealMen, that they would shed thy mercy and show thy handiwork upon the WELL, that it would be whole and healed and made all WEIRD. With every head bowed and every eye closed so that we can't see what the hell is going on, we ask these things in MaleDeadGod'sName, Amen.

The WELL is my shepherd, I shall not have a life.

It maketh me to log on in no clothing;
It leadeth me beside flame wars.
It restoreth my timesink;
It leadeth me in the discussion of the unanswerable for its billing.
Yea, though I packet-switch through the bandwidth of Netcom,
I shall fear no disconnect;
For the WELL is with me;
Its OK prompt and its help menu, they comfort me.
It preparest a controversy for me in the presence of journalists;
It annointest my words with YOYOW;
My cup runneth over in a black bra.
Surely gail and mo will wish I had never logged on all the days of their life:
And I will Muse in the csh of the WELL forever.

by lizabeth@well.com

Found on Cynsa's Home Page: http://www.well.com/user/cynsa/

Ethereal  Newsgroups

Half the fun of visiting these metaphysical Usenet groups is waiting for the hostile, bellowing creeps who don't "believe" to stomp in. I don't understand why they are so angry, but it sure is a hoot. There are usually a few of these interrupters, but luckily the rest of the group cleverly defend themselves and then go right back to the topic that interests them. Most seem really dedicated to the subject at hand, which makes for insightful and truly fascinating discussions.

alt.astrology

This group is loaded with activity. There are all sorts of horoscope questions, and topics like "Romantic Signs" or "Science Attacking Astronomy." You can get a reading here, but be careful when asking for one. You must address the whole group, and not a specific person (which, they say, is a breach of netiquette). There are two distinct groups of people here: expert astrologers (interesting but a little clannish) and complete newcomers.

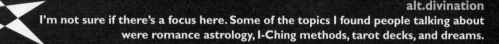

alt.divination

I'm not sure if there's a focus here. Some of the topics I found people talking about were romance astrology, I-Ching methods, tarot decks, and dreams.

alt.dreams

Have a recurring dream and can't figure it out? Maybe you should post it here, where everyone shares their dreams and nightmares and attempts to decipher what certain scenarios may represent. (My favorite: "Why do celebrities make cameo appearances in my dreams?") For more advanced, creative, and in-control dreamers, try alt.dreams.lucid.

alt.hindu

Seems to be a lot of one-person topics here—individuals preaching information about Hinduism or posting upcoming events celebrating the religion. Not much conversation, but perhaps a good place to get some free cultural lessons.

alt.magick

If you want to talk card tricks, you'll be sent over to alt.magic. These magicians are into spells and witchcraft, tarot, and especially Aleister Crowley (natch). To get even more (and more in-depth) topics on this subject, check out alt.magick.tyagi.

alt.mythology

The ancient goddesses and gods of Egyptian, Celtic, Greek, Japanese, and other mythologies are passionately discussed here.

alt.out-of-body

Sharing OOBEs (as they abbreviate it) and lucid dreams are the main topics of discussion. Some skilled astral-projectors also try to teach amateurs how to do it. You get a small dose of hostile nonbelievers here, trying to wreck the fun (but not succeeding!).

alt.pagan

Intelligent and stimulating conversations about paganism.

alt.paranormal

Almost anything considered "paranormal" is covered here, including ghostly dreams, Ouija boards, stuff on UFOs, and channeling.

alt.tarot

Besides comparing tarot decks (Sheesh! I can't believe how many there are) and listing favorite tarot books and FTP sites, these fortune tellers also talk a lot about giving online readings. To my surprise, most of them are really into tarot via the modem, explaining that the energy (electricity) makes readings crystal clear.

alt.wicca

A place for witches to convene. Some are here looking for a coven. Some want to gab about their craft, or to ask how to talk to the goddesses and gods. Christians also come around, many of them ending up in nasty disputes with the wiccas.

feelin' . . .

GROOVY

Someone recently asked me why I was putting a "health" chapter in *Net Chick*, saying that health and computers didn't have much to do with each other. First of all, I answered, nothing that exists in the "real" world is immune to cyberspace, and furthermore, health is just as (if not more) connected to high technology as any other field discussed in this book.

I began my argument with a basic description of the numerous Websites and newsgroups available on the Net that address all aspects of health. This includes both Western and Eastern medicine, spiritual practices (like meditation), physical fitness, and even alternative ways of treating one's mind with tools such as brain machines and smart drugs. While the anarchistic nature of the Net reinforces the old adage "let the buyer beware," where information is concerned, this same source of anarchy allows the Net to be the hottest medium—especially in the conservatively regulated area of health—for fresh, immediate, and alternative ideas.

But using hightech to access information on health matters, I continued, is minor compared to the drastic yet fascinating ways some fitness zealots are using cutting-edge technology as a way to not only improve but extend their health. These immortality enthusiasts (some call themselves Extropians), have faith in the concept of life extension (popularized by *Life Extension* authors Dirk and Sandy Shaw). Ultimately, their goal goes way beyond the common health practice of working to feel one's best and to live a long healthy life; they don't plan on dying at all.

They're working toward this goal by combining the present technology of smart drugs (legal and not-so-legal nutrients and supplements that fight the body's aging chemicals and hormones), with the back-up plan of cryonics (having oneself frozen at the time of death in order to be revived at a later, more technically advanced time). Meanwhile, these Extropians have hope in what the edgiest of scientists are working on right now: nanotechnology—the use of micro-robots (size of bacteria) to perform certain pre-programmed functions, including replicating themselves, the way cells do. This type of tech would allow, among many other applications (see Nanofash, pg. 65) the programmed "cells" to maintain as well as repair any damage or degeneration taking place in one's body.

I must admit I'm extremely captivated by life extension (although I have yet to sign my future corpse over to an Antarctic time-capsule) and even more enthralled with the way the Extropians are going after it. It parallels the whole do-it-yourself, cyberpunk, Net Chick philosophy of taking charge of your own life (literally!). They don't buy into the status quo hypothesis that life equals death. Or that life equals one century. They refuse to turn their backs on a future that most of society won't even consider. Instead, they're using technology and serious, kick-ass determination to test unknown realities. And who knows? They may have the last laugh.

Anyway, by the time I finished my radical health spiel, I think my skeptical friend was too busy digesting this information to remember her original doubts. I left her to ponder while I ran home to write this intro.

If you, too, are pondering over the far-out Extropian concepts of life extension, you'll be happy to know that this chapter spells it out in more detail with author, encryptionist, and Extropian Romana Machado, who'll vouch for me that none of that stuff above is made up ("I think of death and disease as unsolved engineering problems, and I think we'll eventually know how to solve them with the current acceleration of technology"). You may want to warm up to Ms. Machado by first reading the essay on the potential and reality of nanotechnology.

And finally, along with lots of pointers to invigorating newsgroups and Websites dealing with physical, mental, and spiritual health, you'll get a quick lesson on how to protect yourself from the physical hazards—carpal tunnel syndrome, tendonitis, etc.—of sitting in front of your computer (kind of a ironic, don't you think?!).

Although a lot in this chapter may sound a bit bizarre to the health traditionalists (almost everybody, in other words), it makes sense when you read the fine print—theoretically speaking.

ROMANA MACHADO

Better Living Through Technology

Romana Machado doesn't plan on dying. As an encryption software developer (Stego), professional model (even posed for Playboy *in '85!), Cypherpunk, Extropian, and author of a book with the working title* Frequently Questioned Answers: Your Action Plan For A Limitless Future, *she says she's just too busy to give herself up to mortality.*

What most people think is beyond our control—aging and death—Ms. Machado says can be controlled with scientific and engineering solutions. She says it's just a matter of time before humans solve the problem of fatality. In the meantime, she's warding off age by practicing Extropianism, a philosophy that promotes life extension (and freedom), which one achieves partly through smart drug therapy and healthy, optimistic living.

What fascinates me most about Extropianism is its belief in cryonics—having oneself frozen at the time of death in hopes of later being brought back to life with future technology. Before I asked her anything else, I just had to know . . .

Are you a member of a body-freezing company like Alcor?

> Yes, I'm a member of Alcor.

> **Really? Wow. Are you signed up to have your whole body frozen, or just your head?**

> Well just the neuro—that's what they call the head. I see it as a backup measure to preserve the information that is you. It's not really a big deal. It's like setting a button on your car radio. You can set it and forget it, you know? You do have to pay yearly dues, but they're not very expensive, about as much as having cable. And the suspension itself is being covered by an inexpensive life-insurance

policy. So, it's an extreme measure, but it's a way of voting on continuing to exist—what you're saying is, "Yes, I want to live, and I will do that by any means possible."

>**If I were to sign up with Alcor, I think I would rather freeze my whole body.**

>Yes, but it's less expensive to go head-only, and when I have more money or insurance . . . if I actually thought there was a big possibility that I would be frozen sometime soon, then I would care to go whole body. But as it's just a backup, emergency plan-B kind of a thing, just freezing my head is fine right now.

>**And you can switch over later.**

>Yeah, there's no problem switching over later.

>**If for some reason you did end up just freezing your head, when they finally were able to revive your brain, how would they reattach your body?**

>All of the information you need to build an exact copy of your body is in your cells already. By the time they're able to revive you, the cell-repair technology will have to be pretty good in order to overcome freezing damage. So the technology to get you up and running again will be good enough to just create another body for you, if that's what's needed.

>**So they would just grab some cells from the part of you that's been saved.**

>Right.

>**And then how long would it take for the cells to create another you—twenty or thirty years?**

>They may have to wait that long, or they may put you into a very young body—I wouldn't mind that. There are a number of things that can happen, and in my current vision of the future, all of this is very speculative. I think of death and disease as unsolved engineering problems, and I think we'll eventually know how to solve them with the current acceleration of technology. You see, I don't really plan on being frozen. What I'm hoping for is that through taking reasonable measures while I'm still alive, I'll be able to have an indefinitely long lifespan.

>**So if we're frozen, what do you think happens to the energy inside of us—what many call the soul? Does that just freeze along with the body?**

>Yeah, I believe that the energy inside of us is in fact information. The information is written inside of the neurons of the brain, so once you kick start that brain, "you" will be there again.

>**What is the main philosophy of the Extropians?**

>Extropians are both future- and freedom-oriented. We're interested in technology, especially how it relates to making humans more free to do what they wish to

do. Extropianism values self-transformation, spontaneous order, rationalism, and optimism, and we're optimistic about our ability to understand and use the universe and ourselves for our pleasure. The whole philosophy is actually very old and has to do with a healthy mind and a healthy body and almost an extreme materialism—reveling in our ability to control our lives and to control the material universe around us. Extropy is the coined opposite of entropy in a philosophical, if not a scientific, sense.

> **What's entropy?**

> Entropy is the tendency of systems to fall apart, slow down, cool off.

> **What is the difference between an Extropian and your average health nut? How is your philosophy different from that of magazines like *Longevity* or *Prevention*?**

> We're not in opposition to *Longevity* or *Prevention*. We're all of that, and we're technically competent, and we look towards the future. It's not either/or. You can be a total health nut but not be into personal liberty at all—not be a libertarian. You can be a health nut but not be into the abolition of taxation or the end of government. Or you can be into it and not be into future technologies. Or you could be that and not be rational. You can be a total health nut and not be technophilic.

> **How can humans use technology to fight entropy?**

> That's the purpose of technology! Take medicine for instance. In terms of computers reducing entropy, in my life they've been definitely a means for me to write and create value, to become connected to other people, to make money. All of that reduces entropy, because it gives me power.

> **So making money is a way of fighting entropy?**

> Yeah! Definitely, because it's a way of gaining control over your environment. It's a way of gaining control over what you want to do with your life energy and what you want to do with the world around you.

> **Can you think of a way people use the Net for self-improvement?**

> Yeah. I use the World Wide Web all the time as an encyclopedia. I do searches on whatever it is I need to know. To know more is to be more. And you have the opportunity to talk to other people who are trying new things. This whole fat-free eating thing has become much easier for me because I signed up on a fat-free list, and everyone there is into this fat-free eating lifestyle. They give out recipes, and they talk about what it's like to be eating fat-free, and all of that. It's a great way to access a community of people who don't think you're a food nut

Steve Young

just because you don't think you should be eating so much fat.

> **Do you take smart drugs?**

> Yeah, the one I'm really interested in now is deprenyl. Deprenyl is not only a smart drug, it's also a life extension drug. And it's also a pro-sexual drug which means that it has a tendency to be an aphrodisiac. So all three actions are stuff that I like!

> **Yeah, sounds great! How long have you been taking it?**

> I've been taking deprenyl for about two and a half years.

> **Where do you get it?**

> I get it from a friend who gets it from Mexico. It's possible to get it through a prescription here in the United States, but it's more expensive that way.

> **Have you felt any differences since you've been taking it?**

> Well, I'm turning thirty-four this year and people are looking at me saying "My God, you can't possibly be turning thirty-four!" I'm still modeling a lot, my figure is as great as it's ever been . . . I feel great, I look great. As far as I know, my current program of supplementation—not just deprenyl but my whole program—is working really well for me. I've fought off carpal tunnel syndrome, I've fought off arthritis, I've recovered quite well from having a lymph node removed earlier this year.

> **How does deprenyl work? What does it do biologically?**

> It has a number of different actions, but basically it's a selective MAO-B reuptake inhibitor. It prevents brain aging by preventing damage to a center in your brain that produces dopamine—it's called the substantia nigra.

> **You said that cryonics is the backup plan, so what are you doing now to prolong your life?**

> Exercise, eating right, getting enough sleep . . .

HOT SITE: Romana Machado's WWW Headquarters
http://www.best.com/~fqa/romana/

Woo! Check out Machado's Betty Page-style sex-goddess photos that she's entered in the Ms. Metaverse Pageant. (If you vote for her, she may win 10,000 bucks!)

The cypherbabe also goes into grand detail about Extropianism, explaining transhumanism, life extension, cryonics, smart drugs, cryptography, and so much more. If the self-touted "hot-blooded capitalist" converts you to her ways, take a look at the on-sale "Extropian Underground" T-shirt that she designed (the back reads "Better and More Evil").

She may be a staunch capitalist, but when it comes to freedom she gives it away for free. This means you can download her Stego encryption software, which she offers as shareware (no cost!). What a gal!

Some of the edgier stuff in medical science includes brain machines, smart drugs, and cryonics. I've tried different brain machines—some relaxed me, and others only made me crabby. I've also experimented with smart drugs and actually did feel my mind sharpen (with vasopressin). I have not signed up to be a human ice cube with a cryonics company, but I did meet a beagle who was once frozen and brought back to life. To believe or not to believe—that is the question.

MIND GEAR: MENTAL FITNESS TECHNOLOGY

http://www.netcreations.com/mindgear/

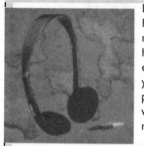

Do you know why people use brain machines? How these contraptions work? Or what entrainment feels like? (What is entrainment, anyway?) It all has to do with altering your consciousness by using either light and sound or electricity. Mind Gear gives you info on how to get your hands (or mind) on psychoactive tapes, books on smart drugs, a catalog with all sorts of brain gadgets, and publications relating to biofeedback and mind-related matter.

A SHORT INTRODUCTION TO SMART DRUGS

http://www.uta.fi/~samu/SMARTS2.html

Originally written for a rave zine, this essay explains what smart drugs (nootropics) are and how they work on your brain. It also describes other brain-boosters like gotu-kola, caffeine, antioxidants, and certain vitamins, herbs, and nutrients. If this titillates your interest in nootropics, you can wallow in the lengthy resource guide that follows.

INDEX OF /DRUGS/NOOTROPICS

http://www.paranoia.com/drugs/nootropics/

For more detailed information on smart drugs, here's a fat selection of articles dealing with the subject. You can even find out how and where to get them (it's illegal to buy most nootropics in the U.S., but legal to take them) and how much they cost.

ALCOR'S HOME PAGE

http://www.webcom.com/~alcor/

If I were going to have myself frozen after life to be revived in the future, I'd definitely choose the Alcor Foundation, which is the largest and most well-known cryonics institute around (they have twenty-nine people in the icebox at this time). Modem in for their literature, as well as for extensive material on cryonics in general, Extropianism, life extension, and nanotechnology. You can even sign up online for "bio-preservation" if you're feeling bold.

> But people have been doing that for hundreds of years and they still die.

> . . . and I'm taking deprenyl and vitamins. Preventing damage is very important, and we know more about supplementation now than we ever have. I'm a real fan of the Life Extension Foundation's publications. The good thing about all this life extension stuff is that it seems like it's all future-oriented and so forth, but the fact is that being healthy makes you feel better right now.

> But you don't think you're going to live for an extraordinarily longer number of years because of what you're doing, do you?

> I might get about a 20 percent boost in life span, and what I'm expecting is that with all of the therapies and so forth on the horizon, that within the next fifty years or so, I'll be able to extend my life another 10 or 20 percent. And so forth and so on. We're in a time of vast technological expansion and I may be able to bootstrap myself into extreme longevity. But I have a back-up plan.

> Ten years ago people were saying the same thing—that they were waiting for technological advances, and in the

meantime were taking this and that. But I haven't seen much of an advance in the life-expansion field within the last ten years, so . . .

> Well, therapy with deprenyl and DHEA is new. My doctor recently prescribed DHEA for me. You go and get a DHEA test to find out what your levels of DHEA are. It's a hormone that steadily declines over the course of your life in both men and women. When it declines suddenly, people get what they call Cushing's syndrome—its effects are very much like rapid aging, very much like progeria. With most of us, these hormones are going through a slow decline, but eventually we get those effects—that's one of the reasons we age. Our hormone systems are slowing down. DHEA is an antagonist to cortisol. Cortisol is a stress hormone—it's something you release in times of stress—and it's a fairly destructive hormone. It's also called the death hormone.

> **That's a creepy-sounding hormone.**

> It is. And DHEA is its antagonist, it's what protects your body from excess cortisol. We had Chris Heward, who's a doctor and an endocrinologist, do two different presentations at two different Extropian conferences about DHEA. He's starting a venture called Youth Quest, in which people get complete workups of all of their hormonal levels—everything that can be tested—once a year in order to try to maintain a balance so that they can supplement where they need to.

> **Does the FDA support any of this?**

> No, but that's not relevant. If you have knowledge and you do your own research, and you're willing to take responsibility for what happens to you, which many people are not, there's no reason you should be interested in what the FDA has to say. As long as you're looking at what they're looking at, as far as research goes, and as long as you have the same information as they do, you should be able to make your own decisions.

> **And probably a lot quicker, too. I was taking the stuff you squirt up your nose . . .**

> Vasopressin.

> **Yeah! And it did clear the cobwebs from my head. Now you're motivating me to get more involved with this stuff.**

> The latest thing I've added to my program is bilberry extract, which is from a Swedish berry. What's in it is this very powerful antioxidant that is supposed to protect collagen, which is one of two things that basically holds your face together—the other is elastin.

David Cellars

> **Ooh, I like that one. Can you get it in an herb store?**

> Yes, you can. The other thing that you want is tycnogenol, which is a grape seed extract. It's also one of these plant-based antioxidants. It's very powerful. It passes the blood-brain barrier and is the protector of elastin. So between these two you may never need a face lift.

Bilberry also increases microcapillary circulation, so it protects you from eye degeneration. So if you have any eye problems of any kind it's a great thing to take.

> **Why is life extension so important to you?**

> Wow. Well I can't even do everything that I want to get done now. There's so much to enjoy!

> **Lots of people who have temporarily died and then been brought back claim to have experienced an "afterlife." Are you curious about that?**

> Well perhaps if I'd had the experiences they say they had regarding the afterlife I would have similar beliefs. But since I haven't had those experiences, I can't say that I'm interested in that, really. Living a long time, you have more experiences, and maybe you'll learn that there's something else out there. In the meantime, I'm happy with what I've got. I don't feel the need to move on. •

NANO

NANOTECHNOLOGY

Can you imagine telling micro-robots the size of atoms to fill in the lines in your face? Or to dissolve any fat that may be clumping up those thighs of yours? You may be scoffing, but scientists are fast and furiously working on this kind of science even as I type. They call it nanotechnology.

The idea of creating these microscopic machines that could conceivably perform any task you program them to do has been around since the 1950s—but when scientists in Zurich were able to actually manipulate individual atoms in 1990, nanotechnology became a real possibility in the eyes of scientists worldwide.

What nanotechnology actually means—something way more significant than the glorious cosmetic fantasies above—is that most hideous diseases would be things of the past. These robots would be able to do stuff like rejuvenate old tissues and organs in your body, scrape fatty deposits off of your hardened arteries, perform brain surgery on specific neurons, and kill cancer cells.

How does it work? Well, in the most simplistic terms, by combining chemistry, physics, and engineering, nano-scientists would build molecular machines that would be programmed to enter an environment (like a human body) on the cellular or molecular level. Although scientists talk a lot about the medical potential, these robots would be able to perform just about any duty, such as cleaning up polluted air or water,

building new kinds of plastics and fabrics with amazing properties, or storing vast amounts of data in a tiny chip.

The beauty of nanotechnology is that these machines would make copies of themselves, so that once the first batch is created, they could perform and then maintain their task on their own. Of course, on the flip side, self-replication also could create some of nanotechnology's biggest nightmares: biological warfare, accidentally releasing the wrong machines into the environment, losing control of these multiplying mechanisms . . . Also, the question that forces itself upon us is, once these machines can reproduce on their own, are they considered living creatures?

Nanotechnology is a fascinating new technology that promises extreme changes in what we call existence. Whether you like it or not, it's on its way. Some say that as soon as the middle of the twenty-first century we'll be seeing some of its first effects. So instead of just flaming or completely ignoring it, it may behoove you to be hip to it. Those with the knowledge are usually the ones with the most influence and control.

For a lot more info, check out these Websites:

DEFINITIONS OF NANOTECHNOLOGY
http://www.nanothinc.com/Definitions/definitions.html

NANOTECHNOLOGY INFORMATION
http://aeiveos.wa.com/nanotech/

"FUTURE QUEST'S" NANOTECHNOLOGY EPISODE (TRANSCRIBED)
http://metaverse.com/futurequest/106.html

LOS ANGELES NANOTECHNOLOGY STUDY GROUP
http://bcf.usc.edu/~tmccarth/nano.htm

Depending on where you live, you may not have access to some of the more alternative health publications. Or you may be in a lazy stupor, not wanting to amble down the block to your local newsstand or bookstore. Either way, no sweat. Just fire up your modem and peruse the following sites.

BOOKS (HOMEOPATHY)

http://www.dungeon.com/home/cam/books.html

Wow! So many books on homeopathy! This huge list is divided up between American and U.K. publishers, with a total of over 800 books. You can find titles like *The Women's Guide to Homeopathy*, *Homeopathic Medicine at Home*, and, if you're not even sure what this medicinal system is all about, *The Complete Homeopathy Handbook*. If you want a book that they don't have, you can add the title to their booklist, and they'll try their darnedest to get it stocked.

BALANCE MAGAZINE
"Fitness on the Net"

http://tito.hyperlink.com/balance/

This is a monthly mag with a columnist, Lisa, who answers women's fitness and health questions. Examples of article topics include *Aerobics—A Living Nightmare; Ginseng, A Root of Controversy;* a fat loss program; and a detailed piece on the benefits of water. These pages aren't graphical, but at least they download quickly.

PAPER SHIPS

http://www.nbn.com/jacob/ship.html

Elaine and David are the nice couple who manage this interesting online collection of alternative and spiritual health books, including a whole section dedicated to goddesses. The books

---more--->

your health

read about it!

LONGEVITY

AOL Keyword: Longevity
If you're hooked with America Online, don't forget to check out *Longevity Online*, which, of course, is the digital counterpart to the pulp

version. They have a whole section of articles dedicated to women's health issues, as well as pieces on food, fitness, beauty, and alternative medicine. The benefits of reading *Longevity* online as opposed to on paper are that you can interact with other readers either by posting messages or by chatting in live forums, and you can obtain articles from back issues with just a click of a button. This is my favorite online health rag—I just wish it were on the Web for *everyone* to enjoy.

come from their twenty-five-year-old bookstore based in the San Francisco Bay Area. Elaine says women make up 75 percent of their customer base. The last time I checked this site I found titles on the Kombucha mushroom, flower essences, a lot of spiritual material, and a few books by Deepak Chopra. You can order by email or phone, and they'll ship anywhere.

BOOKZONE
http://www.ttx.com:80/bookzone/medical.html
Estrogen, AIDS, herbs, homeopathy, pregnancy, and aging are just some of the subjects this shop of health books covers. Under each title is a detailed description of the book; if you want to know more, you can look at the book's table of contents and also read its introductory chapter. Dial in with your modem or phone to order, and in only three to five days you'll receive your package.

VIRTUAL BOOK SHOP'S ONLINE CATALOG
http://www.virtual.bookshop.com./htbin/catalog
I could have browsed through this unique bookstore for hours. It specializes in rare first edition-books. First you have to enter a keyword—either an author, title, or subject of a book. When I entered "holistic," I was only granted three choices, but when I typed in "health," 140 completely varied titles popped up. Some books were published in the eighties and cost between $16–35, while others were from the seventeenth century and cost hundreds of dollars. The most expensive was also one of the most interesting: *Opera Omnia* (1689), by Bontekoe, a famous Cartesian, who recommended plenty of opium, tobacco, and caffeine for a prolonged, healthy life. Those were the days! You can order these books online, but you may want to check first to make sure the book is still in stock. •

HOT SITES:
It's All in the Wrist

Are pins and needles cramping your writing style? All I can say is, repetitive stress injuries suck! Luckily, there are some things a computer user can do to help protect her wrists from the obnoxious disorders. For details, type out—slowly now!—these URLs and find out as much as you can.

A PATIENT'S GUIDE TO CARPAL TUNNEL

http://www.cyberport.net/mmg/cts/ctsintro.html

Dedicated to the ailing wrist, this thorough site provides illustrative maps of the arm and hand and describes the symptoms and treatment of carpal tunnel syndrome. Plenty of photos here. If you have even a hint of CTS, I highly recommend reading these pages.

ftp://ftp.csua.berkeley.edu/pub/typing-injury/typing-injury-faq/

All you need to know about friendly furniture, keyboards, and software can be found in this updated archive of articles. You can jump to hypertext sites from here.

COMPUTER RELATED REPETITIVE STRAIN INJURY

http://engr-www.unl.edu/ee/eeshop/rsi.html

A student named Paul from the University of Nebraska has created this handy site, in which he categorizes and lists the symptoms of repetitive stress injuries and explains some preventative measures to take. He also recommends a list of books on the subject, has links to related Websites, and shows us a variety of stretches that will help keep RSIs at bay. •

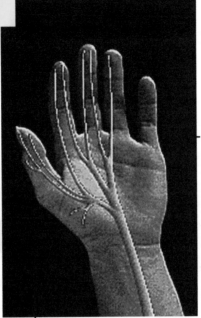

SAFE SURFING

Before you read anything on this page, remember that I am *not* a doctor. I'm just telling you about my personal experience with carpal tunnel syndrome, and what I've learned to do about it. If you have any symptoms at all that could have been caused by using your computer, call a doctor. Now!

As gleeful as Net surfing and other computer activities are, it can turn into a real drag if you don't first set yourself up with the right gear. Even as I type this, for instance, I'm wearing skateboard wrist guards—a little trick Kristin Spence taught me, to ward off the horrible tingling sensation plaguing my hands and fingers.

Using a computer causes some kind of physical pain to more than ten million people every year. This includes repetitive stress injuries (RSIs) like carpal tunnel syndrome and tendonitis, stress, headaches, eyestrain, and back and neck problems. Carpal tunnel syndrome first struck me two and a half years ago (violins start here). I was happily typing away, when suddenly all of my fingers fell asleep. I shook my hands, expecting them to wake up, but the pins and needles wouldn't vanish. I had heard of RSIs before and had a hideous hunch that that's what was vexing me. The hunch turned into a realization when, while continuing to type, my hands became numb, and then even hours after I left the keyboard, it was difficult for me to hold things.

I foolishly neglected seeing a doctor (*not recommended*) until just a week ago, but during the two and a half years of painful keyboarding, I've done a lot of research and have managed to limit my pain to nothing more than light prickles once in a while (my doctor was impressed!).

The most important lesson I've learned is to create a computer-friendly office before anything creepy starts to happen. The following lists, charts, hot sites, and diagram focus on carpal tunnel syndrome but can be applied to almost any computer-related injury.

RSI CHART

CAUSE OF RSI	PREVENTATIVE TIP
• Repeated movement of the fingers on the keyboard.	• If you're a fast typist, try slowing down a little.
• Sitting in one tense position for too long.	• Make sure to take frequent "stretch breaks." (There is software available that will remind you when to break—check out the following diagram.)
• Poor posture.	• Make sure to sit up straight, and don't stretch forward to reach the keys. Relax.
• Positioning the computer too high or too low.	• Keep the computer and chair at levels so that your thighs and forearms are parallel to the floor.
• Resting your wrists on the sharp edge of your desk.	• Don't rest your wrists on hard edges! Make sure it's padded around your key board, and do not bend your wrists!

Growing up in California, I thought of alternative health as the norm. Unless something was majorly wrong, my mom took me to a Vietnamese herbalist rather than to a regular doctor. Tofu and Rice Dream were equivalent to hot dogs and apple pie. That was the '70s. Now I like to blend the philosophies of both Eastern and Western medicine, a combination which makes the most sense to me and which is reflected in this hodgepodge of healthy sites.

GETTING A GRIP WITH REFLEXOLOGY

http://www.doubleclickd.com/reflexology.html

Here's an interesting, lengthy article on reflexology, which is explained as "a science and healing art based upon the theory that there are reflex areas, or specific points in the feet and hands that correspond to all the glands and organs in the body." The piece, written by a reflexology group in Baltimore, lists each section of the foot and its corresponding body part. For instance, massaging or putting pressure to the toes supposedly stimulates the head and neck area, while the inner foot is connected to the spine. They also give information on classes and reflexologists in their area.

MASTER AUSTRALIAN TEA TREE OIL

http://netmar.com/~back2nat/TTOIndex.html

Wow, my only question after reading about the Australian oil's benefits is, what *doesn't* it remedy? The couple who run this site (and own a store called Back to Nature) say this tea tree oil heals acne, burns, nose and throat ailments, and problems with the mouth, ears, hair and scalp, feet, muscles and joints, and even pet afflictions like lice and fleas! Besides informing us on the benefits of the snake, er, I mean tea tree oil (just kidding), the shopkeepers also explain what an essential oil is, how to harvest it, and give info about tea trees and Australia itself. You can buy the oil as well as all sorts of planet-friendly products by logging into their shop at http://netmar.com:80/mall/shops/back2nat/.

KOMBUCHA HOME PAGE

http://www.webcom.com/~sease/kombucha/kombucha.html

I couldn't pass up this page, since I myself am a fan of Kombucha tea, which you make from a very strange-looking flat, slimy, shiny, beige "mushroom." It's pretty creepy looking, but if you marinate it in black tea and sugar for eight to twelve days you get a snappy tea that is even more of a cure-all than Australian tea tree oil. This brew, which people were drinking in Russia thousands of years ago, supposedly helps fight cancer, arthritis, stress, gallstones and kidney problems, memory loss, hypoglycemia, wrinkles, hair loss, gout, menopausal symptoms, and way too many other things to list here. While producing the tea, the mushroom duplicates itself, so you'll be able to make two batches the next time around.

This site lists books, informative articles, a mailing list, and where to get Kombucha starter kits. Since the mushrooms multiply, they are always in

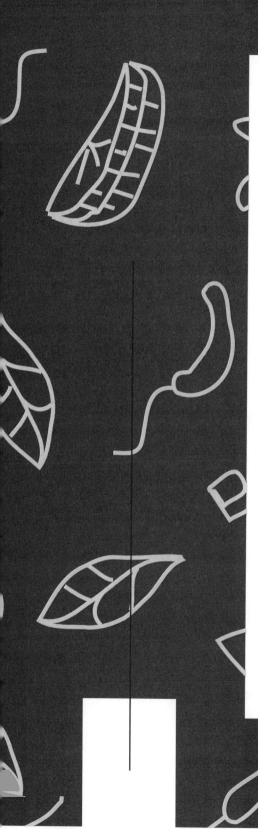

abundance, so you should *not* pay more than forty bucks for a starter kit. (If I'm not throwing mine away, I just give them away for free.) Some people advertise their 'shrooms here for $80. Stay away from those greedy dorks.

ACUPUNCTURE.COM
http://www.acupuncture.com/acupuncture/

I've had acupuncture done, and it's really not as scary as it looks! Read about its benefits here, including what it can do for women in particular (like relieving PMS symptoms), and find out where practitioners and acupuncture schools are. Although this site is titled "Acupuncture.com," these pages actually give just as much information on herbology, Chi Gong (a certain type of rejuvenating exercises that are taught online), Chinese nutrition, Tui Na, and Chinese massage. You can also jump to other health sites from here.

KRISTI'S PMS PAGE
http://ias.rio.com/~nitrous/pms.html

Some chick named Kristi has created smart, lengthy pages that all of us who become bitches when we're pre-menstrual can relate to. She talks in detail about the cause of PMS and what you can do to help relieve the wretched nuisance. For instance, she lists herbs that tackle different aspects of PMS (basil is good for digestive problems, nervous headaches, and anxiety) and explains what you can do for depression and mood swings. (Hint: Increase your intake of vitamin B6, carbos, and magnesium. If you're in a real funk, also decrease your caffeine and salt consumption.)

Besides PMS information, Kristi also lists herbal remedies for bladder and vaginal infections, and herbal forms of birth control, which she suggests taking with another form of control. (Be careful! I sure as hell wouldn't rely on herbal birth control.) Related links, books, and newsgroups are listed as well.

ONLINE PERSONAL NUTRITIONAL PROFILE
http://health.mirical.com/site/form3.html

I always like being analyzed, so this site was fun for me. What you do is fill out a simple form that asks for your age, weight, height, gender, and activity level. In return you get a personal response that lists what your dietary intake of twenty-nine nutrients should be every day, including calories, protein, carbos, various fats, vitamins, minerals, sodium, and water.

FIRST AID ONLINE
http://www.symnet.net/Users/afoster/safety

Here's some basic but essential first aid information that lists what kind of medical supplies you should always have on hand. It also describes the most common injurious accidents (which, they say, happen most often in the home) and explains the best measures to take in case you come across someone who needs your help. •

Marcie Jenner

yoga

Eating right, exercising, finding the right computer chair—none of these routines will make you a happy camper if your spirit is drooping. Keeping your core polished is just as important as maintaining your mind and body. How do you exercise a soul? Yoga is my spiritual elixir, and lucid dreaming is fun, too. Start with the following . . . and stop rolling your eyes!

YOGAPLEX

http://www.gigaplex.com/wow/yoga/index.htm

Do you know how many yoga poses there are, or if Americans practice the same postures as the folks in India? These are the kinds of questions that are answered in the "Advice & Info" section of this site. The other section gives good pointers on how to find the right teacher. I've been a yoga student for many years and still found this site educational.

---more--->

SYMPTOMS OF REPETITIVE STRESS INJURIES

● Stiffness or pain in the arms, wrists, hands, or fingers.

● Pains in the hands or wrist that wakes you up at night.

● A tingling or numbing sensation in the hands or fingers.

● Weakness in the hands that makes it difficult to hold objects.

TREATMENT FOR CARPAL TUNNEL SYNDORME

(*Repetitive Strain Injury*, by Dr. Emil Pascarelli and Deborah Quilter, is an excellent resource for treatment, prevention, and advice in choosing a physician.

Consult a doctor to see which option is best for you.)

- In the earliest stages, a brace may decrease the symptoms. A split keyboard, keyboard pad, and some kind of hand strengthener like Chinese "health balls" will also help.

- Certain anti-inflammatory medications will bring down the swelling of the carpal tunnel and thus decrease the CTS symptoms.

- In more extreme cases, you can receive cortisone shots directly into the carpal tunnel, which will also reduce the swelling and relieve symptoms.

- In the worst case scenario, surgery is sometimes required. But make sure you get a few opinions before making that kind of decision!

YOGA PATHS
http://zeta.cs.adfa.oz.au/Spirit/Yoga/Overview.html

Karma, Bhakti, Sahaja, Hatha . . . I didn't realize so many yogas existed! While Yogaplex covers the basics, you'll get much deeper into yoga's history, philosophies, and cultural background here. There is a special focus on Vedic Culture (Veda means knowledge, and Vedic Culture refers to the Spirituality Aware Society). You can also jump to an International Event Calendar (marking yoga functions, obviously), and a bunch of other yoga sites.

ASTRAL PROJECTION HOME PAGE
http://www.lava.net/~goodin/astral.html

An obese list of hotlinks that will transport you to Webspots dealing with out-of-body experiences, lucid dreaming, and other related topics. Also a "Tips of the Month" page that gives pointers to travelers ready to visit the astral plane. •

injury-free

Here are the office gadgets that I've collected so far to make my Net surfing experience a smooth ride. I've noticed a serious decrease in overall aches and pain (pins and needles in my hands have disappeared completely) since I started my ergo way of life. My biggest piece of advice: Get this stuff before you feel the pain!

GIZMO: WRIST BEAN BAG

What it's good for: Helps to prevent repetitive stress injuries (like carpal tunnel syndrome) by keeping wrist(s) fairly straight and off of sharp desk edges. They also have wrist cushions that run along the front of your keyboard. My bag is called "The Macky Sac."

How to use: Simply place in front of your mouse pad (or keyboard) so that your wrist rests cozily on top.

Approx. price: $10-25

MACKY SAC

GIZMO: SUPPORT GLOVES

What it's good for: Helps relieve hand and wrist pain from computer-related stress by keeping circulation stimulated. I use "Handeze." They look chintzy but they work!

How to use: Just slip them on. Make sure you get a tight fit. I wear my skate wrist guards on top of my "Handeze" for extra support.

Approx. price: $18

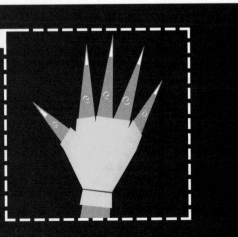

GIZMO: ERGONOMIC KEYBOARD

(a "split" keyboard also works)

What it's good for: Keeps your hands and arms at a more natural angle instead of parallel. Relieves tension in wrists, arms, shoulders, and neck.

How to use: Type the same way you would on any keyboard. The only difference is that your elbows will be pointing outward instead of downward.

Approx. price: $50 – $120

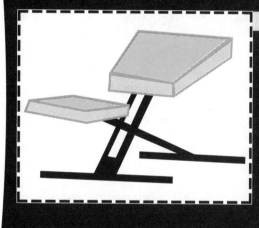

GIZMO: ERGONOMIC CHAIR

(armchair styles also exist)

What it's good for: Conducive to good posture, it helps prevent muscles from cramping up, thus relieving the usual computer-related discomforts caused by tension and strain.

How to use: With the silly one I use (like diagram above) you place your knees and calves on the lower pad so that your toes are facing downward. It's strange, but seems to do the trick. More conventional-looking ergo chairs with all sorts of moving parts are also good.

Approx. price: $150 – $400

GIZMO: HEADSET TELEPHONE

What it's good for: Especially good for yackers who need to use their hands for typing or other activities. If you use your shoulder too long to prop up the phone, expect a mean case of long-term stiffness in your neck.

How to use: Some have cords, some are cordless. Either way, just adjust the headset so it comfortably fits over your head and ears (like a radio headset).

Approx. price: $70 – $350

GIZMO: "TAKE FIVE" SOFTWARE (CD-ROM)

What it's good for: Taking five, or fifteen, from your computer. Besides relieving you from physical discomforts, this will also keep you from becoming a full on bitch. Believe me!

How to use: Pop in the CD-ROM, and at regular intervals (depending on how often you want to chill) your computer screen will either greet you with some stretch exercises, or photos/music to sweep your mind into another place.

Approx. price: $29.95

Invigorating.Newsgroups

Newsgroups serve at least three purposes when it comes to health issues: 1) They offer a chance to share and receive personal health advice, anecdotes, and "family remedies"; 2) They can serve as a meeting place and support group for those suffering with the same affliction; and 3) These groups are filled with health information that may be hard for some to find elsewhere. Obviously if you're illin' you should visit a REAL doctor first.

alt.aromatherapy
Aromatherapists use scents and essential oils from plants and floral waters to improve sleep, concentration, energy level, skin condition, etc. Aroma recipes and related info are given here in abundance.

alt.folklore.herbs
I thought I was over my wowie days of herbs and elixirs, but hanging around these herbal buffs has revived my enthusiasm. I can't wait to dig into my kitchen to see what kinds of potions and tonics I can concoct.

alt.health.ayurveda

This is one area of alternative health I haven't yet grasped. Something to do with hot oil treatments and diagnosis through the pulse. I was happy to see I wasn't the only one confused—lots of people were asking questions, and fortunately some ayurvedic experts were there to answer. It's weird, but I'm curious to find out more.

alt.med.allergy

Just a fraction of the allergy-related topics include side effects from antihistamines, cat allergies, sinus infections, and hives from physical pressure (I hear ya on that one!).

alt.med.cfs

Is Chronic Fatigue Syndrome "real" or not? That seems to be the big debate in this newsgroup. Other conversations revolve around symptoms and possible cures for the disorder.

alt.meditation

More than just the how-tos of breathing and omming. These meditators also discuss the various religions and philosophies behind their discipline.

alt.support.diet

Ugh, I hate the word "diet," but I realize it's a popular one. So here's the place to say it.

sci.cryonics

Fascinating threads on freezing humans for future revival.

misc.health.alternative

What a fat potpourri of health issues! Just a fraction of the dialogues I read pertain to: asthma, maple syrup, panic attacks, taking out a sliver, and fungus treatment.

SMART STUFF

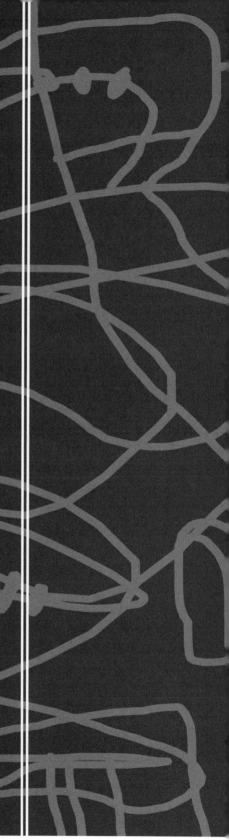

It baffles me when people complain that computers take away jobs. Some fields of work do become obsolete with the implementation of computers, but other positions always form to take their place. As far as the Internet is concerned, we're experiencing a burgeoning new career market that can't obtain employees fast enough. Just some of these coveted positions include:

- Website designers (graphic artists who create and lay out Websites);

1,000,000

- HTML scripters ("programmers" who know how to type the codes that make a Website work);
- Cybrarians (online librarians who find specific information on the Net for paying customers); and
- Teachers (who instruct classes on Net-related topics).

With the boom of the Internet, I've seen more and more women getting into online fields. I think this has to do with two things. First of all, email has lured us grrrls onto the Net because of its interactive appeal. Once we learn the communicative power of the Net, we're hooked! Second, the Web, being as aesthetic as it is, has opened up highly creative opportunities that involve conceptual and graphical design skills. And being the artistic creatures that we are, of course this is enticing to womankind.

As for the more technical side of things, it's beyond me why women were out of the loop when computer hacking first took off almost three decades ago. Obviously women have the inquisitive brains and code-cracking minds it takes to do the job. Take St. Jude (Chapter 4) and

Romana Machado (Chapter 7), for instance, two sharp femmes who enjoy tweaking the innards of cyberspace. And then there's Ada Lovelace, a genius you'll meet in this chapter, who's considered to be one of the first computer hackers ever. The only excuse I can think of for the blatant tardiness of grrrls' entry into the online scene is our country's education system. Girls weren't encouraged in school to pursue a career involving computer science (I even remember being discouraged from enrolling in an auto mechanic course in high school!).

Nowadays, I constantly meet women, many with liberal arts backgrounds, who are taking it upon themselves to learn how to navigate the Internet. I was just talking to an old friend of mine, Nicole, who had majored in English lit, and had been stuck in some "corporate nine-to-five job that was incredibly dry." So last spring she enrolled in a PowerPoint presentation software class, and took some computer graphics and how-to-surf-the-Internet lessons as well. During this time she also quit her job and took a new one that allowed her to use the PowerPoint skills she was learning. In order to upgrade her computer that she hadn't touched since she

,000,000

bought it two years earlier, she spent the whole summer under the hood, adding more RAM, installing a new hard drive, and upgrading the software (all of which she learned by reading the manuals). While upgrading and working at her new job, she's also been diligently reading an HTML book. Within six months, Nicole has transformed herself from a corporate-enslaved Internet-illiterate (except for the use of email) working stiff, to a Net Chick who just landed a gig as a Web page designer and will be starting a new position as a teacher of PowerPoint and Microsoft Word. When I asked her if she felt overwhelmed she said, "You should feel overwhelmed every day, so that you don't become stale."

If a Net-related career sounds interesting to you but you're confused as to how to prepare yourself or how to go about a job search, you may want to start by nosing around the Web for schools and employment opportunities. (For example, MIT has a site at http://www.mit.edu/ which may have some good leads.) You should also see what kind of information you can pick up in newsgroups.

"Smart Stuff" will give you a head start in becoming a pro Net surfer by supplying you with some handy occupational addresses. But even more inspiring are the two modem-smart women featured here who have created their own prestigious Internet positions. So give a warm welcome to: professional dancer-cum-Director of African American Networking, Deborah Floyd ("When I dance I'm using movement, and when I'm online I'm moving through people, I'm moving with people. I'm getting people to move"); and author, *Computer Life* columnist, and professional data surfer—or cybrarian—Reva Basch ("It's very tempting, especially on the Net, to just get out there and 'surf,' and you'll spend three or four hours just finding interesting things…and then you'll log off and discover you never did get the answer to what you were looking for").

Even if you don't want a career in the digital world, you can still take advantage of your modem to find an offline job or non-tech college. You can use the Net to teach yourself how to write a resume or to discover the latest job trend. "Smart Stuff" isn't just about working on the Net; more importantly, it's about networking for empowerment. •

ADA LOVELACE: THE WORLD'S FIRST HACKER

The image of hackers is usually that of stiff, pale, bespectacled boy-nerds with greasy hair and crushed Pepsi cans lying at their feet. It's true that this type of human has dominated the world of computers for the last several decades, founding multimillion dollar companies and creating ingenious programs. With that kind of track record, it's no wonder most of society equates the birth of hacking with men. What we need to get straight, however, is that, au contraire, the world's first hacker was a woman! A beautiful Victorian countess, to be exact.

Ada Byron, also known as Lady Lovelace, was born in 1815 to British aristocrats Anne Isabella Milbanke and poet Lord Byron. She was already a scientific whiz kid and visionary at the age of thirteen, coming up with brilliant concepts like scientifically sound ideas for a flying machine. Unfortunately her mother never appreciated Ada's amazing gift and discouraged her from becoming an inventor. She thought her young daughter was spending too much time on wasteful notions when she should have been tending to her more traditional school studies.

Thus Ada didn't enliven her blueprints of the flying machine, but she couldn't stifle her highly charged scientific aptitude. At seventeen she met and became lifelong friends with scientist Charles Babbage. After he had

INTRODUCTION TO NEW ADA PROGRAMMERS
http://lglwww.epfl.ch/Ada/Discover.html
Did you know there's a programming language named after Ada?
Modem in for an introduction, history, and free online Ada '95
tutorial of the language.

THE ADA PICTURE GALLERY
http://www.cs.kuleuven.ac.be/~dirk/ada-pictures.html
This gallery is divided into three categories: images of the Ada language, portraits of Ada Lovelace, and miscellaneous. I don't give a hoot about the programming graphics, so I immediately zeroed in on the Lady. What a beaut!

invented a calculating machine called the Difference Engine to gather tables of logarithms, it was Ada who passionately pored over math books day and night to come up with a sixty-four-page article that outlined her concept for the Difference's successor, the Analytical Engine. This was a machine that is now thought of by many as the first computer, which she envisioned to one day be used not only to crunch numbers but to compose music, produce graphics, and help create art as well. While Charles was busy constructing their new machine, Ada devoted all of her time and energy to writing the instructions that explained how to program it on punch cards to calculate any kind of math problem. In other words, this hacker chick wrote the world's first computer programs.

So you see, the image of hackers as whiskered, testosterone-laden boys isn't quite right. Next time hackers are the topic of conversation, let us picture curves, corsets, and countesses! •

Ada, The Enchantress of Numbers: A Selection from the Letters of Lord Byron's Daughter and Her Description of the First Computer, by Betty Alexandra Toole, Strawberry Press, ©1992

Ms. Toole did research for more than eight years, burying herself in British archives and libraries to narrate and edit this extraordinary collection of letters written by Ada Lovelace. Not only do they outline the evolution of Ada's ingenuity for the sciences, but they also enlighten us on all aspects of Lady Lovelace's multidimensional life: her passionate desire to flourish in "a man's world," her battle with drug addiction and chronic sickness, and her efforts as a mother and wife. Lovelace has also had a reputation as a wild gambler and lover. What can tell us more truthfully about Ms. Lovelace's life than letters from the Lady herself?

I didn't realize information was such a hot commodity, but Reva Basch can sell it at $1,000 a crack. No, she's not a private detective (although she sometimes acts like one) but a "cybrarian," someone who uses a high-powered modem to find information for clients. And with approximately 5,000 cybrarians roaming the outer boundaries of the Net, she's not alone.

Basch wasn't always a data surfer, however. With a Master's degree in Library Sciences, she used to be a paper-perusing librarian.

RevaBasch

Data Sleuth Know-bot

Then the commercial databases (searchable electronic warehouses of news stories) caught her eye, and before she knew it, she became a "hardware junkie" who constantly wants more RAM, more speed, and more software.

When not sniffing around for facts, she writes the Cybernaut column for Computer Life magazine and hosts the WELL conference known as WOW (Women on the WELL). She's also working on the tentatively titled Secrets of the Super Net Searchers, an online project modeled after her book, Secrets of the Super Searchers (1993), in which she interviewed about two dozen expert cybrarians who disclosed the tricks of the trade. I got Ms. Basch to share some of her secrets with me.

Are there many female cybrarians, or are you one of the few?

> There are actually a lot of us, I think because the library profession has been a traditionally female one, and librarianship has fed, naturally, into cybrarianship.

> **If I want to look something up on the Web, I just use a search engine like Yahoo or WebCrawler. Why do people need to pay a cybrarian to find stuff for them?**

> The kind of research I mostly do isn't really on the Web or the wider Net. It's in the commercial databases, the ones that usually cost a lot of money to search, like Dialog and Nexus Lexus and Dow Jones News Retrieval. I do use the Web for

Tracy Johnson

some things—I usually use it to find experts, or to get information that hasn't been published in the commercial databases. But the Web and the Net are really a supplement to what I do, which is the heavy duty professional database services.

> **So when you use a service like Nexus Lexus you have to pay them a fee by the hour?**

> Yeah, in fact most of them charge by the minute. Nexus charges by the search, about $6 to $50 every time you put in a search query.

> **Yikes!**

> Yeah, and Info Seek on the Web is only twenty to forty cents a search query, so I just laugh when people say "we shouldn't have to pay for information on the Net," when that is so minuscule compared to what something like Nexus or Dialog charges. Typically you'll pay anywhere from twenty bucks to several hundred, or sometimes even $1,000 for a big online search on one of those commercial services.

> **What kind of client would pay $1,000 for an information search?**

> Usually companies that really need the information. A lot of business people, companies that are making strategic decisions based on the information you can get for them. Sometimes it's someone who needs information on a medical topic. It might be someone who's job hunting and wants to be really prepared to go into an employment interview, so they want background on the company they're interviewing with and its products. Very precise targeted information that you can't find—at least not yet—on the Net to the same extent that you can find it on the commercial databases.

> **If these databases aren't on the Net, where are they?**

> You can telnet to them, and they have Websites, but there's a gateway. You can only get to the information itself if you've already made an arrangement to open an account. So they're on the Net—kind of—but they're not really part of it.

> **What's the most common type of search for you?**

> I get a lot of marketing people who will come and ask "What's the market for designer sunglasses in the U.S.?" or "What are trends in expensive upscale fountain pens?" or "Tell me about how coffee bars or coffeehouses are developing in different cities, who's combining them with Laundromats…?"

> **And it's mostly articles that come up?**

> Yeah, mostly articles. See, the difference between most of what's on the Net and what's in the commercial databases is that the commercial databases tend to be electronic libraries. It's the ASCII version of print publications, like the *LA Times, New York Times, San Francisco Chronicle…*

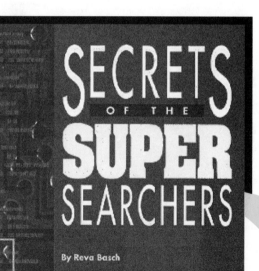

> **Do you ever get strange requests?**

> Oh, I get weird stuff, so much of it is weird. They'll ask for background information on a person. Now and then I'll get something where there's a divorce suit happening, and the guy will say he has absolutely no assets to give his ex-wife. Then I'll search for society pages, and it'll turn up that he's just returned from an around-the-world cruise and jetted in from Vail for a debutante party or something.

> **I love it! You get to play spy!**

> And some of the stuff I do that's really straightforward for the person that's asking for it sounds weird to outsiders because they're just not in that field. Like I had this engineering company that wanted to know about sports stadiums throughout the world—whether any of them had problems with a particular kind of rust where the metal parts would rust and drip down and discolor the concrete, and to someone who's not an engineer it's like, "How bizarre!"

> **Do you ever fear that agents [software "agents" that search for data] will replace your job?**

"how bizarre!"

> Uh, I think what's starting to happen is that we are becoming the agents and we're designing the agents. One of the best things I've read in *Wired* is something Paul Saffo published a couple of years ago about how the commodity that is going to become important on the Net is point of view. That means that people will pay for a filtering agent they trust, whether it's a person or a piece of software that reflects their own priorities and their own point of view. They know they're not going to be able to get everything that's appeared out there on a subject, but they want a device, or whatever that agent is, that will consider the same things to be important.

> **Yeah, I also read in *Wired* about the idea of having, say, a Rush Limbaugh know-bot…**

> Yeah, right, versus the, whatever…

> **Versus the Howard Stern know-bot!**

> Oh yeah, right. God, that's one concept of Hell. Howard Stern as your filtering agent.

> **Would you ever become an agent with a viewpoint for somebody?**

> I do it to a certain extent now. I have regular clients who I know are interested in certain things, and when I happen to run across those things I snarf them down and send them to the client. I think a lot of my colleagues, especially people just starting out in the business, are going in that direction.

> **What are some of the secrets of searching that you talk about in both your book (*Secrets of the Super Searchers*) and your upcoming Net publication?**

> I think probably the single best piece of advice I could give—and there's a lot of advice—is to know what you're looking for before you start. See if you can boil it down to one sentence. It's very tempting, especially on the Net, to just get out there and "surf." And you'll spend three or four hours just finding interesting things that lead to other interesting things, and then you'll log off and discover you never did get the answer to what you were looking for. So to stay focused, really have a good idea of what you're looking for before you go in.

> **Sounds like a very good tip. I'm horrible at staying on track, I always go off on these wild tangents.**

> Yeah, me too!

> **Even when you're searching for someone else?**

> I do, more on the Net than on the commercial databases. And the reason for that is quite simple.

> **The money?**

> Yeah!

> **How much time do you spend online each day?**

> Oh, (laughs) do I have to tell you? All inclusive, I would have to say my modem is hooked up—connected—probably six or seven hours a day. Some of that is answering email—I couldn't live without email, both personally and professionally—and I get a ton of it. Some of it is researching, for sure, and some of it is gathering background info for an article I'm writing, and I spend a lot of time on the WELL. So it adds up.

HOT SITE: Reva's Home Page
http://www.well.com/user/reva/

*T*o find out more about Ms. Basch and her own cybrarian business (Aubergine Information Services), cruise over to her Home. After reading her bio, she'll kindly take you to the WELL (where you can sample some conferences) and *Computer Life* (make sure to read her articles!). If you want to see a sliver of her real life, take a peek at her photos.

> **What is it like to be online for so long and then to have to go back to your "real" life?**

> That's a really good question. For one thing my distance vision is shot. I'm so used to seeing this screen that's just eighteen inches away that things in the distance are now blurry.

I'm so used to being in "browse" mode when I'm online, just looking for little bits of information or interesting conversations or whatever and picking out the good stuff, that I really have to force myself to slow down when I'm dealing face to face with someone. I have to think, "This is a conversation I'm having with someone, I'm not reading for information, I'm participating in a conversation." I think that's the most important thing—reminding myself to slow down and be "in the moment." Because being online has a way of accelerating things like crazy.

> **I read the interview with you in _Wired_, where you said you go to parties and just scan the room, from person to person, browsing...**

> Yeah, and it's a bad habit. There may be a reason why the people I consider to be my closest friends now—just about all of them—are people I've met online in the first place. You know, I wouldn't have met them if it hadn't been for online. Most of them live in my general area—in Berkeley or Oakland or in the city [San Franciso]—but in a way we kind of chose each other because we understand the online environment and what it's like, and how hard it is to shift over to this other mode of interacting.

> **Why would there be a different understanding between people who are online?**

> Well, they've been there, you know? They know the kind of mindset you fall into when you're online. They also know the jargon, the abbreviations and acronyms and all that stuff. And they also know—let's face it—the same cast of characters, so if you're gossiping, everyone is sort of plugged into the same events that are happening.

> **Tell me about Women on the Well (WOW). I'm so embarrassed that I haven't checked it out.**

> You're probably on the Ulist already, but I'll check. WOW is probably the second oldest private conference on the WELL. I'm not sure of that, but it goes back to 1986, and the WELL started in 1985. It's private in so far as it's limited to women only. It's a big conference, over 400 people, with about 100 active regulars, and we talk about everything. It's not really a feminist or women's issues conference. There is some discussion of women's politics, but there's also a lot of chat, even talk about clothes and shopping.

> **Do boys ever sneak on?**

> Not that I'm aware of. Nothing is foolproof, but we do a nominal check...

> **What are your favorite topics in the WOW conference?**

> I like what we call the Check-In topic, which is like, "Hi, what's happening with you today?" It just lets people know what's going on with your life. Other good topics deal with what's stressing us out, or what particularly good things have happened in one's life...

> **How come this group wants it to be all women when you're talking about things that could involve men as well?**

> Just because it feels different. I mean, there are topics in WOW that have their direct equivalent elsewhere on the WELL. For instance, there's a topic where people can ask technical questions, and a lot of them could be answered in the IBM or the Mac conference, but there are a lot of guys— I'm sure you've seen this—who have a vested interest in showing how much they know, and who needs that? There are a lot of women in WOW with pretty heavy-duty technical chops, and if you can get a straightforward answer to your question without having to deal with the attitude, why not ask in WOW first? It just feels different.

A lot of women who are new to cyberspace ask to join WOW after they've been blown away, or blown off, completely ignored in another conference. They'll get some support and attention in WOW, and then they can go out into the larger Net and attack. •

DEBORAH FLOYD: DANCING THROUGH CYBERSPACE

W hen I asked Deborah Floyd how she went from being a professional dancer to being Program Coordinator for an online service provider (two careers I thought to be worlds apart), she surprised me by saying she became attracted to computers because of the parallels she found between dancing and using the Internet. Parallels? Please explain. "Movement is one. When I dance I'm using movement, and when I'm online I'm moving through people, I'm moving with people. I'm getting people to move."

She says communication is another link between her two passions. She used to choreograph dance pieces that dealt with sociopolitical issues that mainly revolved around women. For instance, one piece addressed women's addiction to drugs and alcohol ("But I did not give opinions as to whether addictions were right or wrong"). She created the piece as a way to reach out to women who were in need of help. Now she's "using this service, the Internet, to reach out to African-descent people. Using it as a unifying tool, as a way of talking to each other, of coming together, of knowing what we

Deborah Floyd

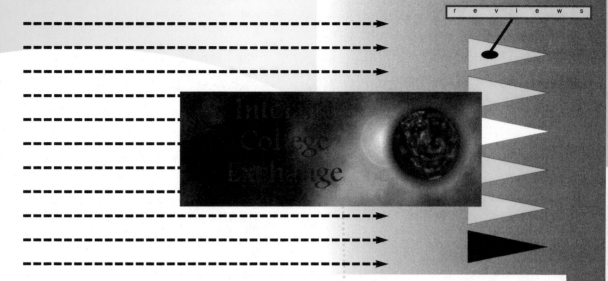

are doing across the waters, across the land so that we can continue to work together as a unit and stay in contact with one another."

Floyd, one of the founding members of CitiCentre Dance Theatre (a dance company in Oakland, California), was first attracted to the Net around seven years ago, when she discovered live chat rooms, email, and research capabilities via online libraries (which came in handy for the Women's Studies classes she was teaching at San Francisco State University). She then enthusiastically volunteered for IGC (Institute of Global Communications), a nonprofit full Internet service provider that's been around for more than a decade. Here she was able to see firsthand the Internet's powerful ability to touch and influence others.

After realizing she'd found her calling (her most important online mission is to "make African Americans aware of the Internet and how it can service them"), she applied along with eighty or so other applicants to be the coordinator of their five networks: PeaceNet, Women'sNet, EcoNet, ConflictNet, and LaborNet. When she got the job, she immediately set forth on her mission by also becoming Director of African American Networking (see sidebar), a service she created herself that now resides on PeaceNet.

Although Floyd feels that IGC offers an invaluable service for marketing social, political, and ecological types of issues, it doesn't offer what she thinks is equally important: marketing and unifying small businesses which cater to African Americans on the Net. So on top of her all-consuming work at IGC, she also works with MELANET (http://www.ip.net/melanet/), a

When I was deciding which university to go to, I bought this heavy, clunky guide-to-colleges book that was confusing and cumbersome, to say the least. It brought out the raging beast in me more than once. If only the simple-to-use college-related sites on the Web would've been available at the time. But they're here now! Makes me want to apply all over again... (not!).

INTERNET COLLEGE EXCHANGE
http://www.usmall.com/

Academics from all over the country can enjoy this online student center. Check out their bulletin board (where people can discuss any school-related topic they want, the most popular being about university programs), online bookstore (a place to order merchandise from universities nationwide), and their searchable school database (type in the area, size of campus, kind of college, and tuition range that you're looking for, and a list of your possible school options will appear on the screen). They also have a newsletter, but unfortunately it was down when I visited this site.

--more-->

DEBORAH FLOYD: DANCING THROUGH CYBERSPACE

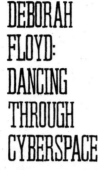

continued

commercial online site that connects people to all sorts of businesses that focus on African American needs. She helps to get clients their own Websites, online conferences, links, etc.

When I asked her if she still had fun on the chat lines, she laughed, saying they had only held her attention for a day or two. Then, in a more serious tone, she told me, "African Americans don't tend to look at this in terms of chatting. This is not a device to chat—we can chat on our own. It's about networking. It's about business."

Ms. Floyd says she's seen progress in getting more African Americans online, but wants to become involved with the actual nuts-and-bolts of things. "But aren't you already doing more than one woman's share of work?" I ask. "Yes," she answers, but says she's enthused by the organization Play to Win (PTW), which goes to under-privileged communities and sets up computer centers. These centers are not just in the schools but in buildings that aren't formal education–based, so the kids can go in and do their own projects. She wants to collect used modems and other computer gear to contribute to the group.

Although Ms. Floyd expresses fear of the Internet being used as a device "to keep us separated once again" (it won't be with sharp people like her choreographing things!), she did empha-size that she's trying not to focus on what African Americans don't have. "I'd rather focus on how this is a useful tool, and how this can move people ahead. All people." •

If you're interested in signing up with IGC, it's $12.50 with six free hours per month, and then $2–4/hour. For more information on IGC, log in to IGC's "Progressive Directory" (http://www.igc.apc.org/igc/).

HOT SITES:
Deborah's Hot Sites

IGC'S AFRICAN AMERICAN DIRECTORY
http://www.igc.apc.org/africanam/africanam.html
Within just the last couple of weeks I've seen Deborah's online directory of black resources really expand. Among her vibrant pages you should definitely check out:
• The African American News Service.
• "In Our Words," a page of quotes from anonymous African Americans.
• The index to educational articles.
• A Northern California African American events calendar. (Now that Deborah has relocated to the DC area, perhaps the calendar will relocate as well …)
• Links to other pages related to African American culture, like "Afro-American Newspapers," "BET" (Black Entertainment Television), "African American Issues," "MELANET," and a whole lot more.

DEBORAH K. FLOYD'S HOME PAGE
http://www.igc.apc.org/dfloyd/
If you want to see who owns the brains and sweat behind it all, visit Ms. Floyd at her Home Page. She gives us a short bio, a few photos, and a couple of links. It's a nice start, Deborah, but I wanna see more!

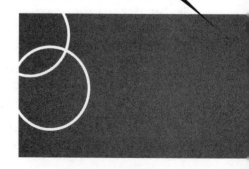

NetChick@smart.stuff.200-201

an authentic dorm room

CHRISTINA'S COLLEGE AND UNIVERSITY HOME PAGES

http://www.mit.edu:8001/people/cdemello/univ.html

Christina, who comes from MIT, says "I spend way too much time online." She ain't kidding! She's created this humongous database of college Home Pages from all over the world. Just click on a letter from A to Z, and a list of links to schools beginning with that letter will pop up. For instance, I clicked on B and received 62 schools, from Bangkok University to Boston College. If you're confused about what school you want to go to, bookmark this page!

STUDENTSTUFF'S HOME PAGE

http://www.geopages.com/SiliconValley/1323/

This stimulating and educational college playground is made up of links that will take you all over the place: Hispanic, Persian, Bosnian, and other cultural pages; religious spots (Jewish, Islamic, etc.); chat lines; and "Fun Stuff" that includes astronomy, a look at Earth, remote and robotic telescopes, and more.

PRINCETON REVIEW

http://www.review.com/index.html

Preparing for college? This online (and paper) newsletter, which has been around since 1981, gives you the skinny on various Business, Law, Medical and Graduate schools, as well as test preparation tips, financial aid requirements, career advice, and "educational links." And no, this isn't related to Princeton University.

--more-->

Schoool Grrl Hot Sites continued

WOMEN IN MATHEMATICS

http://www.cs.umd.edu/~gibson/wim.html

Sponsored by Women in Math (WIM), this page is for women who are turned on to math, computer science, physics, and engineering. They'll point you to all sorts of related sites, as well as to those that deal with women's issues and WWW information. WIM also has an electronic newsletter; you can subscribe to it or read excerpts from it here.

WOMEN UNDERGRADS IN COMPUTER SCIENCE

http://www.science.unimelb.edu.au/cielle/women/wucs.html

For chicks into computer science, you'll be able to find out about academic internships, scholarships, conferences, mailing lists, and grad-related stuff. They also have a "cool information" section that has lots of facts and various articles about women in computing (like "Why Are There So Few Female Computer Scientists?"). •

Educated.Newsgroups

School is about so much more than just learning: the whole application process, paying tuition, finding room-mates, fitting in, adjusting to dorm food. ...If you need help or an area to vent your frustrations, give these groups a try.

alt.college.sororities

No, I was never a sorority gal, woe is me. But if you're thinking of joining a house, these nice sisters will answer anything you want to know about turning Greek.

alt.college.us

A wide-open arena for college talk. Look at the range of topics: "Need Housing Near CSU Sacramento," "Law Schools," "Paying Too Much for College?" and "Electric Resume."

alt.grad-student.tenured

A bunch of academics discussing faculty careers, post-doctorate work, student loans, and other grad life–related issues.

alt.grad.skool.sux

Everyone is so cranky here, it's great! These stressed-out students viciously bicker about the lamest matters, like whether a tomato is a fruit or a vegetable. See what college tuition will buy you?

alt.radio.college

DJs and listeners of college radio exchange technical and musical information in this newsgroup.

rec.arts.marching. band.highschool

When I was in high school I avoided the marching band, being an orchestra geek myself (violin, if you care to know). But if you're a teenager who can march with her instrument, here's your group!

soc.college.admissions

This seems like an excellent forum for anyone with questions about getting into college. Lots of smart talk about SATs and GREs, Ivy League programs, filling out applications, etc.

soc.college.financial-aid

Scholarships, getting aid with bad credit, taxes owed on loans, and financial aid for schools in the States as well as abroad are just some of the money topics discussed.

soc.college.grad

A general issues group for graduate students looking for roommates, financial aid, and jobs.

∫≈ç∂

f´d

ßßß

The thing I like about online "help wanted" classifieds as opposed to the ones found in the papers is that you can send your resume and cover letter instantly (it's too easy to mark up a newspaper with an orange highlighter, only to then recycle it as a TV tray). Along with some Webspots that post fresh job openings on a daily basis, most of these sites will also give you career tips and advice to make your search a little less awkward. (Some will also try to sell you books and stuff, but that's easy enough to click around.) Good luck!

JOBS
http://none.coolware.com/jobs/jobs.html

Ooo, I like this job searcher. It's so easy to use—just type in the kind of work you're looking for, and a list of available jobs pertaining to your field will then show up on your screen with contact info. I typed in "graphic artist" (just for grins) and three openings immediately popped up. When I typed in "teacher" I found open positions for ESL and elementary teachers, and even one for an au pair/tutor. You can also place an ad here (as employee or employer) for $10 to $50, depending on the size.

WORLD WIDE WEB EMPLOYMENT OFFICE
http://www.harbornet.com/biz/office/annex.html

For $10 per year this virtual employment office will post your resume, and for $20 per month they'll display a job-wanted ad for you. They also have tons of links to other employment sites.

--more-->

POWERGRRRL.

Whether you want to show off your sass and muscles or reach out for help on a particular issue, I found some spots that may work for you. But if it's support you need, sit in on a group first. Nothing wrong with lurking. Then, join the party only if and when it feels right for you.

alt.abuse.recovery
All kinds of abuse—including physical, emotional, and drug—are talked about here. The group seems like a safe place, filled with warm and compassionate people.

alt.feminism.individual
A lot of hostile macho boys screaming at the feminists in this uncomfortably interesting spot. It's amusing to see how the tough chicks defend themselves, but it's also disgusting to see so many peaheads up in arms about something they don't know much about.

alt.support.abortion
Debates and discussions on typical abortion topics: the constitutionality of it, the Catholic stance on birth control, etc.

NEWSGROUPS

alt.support.breastfeeding

The bottle vs. the breast. Women exchange opinions, advice, and information on feeding their babies.

alt.support.eating-disord

This seems like a friendly, supportive bunch of folks who have eating disorders (anorexia, bulimia, etc.). They share their fears of food and fat, suggest support groups and books on the subject, and talk about solutions.

alt.women.attitudes

Now this is a group with attitude—a group for Net Chicks! Intelligent angles on topics, and even smarter comebacks to any Macho 101 grad who tries to put a grrrl down. Gotta love it.

soc.feminism

A huge variety of conversations going on, including "Women and lifting boxes," "Is being a housewife a choice?" and "Gloria (Allred) and Camille (Paglia)," as well as more serious issues surrounding rape and violence.

soc.women

A very popular salon where both grrrls and boyz talk about orgasms, other women, marriage, lesbians, Miss America, and anything else that involves women.

CAREER ADVICE HOME PAGE

http://www.review.com/career/8000.html

As part of the online publication *The Princeton Review*, these fresh-out-of-college students focus on the trials and tribulations (along with solutions) of post academia. Their easy-to-relate-to articles include "How to Survive Without Your Parents' Money," which deals with the struggle between what you want versus what your parents want, chronic procrastination, and entering the Real World. Also, check out their excerpt from *America's Top 100 Internships* (yes, it's promoting a book, but it's also handy information).

NCS CAREER MAGAZINE

http://www.careermag.com/careermag/

With new material coming in every day, this career mag offers a look at job openings, employer profiles, job-related news, resume help, and much more. Some of the articles in the issue I read include "Be Your Own Headhunter," "How to Find an Online Journalism Job on the Web," and "Write a Great Resume: Tips to Help Your Profile Stand Out."

CAREERWEB

http://www.cweb.com/

Here's another site with job listings (you can never have too many!) and profiles of employers. You also get access to the CareerWEB library—a list of books, some of which you can order online, that teach career search strategies. You can take their online Career Fitness Test (suspicious alert!) to see what kind of shape you're in as an employee on the lookout (if you only score one out of four stars, like I did in my half-assed attempt at the test, they try to push a book on you).•

If you're in a situation you don't like, don't let anyone bully you into feeling weak and helpless. As a warrior, find your strength and take charge. If you need help finding the mighty power that you possess, these sites may be a good place for you to start. Besides getting information on what you can do to make a change, you can also get understanding and support from other women who are going through the same experiences as you are. Go girl!

BODY LANGUAGE
http://www.the-body-shop.com/
index.html

Being that this E-rag is created by the popular soap store The Body Shop, I had saved a chunk of white space in the Stylin' chapter to review what I had thought was a mail-order catalog for pampering products. So imagine my surprise when the articles listed in the table of contents were titled: "Welcome," "Human Rights Issues," "Stop Violence Against Women," "Community Projects," "Endangered Species" (special focus on elephants), "Missing Persons Helpline"… and finally, one article about proper shaving techniques.

I knew that The Body Shop had a social conscience, but not to this extreme. I didn't see one mention of their products or shop locations. Instead, I found their material to be spiritually uplifting and motivating. They have a cute image map with boxes on which you can click to get articles on topics such as, "What Is Empowerment," "You've Got the Power," and "Imagine What You Can Do." Not only is this site intelligent and informative, but the bright cartoonish graphics make it stimulating to look at as well. Having read this from "cover to cover," I now anxiously await the next issue.

Women's Wire

WOMEN HOMEPAGE

http://www.mit.edu:8001/people/
sorokin/women/index.html

A fat collection of articles and
resources by/about/for women. Find
out about women's centers and studies programs, women in academia and
the workplace, gender and sexuality
issues, etc. A handy URL to store in
your E-address book.

SAFETYNET

http://www.cybergrrl.com/dv.html

Hosted by Cybergrrl (Aliza Sherman),
this site offers women a vast amount
of information pertaining to domestic
violence. Sherman replaces myths with
facts, and has put together comprehensive lists of hotlines and referral
numbers nationwide, shelters, reading
resources, suggestions for help, and
much more. She also gives us statistics
on different aspects of domestic violence, taking care to make sure her
figures are as accurate as possible. Two
thumbs up for Cybergrrl!

BAY AREA MODEL MUGGING/
IMPACT

http://www.ugcs.caltech.edu/~rachel/
bamm.html

BAMM offers classes that teach
women how to defend themselves.
They say it's not a woman's size that
stops her from successfully protect-
ing herself from an attacker—instead
it's "the internalized cultural role
which restrains them from taking
action." Learn about the self-defense
instructors, their training techniques
(students work with a padded "mug-
ger"), and the various classes taught
across the country, including some
for kids.

META-INDEX FOR NON-PROFIT
ORGANIZATIONS

http://WWW.AI.MIT.edu/people/
ellens/non-meta.html

You'll find a humongous list of links to
non-profit issue-oriented services
here, including pages on human rights,
civil liberties, health and human services, environmental issues, animal
rights, and tons of other miscellaneous
helpful spots. This site is updated and
maintained by Ellen Spertus.

NATIONAL ORGANIZATION
FOR WOMEN (NOW)

http://now.org/now/home.html

NOW is dedicated to helping women
climb into powerful positions by fight-
ing for economic rights, abortion
rights, eliminating racism, lesbian/gay
rights, and everything else under the
equal rights amendment. Find out
about their nationwide chapters, the
history of NOW, and how you can
become a part of this organization.
You can also read their monthly online
newspaper, *The National NOW Times*,
and check out their links to other
feminist resources. •

I f you're reading this chapter, I assume you need some help getting online. Cool! I'm glad you're asking. I think two of the biggest obstacles a lot of non-tech people have to logging on are 1) being afraid or embarrassed to ask for help, and 2) thinking that because it's technical it's going to be too difficult. But I swear, if I can tap into the Net, so can you!

I was *not* a technical girl growing up, and I never imagined myself as a computer chick. First of all, I idiotically thought it was just a boy thing, and second of all, I thought I'd have to know all sorts of secret codes and calculations to be skilled enough to hop onto the Internet. It wasn't until I realized how easy it was to write a school paper using a computer and how accessible

the world would become once I made friends with my modem that I timidly decided to enter the digital universe.

The first places I dialed up were local bulletin board systems (BBSs), where people in and around Boulder, Colorado, could participate in all sorts of online discussions. Some were just friendly get-to-know-you chats, while others focused on specific subjects, such as pop culture or politics. I was so enthused when I first read a response to something I had written. I was communicating with strangers through my computer! It was as if these strangers were sitting in my bedroom. Back in the late '80s this seemed like magic to me.

Then I joined the Whole Earth 'Lectronic Link (WELL), a BBS with thousands of users, and information just poured through my computer screen. I was sitting in on fascinating discussions every night (and once in a great while I got the nerve to pipe up). The people on the WELL were so brilliant and intellectually stimulating (they still are) that when my husband, Mark Frauenfelder, and I started our zine, *bOING bOING*, it was through this Sausalito-based online BBS that we were able to garner a lot of our ideas and cutting-edge material.

Now I can't imagine not having access to the infinitely vast source of art, literature, up-to-the-minute news, social happenings, politics, and any other kind of info you can think of that floats down the roads of the Internet. It's amazing how perceptive Marshall McLuhan was in the '60s when he talked about the world becoming a global village. And it's even more amazing how something so seemingly complex can be so simple to use. It's a cinch!

qrstuvwxyz

This chapter will explain the main steps needed to get onto the Net. This includes:

- What you need to go online. It ain't much!
- Choosing an online service. Signing up with a service will allow you to send and receive email and will, in many cases, give you access to the thousands of Usenet groups (areas on the Net where people discuss topics) and the World Wide Web (where all of the Hot Sites listed in this book reside).
- Selecting and hooking up your modem. The speed of your modem determines how long it takes for stuff to appear on your screen. If you're going to be playing on the Web, you want to make sure not to get stuck with a slug of a modem.
- Accessing the World Wide Web. Once you get your modem all set up, you'll need to get another goody or two to get on the Web.

That's it!

I've also included some recommended hotlists (lists of Internet addresses other people have created that point you to topic-related spots on the Web) and my favorite books, some of which will give you more detailed lessons on navigating the Net. Finally, you'll find a glossary of all the fancy words used in this book, so that you'll not only be a Net siren, but you'll sound like one, too!

TEN

WHAT IS THE NET?

M any people use "Net" and "Internet" to mean the same thing. When I say "Net," I mean the entire online world: services such as America Online and Prodigy, the thousands of local and regional bulletin board systems, and the Internet.

The Internet is a collection of millions of networked computers linked together in a global supernetwork. This network of networks creates an interactive electronic medium in which people can share information, art, photographs, video clips, music, and software. The fascinating thing about the Internet is that, as huge and complex as the system is, no one is in charge. It isn't centrally located anywhere. When you send an email message from Los Angeles to a friend living in New York, it doesn't have one standard route to follow, as regular snail mail does. Instead, the email is broken down into little digitized packets that shoot off across phone lines and cables from one computer network to another until it finds its destination. If one computer system is down, it will bypass that area and find another, until it arrives at its final stop. Each packet may take a different route to reach its destination, but the Internet software ensures that the message gets reassembled correctly at the receiving end.

You may be wondering, if no one is in charge, who designed the system to perform such a task in the first place?

The Internet was started in the '60s by the U.S. military as an instantaneous communication system that could survive a nuclear attack. If military officials wanted to send an urgent message from Kentucky to Arizona, they could use the Internet to send large amounts of data in seconds; if a computer system en route had been destroyed, the message would just find an alternative path to get to its target. (Ironically, this also makes it very difficult for the government to censor information on the Internet. As the popular saying goes, "The Internet interprets censorship as damage and works around it.") Eventually, private businesses and universities began using the Net. Now over twenty million people around the world with computers and modems regularly access the Internet.

While much of the online world, including the World Wide Web (I'll get to that later on in this chapter), is on the Internet, some parts of cyberspace stand on their own, such as bulletin board systems. These are online forums in which members post messages to ongoing conversations, or conferences, as well as swap graphics, games, and software. There are two main differences between BBSs and the commercial online services. One, the larger services often have Internet "gateways" that allow users to send email to other people with Internet access, and two, BBSs are usually run by individuals using one or two personal computers set up in a room. A good number of these BBSs contain nothing but sex pictures that horny geeks download (after they input their credit card numbers for access), but many BBSs are dedicated to local events and special interests, such as sports or politics. One of the best ways to find out how to locate local BBSs is to scroll through the Usenet newsgroup alt.bbs.lists, or to look in the classifieds section of your local newspaper.

If you're still a little fuzzy as to the big picture, you're not alone. Most people who use the Net don't completely understand how it works, and, frankly, it doesn't really matter. The important thing is taking advantage of what the online world has to offer. And, like driving a car, you've got to actually sit in the driver's seat and go around the block a couple of times before you begin to understand what it's all about.

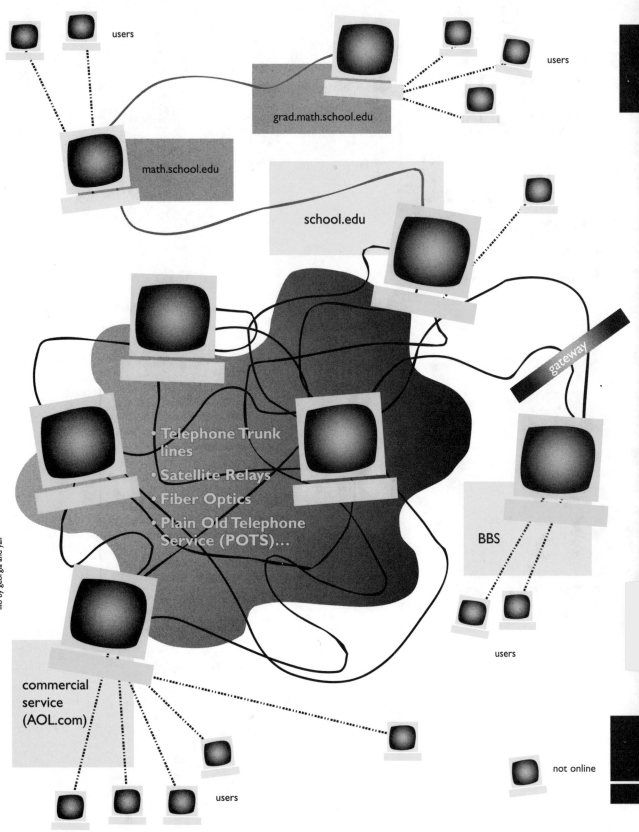

users

users

grad.math.school.edu

math.school.edu

school.edu

gateway

• Telephone Trunk
lines
• Satellite Relays
• Fiber Optics
• Plain Old Telephone
Service (POTS)…

BBS

users

commercial
service
(AOL.com)

users

not online

illo by georgia and yair

NECESSARY GOODS TO GET ONLINE

Jumping onto the Internet is really a simple process. All you need are four things:

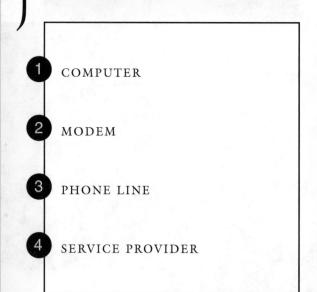

1 COMPUTER

2 MODEM

3 PHONE LINE

4 SERVICE PROVIDER

Obviously you need a **computer**. Either a Macintosh or DOS/Windows PC is fine. If all you want is email, then you don't need to worry too much about the type of computer you have. If you want to access the World Wide Web (which you should!), however, you'll need at least 8 MB of RAM (random access memory) to make your online experience pleasant. The more megabytes the better, especially if you want to take advantage of all of the Web's photos, sounds, and video clips. If you have a PC, you'll need to get an additional

1.

LOGIN: SMARTCHICK
PASSWORD:

YOU HAVE 5 NEW
MESSAGES GRRRL

sound card to hear
anything on the Web.
And since the WWW is so
color-intense, a color computer
monitor is highly recommended.

If you're shopping for a computer,
you may want to consider spending more for a
laptop. They're portable, which means you're not anchored
to one spot in your office or home. It also means you can take
it on business trips and even vacations, if you so desire. Laptops
can perform the same online functions as those of big clunky
stationary computers, and as long as there's a phone line
around, you can jack into cyberspace from virtually anywhere.

A **modem** is your pipeline to the Net. It's a device
that allows you to transfer data over an ordinary telephone
line from your computer to other computers. There are two
important factors to consider when shopping for a modem:
speed and whether it's external or internal.

The speed of your modem determines how fast information will be transferred to and from your computer. For email
only, 2,400 bits per second (bps) will do the trick and will
cost you less than fifty bucks. But to do anything else online,
especially on the Web, you must use a modem with at least
14,400 (14.4K) bps—unless you're a glutton for misery. Even
a 14.4K modem can sometimes seem frustratingly slow when
you're trying to access large graphic, video, and sound files.
You might as well spend a little bit more money, around $100

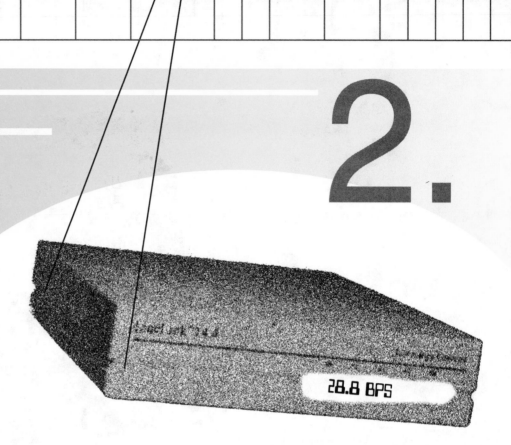

2.

28.8 BPS

and get 14.4 bps, or splurge for over $150 on a 28.8 bps, which is the fastest standard modem at the moment.

Besides the speed, you need to decide whether you want an external or an internal modem. An external modem sits on your desk, and you plug it into a serial port in back of your computer. An internal modem, on the other hand, fits into a slot on the inside of your computer.

The advantages of an external modem are that it's easier to install (since you don't have to open up your computer), and it has blinking lights that tell you if and when it's connecting. Also, if you have more than one computer, you can easily switch your external modem from one to another (even between Macs and PCs). Disadvantages? External modems take up desk space, adding to the clutter around your computer. They also tend to be more expensive than internal modems. Besides being cheaper, internal modems are nice because once they're installed, you only need to plug a phone line into the back of your computer.

Don't worry about installing your modem. It will come with a manual (along with software that you'll need to install), which will tell you step by step how to get everything in working order. If you're a Mac user, I

highly recommend a Global Village modem, which is very easy to install and use.

Your modem needs a **phone line** to obtain access to other computers. Either use your existing phone line to switch back and forth between your telephone cord and your modem cable (which means you can't receive phone calls when you are logged on), or get a second line. Once you've paid the phone company's extortionate (usually $150) set up charges, this will only cost you around $10 more per month (not including any long-distance charges, of course), and will be more convenient if you plan to spend a lot of time online.

Finally, you need an account with a **service provider**. Without one, the only thing you can do with your modem is dial into free bulletin board systems. Don't get me wrong, BBSs can be extremely stimulating and entertaining. But a subscription to a service allows you so much more, since it gives you access to the Internet, thus opening up the gates to email, the Web, Usenet groups, thousands of text files (gophers), and more. To get an account you must go through: commercial online service, an Internet Service Provider (ISP), or a university.

3. ■ YOU HAVE A PHONE

4 ■ GET AN ACCOUNT

America Online (AOL), CompuServe, and the WELL are examples of commercial online services. Although they all provide email and other perks, such as conferences (which are like BBSs), live chat rooms, digital publications, or online shopping, only some of them offer access to the World Wide Web at this time (see pg. 233 for more details, including costs). If you decide to go this route, take advantage of the free trial periods that most commercial services offer so that you can get a chance to test drive these various vehicles before committing to any of them.

If you go with an Internet Service Provider, ask for a SLIP or PPP account, which will cost between twenty and fifty dollars a month. They will then furnish you with an email account and access to the Internet, meaning you'll be able to play on the Web, participate in Usenet groups, and check out gopher files. The difference between an ISP and a commercial service is that the latter creates all sorts of resources that are available only on their particular service. For example, services like the WELL and ECHO offer hundreds of entertaining conferences, a few of them for chicks only; these are really fun, but they aren't open to anyone except members of the service. An ISP, on the other hand, only offers its members access to Net spots that anyone with any kind

of service can check out. In other words, you don't get anything extra. But the Web is already way too packed with stuff to ever keep you from getting bored, so those extras may not be important or necessary to you.

To put it another way, you could think of commercial services as private country clubs and an ISP as a big anarchistic park next to the clubs. The country club is private and offers its members cozy social lounges, special publications and boutiques, private events, and other unique services, as well as a key that will give you entrance to the wild park outside their gates. ISP members also have access to the wild park, which is full of fantastic sights, sites, art galleries, people, and even businesses, but they don't get a key to any of the country clubs.

If you don't have the bucks to pay the monthly fee for a service (or a computer, for that matter), *and* if you're a student, you may want to see about the possibilities of getting a free university account. Check with your computer studies department to see what they offer. Also, if you work in a big company that has Net access, you may be able to get a free account there. Find the company's "alpha geek" and ask them.

Once you've got these four online essentials set up, you're in! •

CHOOSING AN ONLINE SERVICE

echo?

the WELL?

Prodigy?

aol?

Mind Vox?

Women's Wire?

CompuServe??

It's smart to investigate before signing up with an online service. Like cars, each service fulfills different needs. If you're the kind of chick who wants:

● An easy ride with total comfort

● Lots of features (with just a push of the button)

● Paved roads (no seedy regions, please!)

● Perky, conservative, and not necessarily hip

then you might want to consider one of the big three—America Online, Prodigy, or CompuServe. These more corporate mega-services have millions of subscribers and are user-friendly, which is encouraging for the newcomer. If, however, you're a grrrl who craves:

● Something sporty but perhaps a little rough

● Lots of adventure (no closed gates)

● An off-road machine made for tougher terrain

● Bold, smart adventures and sometimes daunting territory

then perhaps you'd have more fun playing with one of the smaller, more personable services. These usually don't have an intuitive interface, but, like driving stick-shift cars, once you learn how to navigate them it becomes second nature.

Since there are dozens of smaller services, I'll just talk about four that I find most interesting: ECHO (East

Coast Hang Out), the WELL (Whole Earth 'Lectronic Link), Women's Wire, and Mind Vox.

Let's start with the toughest gig of the bunch: Mind Vox. I considered not even listing this one, which is hard to learn and not any kind of a place for a lady. (Ladies, scooch back over to Prodigy! Or better yet, use a phone.) But let me tell you, the Webgrrls whose Home Pages give me the biggest charge always seem to be from Mind Vox. These Voxxen (as women on Mind Vox refer to themselves, named after their private women-only conference) are the epitome of riot Net grrrls. They're brazen, combative, clever, personable, and sexy. When I asked Voxxen Marjorie (did you read her romantic essay in the sex chapter?) why these chicks are so damn cool, she said it's because in order for a woman to survive in Mind Vox, which can be very hostile and male-chauvinistic, she must be technically savvy and have a "high level of toughness and hipness; she must have a real sense of sisterhood because it's not a girl-friendly place." So the Voxxen stick together, like a clan of women warriors, and learn how to use their feminine goddess-power to fearlessly infiltrate any Net space they please. Of course, I highly discourage this service for the weak or feeble.

Even in 1989, when I first signed up, I always thought of the WELL as a warm, closely-knit group of people, and it didn't really matter in most cases what gender you were. Some of the conversations did bore me, since they were so nerdboy-oriented, but there was always enough intellectual juice flowing to keep me excited. The WELL does have some great conferences for women, including Women on the WELL (WOW), and a couple of chick-only private rooms called "Blow Me" and "FemXPri." And as always, you'll find high-energy discussions on any subject you can think of. You're assured to get good information, and you'll lock horns with some of the smartest intellectual combatants you'll ever meet.

New York-based ECHO and the West coast's Women's Wire were both started by women. ECHO's founder, Stacy Horn (check out the interview with her that follows), had to expend a lot of energy trying to get women to sign up, but by giving them free accounts for the first year and by offering women-only conferences including WIT (Women in Telecommunications) and BITCH (Babes in Their Cyber Hangout), as well as a conference hosted by *Ms.* magazine, the service now enjoys almost a 40 percent female membership.

Co-founded by Ellen Pack and Nancy Rhine, Women's Wire is the smallest in terms of membership, with only 1,500 subscribers, but its membership is 90 percent women—definitely female-friendly. The cool thing about Women's Wire, ECHO, and the WELL is that they regularly host meetings in cafes and bars so that their members can meet one another in the flesh.

As far as the big three go, they're all about the same at this time. However, Prodigy seems to be the most conservative and family-oriented (corny is more like it), while America Online (AOL) is my favorite. Although I use the WELL for info-gathering and stimulating conversation, I like using AOL for business, because they make sending and receiving documents so easy. CompuServe may win me over, however, with their new feature called WorldsAway, which offers real-time chat in a 3-D world. You select a character (from a variety of cute cartoony girls and boys, some of them wearing silly masks) to represent yourself in the virtual universe. In this alternate world, there are cafes, houses, and outdoor areas where you can "walk" around and visit with friends. At this time I only have a demo tester, but it's supposed to be out by the time this book is published. And I must say, if all goes as planned, this new groundbreaking feature could completely revolutionize online social interaction.

AOL, Prodigy, and CompuServe have easy email, up-to-the-minute news, chat rooms, and other useful services like online shopping and ordering airplane tickets. But the biggest problem I have with them is censorship. They won't let you find out about certain newsgroups that are too "racy," and you have to watch what you say in the chat rooms (or else an invisible lurking "big brother" will tap you on the shoulder and eighty-six you). Also, their World Wide Web access isn't as good as using the Netscape browser with a direct or SLIP/PPP connection.

If you still need more details, take a look at this chart. And then just log in already, wouldja? •

	PRICE	PERCENTAGE OF WOMEN USERS
WELL 415/332-9200	$15/month + $2.50/user hour (after 5 free hours) or $35/mo. + $2.50/user hour (after 20 free hrs.)	20
ECHO 212/292-0900	$19.95/month + $1.00/hour (after 30 free hours)	Just under 40
WOMEN'S WIRE 800/210-8998	$9.95/month + $3.95/hour (after 3 free hours)	90
MIND VOX 212/989-2418	starts at $17.50/month + $1.00/hour (after 60 free hours)	30–35
AMERICA ONLINE 800/827-6364	$9.95/month + $2.95/hour (after 5 free hours)	25–30
PRODIGY 800/776-3449	basic plan: $9.95/month + $2.95/hour (after 5 free hours); alternative plan: $30.00/month + $2.95/hour (after 30 free hours)	40
COMPUSERVE 800/858-0411	$9.95/month (unlimited use of CompuServe's services) + $2.50/hour for use of WWW (after 3 free hours on the WWW)	20

ONLINE SERVICES

MOST POPULAR TOPICS	NUMBER OF USERS	ATTITUDE	IN A NUTSHELL
Women on WELL (WOW); Internet conference; News/Media conference	11,000	Bay Area Intellectual, Dead Head Techie	Digital Berkeley
Pop Culture (books, films, etc.)	3,500	Intellectual, Well-read, New Yorky	Coffee House
Relationships, Health, and Career	1,500	Smart, Savvy, Friendly	Pheromone-synched
"Bandwidth"—collective stream of consciousness from the community	3,500	Tough, Combative, Fighter-girlish	Tank Girl
General Chat Rooms, Email	2.5 million	Happy Shiny People	Yupville
30-something; Teen Stuff	2.3 million	Conservative-trying-to-be-hip, Fun for Everyone!	Family Sedan
Email, Forums, Chat Rooms	3.2 million	Leader of the herd, Preppy	Cutting-Edge Vanilla

Kevin Walker

S T A C Y   H O R N

Just because Stacy Horn is a woman doesn't mean her online service is politically correct or all femmed out. In fact, she started ECHO (The East Coast Hangout) to be a virtual salon where anyone could gab about anything, especially both lowbrow and highbrow culture, her favorite subject areas. Right now some of the hottest topics on ECHO are Film, Body Modification, and a conference called "Connoisseurship of Everyday Moments," in which people post their most incredible experiences.

For the last five years, Ms. Horn has been running her online service out of her apartment. "It was fun at first," she says, "but now it's a nightmare." So she's moving it to some beautiful offices in Tribeca, where the busy view reminds her of the movie Rear Window. *She says that although she's overworked, her company is making a profit, and she's having the time of her life.*

Okay, the big question first: Why did you start ECHO?

> Why? (Chuckles) To escape corporate America. I was working for Mobil at the time. I was miserable.

> **For Mobil.**

>It's true!

>**So how did you go from there to starting ECHO? Seems like such an extravagant move.**

>I was a graduate student at the time, at a place called the Interactive Telecommunications Program at New York University. It's a program in new technology and interactive media. I had an assignment to call the WELL in California, and I just took to the whole medium instantly.

>**Had you ever been on the Internet before?**

>No, never.

>**So did you sign up with a service at that time?**

>I tried a bunch, but the only ones I liked were the WELL and Meta Network [an online service in Virginia]. They were both fun places to visit, but not places that talked about stuff that I was interested in. I'm more interested in books, films, movies, very arts-oriented stuff. So I started ECHO to have that kind of bent.

>**Was starting ECHO hard to do?**

>It was very hard, because I started in 1990, and in New York at that time, there were very few people who were online or who had even heard of it. So getting people online was literally one at a time.

>**How did you do that?**

>Um, just went out and begged people to try it. (laugh) Literally, I did! I'd go to parties and openings and anyplace that had people who I wanted to get online. I would go, and then try to corner people.

>**That's amazing. I wouldn't know where to start!**

>I didn't know how to start either! I didn't know what the hell I was doing. I remember I used to just end my days moaning, "Oh, if only I knew what I was doing, it would be so much easier …"

>**Tell me about the BITCH conference on ECHO.**

>BITCH is really great. BITCH happened because in the WIT conference, two of the women started two topics. One was "Five Guys on MOE (Men on ECHO), Who Would You Do?" It was just hysterical! And the

Echo has a weekly exchange between BITCH (Babes in Their Cyber Hangout) and MOE (Men on Echo). Every week a woman is chosen as BoTW (Bitch of the Week) and a man is chosen as MoTW (Moe of the Week), and they agree to answer whatever questions are thrown at them. Ms. Horn was kind enough to send me some samples of questions from Moes, along with the Bitches' answers (typos included):

The Strange Apparatus (jet66) 29-OCT-94

Dear BOTW:
Do women notice nose-hairs creeping out of a guy's honker?

Dear Jack,
You bet we do, and we wonder why the fuck the guy doesn't go out and buy a pretty little set of scissors (you know, you get them at Duane Reed—they're in the manicure implement section, but they're not scary looking at all).
anyhow, we wonder why the fuck you guyz don't go out and invest in a set of those cute l'il scissors and trim those hairs.
I mean, face it. They're ugly. They're distracting. Sometimes they tickle a gal when you're kissing her. And worst of all, sometimes they collect dried spooge.
But even more than nose hair, we notice the hair on your knuckles ...
Wishing you'd go shopping,
Janet

Jelly Donut (aka P. Driftwood) (peterme) 30-OCT-94

Dear Tingey-one ...
Do women bitch about all the "cute and intelligent" men being taken as much as men do about all the "cute and intelligent" women being taken?
If so, shouldn't there be an obvious remedy to this problem?

other one was "Ask Trashed and Tanked." Those were their online nicknames—one calls herself Trash and one calls herself Tank Girl. It was an advice column, except it was a bitch advice column. You had to be there. It wasn't like this lovely supporting stuff, it was with attitude. I loved those two topics so much, and I said I would love to have a whole conference entirely with this flavor, with this style, and then they went, "why don't we?" So these two women who had started these two topics started the conference called BITCH. It actually stands for Babes in Their Cyber Hangout. It's a place where you don't have to be nice.

> **How wonderful! So, how important do you think it is for women to learn about the Net and to get on it?**

> I'm not very political, and I'm not much of an activist. The only time I do get very active is when I'm up against the wall, and that happened to me during the Anita Hill hearings. I found it so upsetting to see this panel of guys judging this woman. So I started this conference called WON (Woman's Online Network), and the whole purpose was to get more women voted into public office. But it didn't really go anywhere, because I'm not really political, and I'm not good at organizing in that way. So I asked the people at *Ms.* magazine to take it over, so now they're doing that. The only reason that I work hard in this respect is that it's a very powerful medium, and I would hate to see women not use it, not take advantage of this thing that's right in front of them.

> **I've read that you tried really hard to get women to join ECHO.**

> Yeah, well I did it not as a political reason, but the only reason I did it was because I thought it would be a cooler place if there were women there. I mean, who cares to talk to twenty-year-old white guys all the time? It's just better when you've got more diversity.

> **So has ECHO actually changed as more women have joined?**

> You know, it has, but it's a difficult question to answer, because it's hard to put your finger on just why it has. Like if you get on ECHO, you'll see instantly that it's different, everything is different. But just how the women have made it different, and what that difference is, it's impossible to say. It's very infuriating. Just a different feel, but to say that feel is feminine—I wouldn't want to make that statement. But to reverse the question, how could it not be different? How could a system that is just under 40 percent female not be different, when most systems are only 10 percent female? You want to say it's more civilized, but it's not—as a girl you know that's bullshit.

> **Maybe it's smarter.**

> I think so! That's it! (laughs) The conversations are definitely much more intelligent on ECHO than in most places •

Dear Jelly-one,

From time to time I may be found on a Sunday evening, in a depressed huddle, whining pitifully to my cat that "all the good ones are taken" (tho I would never go so far as to limit "good ones" to just the "cute and intelligent" ones).

Since my cat is an unsympathetic listener, I am left to talk myself out of my depression, which I do by reminding myself that while it's sort of fun to imagine that evil, mysterious forces in the universe are whisking the "good ones" away before I can get at them, it's really not very productive.

It is much more productive to remind myself (quoting from my best friend's grandmother) that men are just like city busses, and there'll be another one along sometime soon.

Then I'll go read a good book, or watch an interesting movie, or call a friend, or do SOMETHING that makes me feel like I'm living my life, not being controlled by forces beyond my will.

which is very helpful, because if I live my life, I'm bound to have something interesting to say the next time I happen to stumble across a "good one" who hasn't been taken away.

one of the "good ones" who isn't taken,
Janet

Ne'er-Do-More (*craaawwwk!*) (dandy) 02-NOV-94 12:27

Dear Janet,

Boxers or briefs?
-Ne'er-was-just-speaking-hypothetically-and-with-a-certain-degree-of-exaggeration-that-he-considered-appropriate-to-this-item

Dear Ne'er,

Actually, there is no cut and dried answer to this one. It really depends on the physique of the guy at hand (so to speak).

I like boxers. I like briefs. Actually, I just really like men in various states of undress, especially below the waist.

The only thing I really don't like are those zebra-striped bikinis, which make any man look impossibly silly.

wondering what YOU'VE got on under the jeans.
Janet

Dear Topper,

What do women care about?
Why can't they care and talk about the same shit as guys? Wait, scratch that. I can't talk to guys either.
Sincerely,
Too luststruck to speak.

My reply:

One Dozen Popular Female Discussion Topics (in order): 1. Feelings; 2. Relationship with current beau; 3. My Job From Hell; 4. Relationship with mother; 5. I need to lose 10 pounds by next week; 6. Feelings; 7. Politics; 8. Where Did You Get That New Lipstick?; 9. Feelings; 10. Relationship with Sister; 11. He's Hung Like A What??; 12. Feelings.

Sorry. My first reaction to these questions is to be entirely flippant. Do you want to know what women care about so you can talk TO/WITH them or do you just want to talk them into something (you signed your letter "luststruck")? You'll have success with the latter if you concentrate on the former.

FASTER THAN MODEMS: FROM ISDN TO ADSL

The fastest standard modem on the market today is 28.8K, and I'm sure most people are quite satisfied with theirs. I was about to get one myself (just six months ago I was strapped with only a 14.4K modem), but when I found out there was something twice as fast as the 28.8, I had to have it. I'm talking about a Home ISDN line.

To refresh your memory, the speed of a modem determines the time it takes for your computer to receive text and images (and sound) from the Net. I'll admit that I'm a bit of a rushed woman. People tell me I talk quickly, and I usually walk at a pretty fast clip as well. So I can't help it, I need my computer to move full speed ahead.

A Home ISDN line is different from a modem because it isn't a gadget you need to attach to your computer; it's just a phone connection that requires a larger-than-usual jack that plugs into your wall. You also have to buy an ISDN terminal adapter, which costs around $400. The (regional) phone company has to install it. Besides being the speed-champ of the modem world, the advantage of an ISDN connection is that you get an added voice line so that you can receive phone calls while you're online (without paying for an extra line).

As happy as I am with my almost-instant Net connector, a Home ISDN is by no means flawless. Let me warn you that the phone company charges $28 per month, plus business rates, even if it's installed at your home, which means your voice-line bills could be a bit higher than usual. Also, not all service providers have ISDN-connection capabilities. For instance, AOL won't

let me dial directly with my ISDN line (so I still have my old modem attached as well—lame, I know!). The WELL, however, is (and always has been) much more on the edge, and I can dial them up with my ISDN. So you need to be aware of what your online service provider actually offers before leaping forward with an ISDN.

The biggest reason *not* to get an ISDN (unless you're as manically impatient as I am) is that it may become obsolete within the next year. Two contenders are vying for its spot: the cable modem and the ADSL modem.

Cable modems are actually being used now on a trial basis in certain cities, and may be available by next year. They're much quicker than the Home ISDN, and your Internet connection would be supplied by your cable company instead of your phone company.

ADSL, on the other hand, would be one hundred times faster than a Home ISDN. AT&T has just uncovered GlobeSpan, a technology that uses an ADSL modem that would transfer online data through ordinary copper telephone lines. AT&T says GlobeSpan may be ready for use in most cities nationwide by 1996, and wouldn't cost much more than your regular phone service.

If, after all the cons, you're still chomping at the bit for higher speed and just gotta have a Home ISDN connection, then call your local telephone company. If your area offers this type of service, they will connect you with your town's ISDN Kahuna. Just tell them to hurry! •

go>fasta

Getting into Newsgroups

It's easy to access one of the thousands of newsgroups on the Internet. Also known as Usenet groups, they cover discussion topics from music to food to politics, to almost anything else you can imagine. Here are the three basic access methods:

1. If you belong to an online service, there's a good chance you can check out Usenet groups from there. Investigate.

2. For those who have an Internet service provider, you can get Nuntius freeware (meaning it's free software!), which will connect you to any newsgroup you want.

3. Netscape users just have to click on the "Newsgroups" button on the Home Page menu bar, and voila! You'll be a groupie in no time.

Netiquette

Every grrrl should learn some Netiquette before she makes her debut into cyberspace. Here are my three cents:

1. Don't type in ALL CAPS. It's obnoxious and loud, and you'll get on everyone's nerves.

2. When responding to a point in someone's message, it's best to copy the part of their message that you're reacting to and paste it in your message with a > in front of each line (which is the Net's version of putting something in quotes). This way, no one will be confused as to what you're talking about.

3. If someone has sent you a questionably offensive message, whether it's private email or in a public forum, make sure you understand the tone of said offender. Sometimes with text-based dialog, intentions can be misunderstood. If you are sure, however, that said offender is actually being crass, rude, or downright evil, don't scamper away in a tearful rage. No one likes a sissy. Better ways to handle it are: a) If the creep is known as such, it may be best to turn the other cheek and completely ignore what was said. You will be respected and the jerk will continue to be known as a jerk. b) If, on the other hand, you can come up with a smart, witty, cutting comeback and want to show off your muscles, by all means flame away. It's part of life on the Net, and sometimes it's the only way to squash the idiot and make yourself feel better. Be careful though—you could find yourself in the middle of a full-fledged flame war! •

hot

It's impossible to cover every smart site on the Web—there are just too many, with new ones popping up every day. So sniff through the following collections of links, jot down the good ones I missed, and pretty soon you'll have an obese hotlist of your very own. Happy hunting!

ELECTRONIC NEWSSTAND
http://www.enews.com/

Hundreds of electronic magazines and zines are listed here, with subjects ranging from business to health to travel to sex.

THE INCREDIBLY EXPANDING HOTLIST
http://www.euro.net/5thworld/women/hotlist.html

Very hip links to all sorts of cultural hot spots for women. A feminist guy named Leo runs this joint.

PREVIOUS COOL SITES
http://www.infi.net/

Pretty conservative and straightforward stuff by InfiNet.

A WEB OF ONE'S OWN
http://www.best.com/~jtmax/wmnpage.html

An A–W guide to womanly sites. For example, one of the many links you'll find under 'A' is "American Women Writers." Under 'B' you'll find "Biographies of Women in Congress," and so forth. Part of Judith Meskill's jam-packed personal Home Page.

My Favorite Books

Actually, my favorite books are from the cyberpunk, slipstream, and gothic romance genres. But it would probably be more behoovable for you to read my hotlist of computery self-help books. So here they are:

- Line of QuickTour books by Ventana Press, including:
  Netscape QuickTour, by Stuart Harris and Gayle Kidder
  Mosaic QuickTour, by Gareth Branwyn
  Internet Chat, by Donald Rose
  Internet Email, by Ted Alspach
  These are all easy-to-read, easy-to-follow guidebooks to cyberspace.

- Line of Pocket Tour books by Sybex, including:
  Music on the Internet, by Colin Berry
  Celebrities on the Internet, by Colin Berry
  Money on the Internet, by Mark Fister
  Health and Fitness on the Internet, by Jeanne C.Ryer
  Games on the Internet, by Scott Taves
  Travel on the Internet, by Savitha Varadan and Kenyon Brown
  These are fun guides to online Hot Sites.

- *Mondo 2000: A User's Guide to the New Edge* (HarperPerennial), by Queen Mu and R.U. Sirius. A great introduction to the wired world. Even though this book is a few years old, it's still ahead of its time.

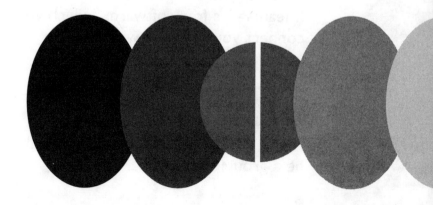

- *Happy Mutant Handbook* (Riverhead), by Me! and Mark Frauenfelder, Gareth Branwyn, and Will Kreth. Beautifully designed by Georgia Rucker.
    A full-color, peppy guide to do-it-yourself fun. Of course I'm gonna plug my own book! (Tee-hee!)

- *The New Hacker's Dictionary* (MIT Press), by Eric Raymond

- *Jargon* (Peach Pit Press), by Robin Williams.
    Don't be a priss. These books will get you hip to virtual street-slang.

Oh...I can't resist. I've gotta tell you my all-time favorite books:

1. *The Secret of Life* (Blue Jay), by Rudy Rucker.
   A cyberpunk classic.

2. *Slam* (Bantam), by Lewis Shiner.
   Slipstream at its finest.

3. *Wuthering Heights*, by Emily Brontë.
   I'm getting goosebumps just thinking of it! •

WHAT'S COOL
http://home.mcom.com/escapes/whats _cool.html
This constantly updated list of links really *is* cool!

WHERE THE GIRLS ARE
http://www.eskimo.com/~susan/ girls.htm
Visit this sassy hotlist of sites by, about, and for chicks. Created by a woman named Susan, these links will give you the lowdown on the ladies who pioneered the foundations of the Net. •

HOT SITES:
Help!

Once you're savvy enough to get on the World Wide Web, you'll be able to check out these instructional spots, which will further your Web wisdom in areas like surfing for live chat rooms, maneuvering around the Net, and designing your own pages.

EXPLORING THE WORLD WIDE WEB
http://www.gactr.uga.edu/exploring/toc.html

If you're still confused about the difference between the Internet and the World Wide Web, or if you need further explanation as to what kind of software you need in order to access the Web, you should find this site helpful. It's created by the University of Georgia Center for Continuing Education, which does a nice job of spelling out the ABCs of the WWW.

A BEGINNER'S GUIDE TO HTML
http://www.ncsa.uiuc.edu/demoweb/html-primer.html

For the grrrl who likes to get under the hood, this guide will teach you the basics of HTML so that you can create a Web page on your own. You should have at least a passing knowledge of how to use a Web browser (like Netscape or Mosaic) before taking your first HTML lesson.

--more-->

Nancy Bennett Evelyn

What is the World Wide Web

The World Wide Web (WWW) is the most versatile, dimensional, vivid area on the Net. This is the spot where you can listen to riot grrrl music, find photos of Sandra Bullock, watch short videos, buy coconut oil, and read what the gal-next-door has to say about her sex life. And this is where the "Hot Sites" covered in this book reside.

What makes the World Wide Web unique from the rest of the Net is that it offers "hypermedia browsing." This means that you can jump from one Website to another just by clicking on a word or image. For example, let's say you go to Jane Doe's Personal Web Page (Web documents are referred to as pages), and you read, "The best date I ever had was when I went to the Liz Phair concert with a guy named John. Before we went he surprised me with passionfruit bubble bath from The Body Shop and a pair of red stockings from Nicole Miller. He's so fine! . . ." You could either continue to read Jane's account of her dreamy rendezvous, or you could click on one of the highlighted words and be transported to a whole new site. Even if Jane's site is based in Singapore, if you click on <u>Liz Phair</u>, within seconds you may have an American Web page in front of you created by a Phair fan, from which you can read all about the singer and access photos and sound samples. From there, you may be able to click on a word or photo which will transport you to yet another site. Linking your way from site to site is what people call "Web surfing," or "Net surfing."

A Website is made up of one or more Web pages. A page is simply what you can see on your screen, though you may have to scroll down to see everything on it. Some sites only consist of one page, while others may contain fifty pages or more. To get from one page to the next you just click on a highlighted word (or a clickable image). If nothing on the page is highlighted, then you've come to a dead end—there are no more pages in that document. If you click on a word that takes you to a completely different site (like the Jane example above), then you've been escorted—or linked—to a whole new Website—often a "Home Page." A Home Page actually has two meanings: 1) The first page of a Web document, or 2) Somebody's personal Website. (Jane might email her friends and say, "Hey! Have you seen my new Home Page?")

The WWW hasn't been around too long. It was created in 1991 at the European Particle Physics Laboratory (CERN) in Geneva as a way for European physicists to exchange documents on the Net through a hypertext system. When computer programmers got wind of this they enthusiastically took the idea and, based on the same principle, expanded it to include more than just text. Being a global system, it's now called the World Wide Web.

GLOBAL INSTITUTE FOR INTERACTIVE MULTIMEDIA
"How to Publish on the Web"
http://www.thegiim.org/
From a list of sample Web pages, choose one that most closely resembles what you'd like to create for yourself (Personal Home Page, small-business page, online community project, etc.). Then get a tutorial that will explain design considerations, technical details, costs, and other Web resources to help you with your online venture.

LYNDA'S HOMEGURRLPAGE
http://www.earthlink.net/~lyndaw/
Lynda Weinman, a teacher at the Art Center College of Design in Pasadena, has a warm, welcoming Home Page full of links to various tutorials (some taught by her, some by other teachers). One of the links I like a lot is Web Design-O-Rama (http://www.the net-usa.com/mag/design/design.html), where Lynda interviews art directors of pretty Websites, and then tells you in plain English how to create a similar one yourself.

Other examples of helpful links on the Homegurrlpage include "Top 10 Web Design Tips," "How to Do Image Maps," and "Find Out How to Do Cool Netscape Tricks."

--more-->

Lynda's Homegurrl Page
http://www.earthlink.net/lyndaw

NETSCAPE TUTORIAL

http://w3.ag.uiuc.edu/AIM/Discovery/
Net/www/netscape/index.html

You need a Web browser—software that allows you to roam through the World Wide Web—if you want to have full access to this part of the Net. Netscape has become the standard browser, so if you're a Netscape Newbie, you may want to peruse these pages. You'll learn how to easily navigate the Web through Netscape, as well as how to take advantage of their "extras," like using their search engine to find what you're looking for, printing out Web documents, etc. It's such a cinch that you'll be a Netscape expert after only one visit.

INTERNET RELAY CHAT

http://www.kei.com/irc.html

Find out how you can elbow your way into the live Internet Relay Chat parties, where people from all over the world gather on the Net and talk about everything, in real-time. You'll also learn the history and meaning of IRC. •

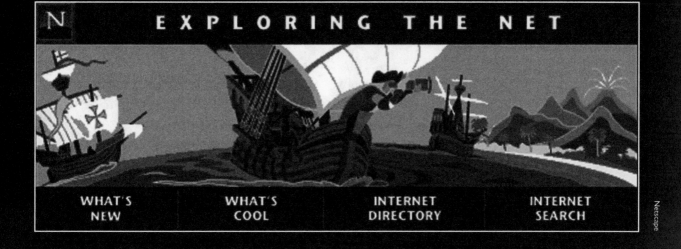

N EXPLORING THE NET

WHAT'S
NEW

WHAT'S
COOL

INTERNET
DIRECTORY

INTERNET
SEARCH

Netscape

GETTING ON THE WORLD WIDE WEB

Before you can party in the fancy part of cyberspace known as the Web, you first need "browser software." This allows you to obtain from your computer the colorful multimedia documents I've been gushing about. Mosaic used to be *the* Web software, but today the standard browser is Netscape, and I highly recommend it.

If you belong to an online service, however, you may not need to worry about installing a browser, since many of them provide Web access for you. For instance, **IGC** (Institute for Global Communications) is a service that uses Netscape to get you on the **WWW**. Other services, like America Online, also get you on the Web. Unfortunately, they currently use their own browser, which doesn't incorporate all the nifty features that make Netscape so useful. If you're unsure of your Web status, call your service and they'll set you straight.

If getting on the **WWW** through an online service isn't working for you, another option is to get a **SLIP/PPP** connection through an Internet Service Provider (which, contrary to an online service provider, only supplies you with software for and a connection to the Net and Web and does not offer chat rooms, newsgroups, etc.). One of the largest ISPs is Netcom (800/501-8649). Although the provider will cost a low monthly fee, the actual **SLIP/PPP** software is "shareware," which means you can try it out for free and send in a registration fee if you like it. Note that **AOL** and Compuserve have begun offering **SLIP/PPP** connections.

But don't do any of the above until you check in with your university, workplace, or library. You may already have free access to the Web and not even know it!

glossary

BBS (Bulletin Board Service)
An online clubhouse with discussion groups, email, and sometimes games and libraries. Most BBSs are run as hobbies and are free. You can modem into many BBSs even if you don't belong to a service or have Internet access.

Bookmark
To save a Web address in a special file so that you can fetch it at a later time.

Chat Rooms
Social hangouts on the Net. They are easiest to access from an online service such as America Online, but one can participate on these types of salons on the Net as well.

Chick
A woman with sass and attitude who's eager to explore the Net.

Cyber
As verb: To self-pilot. As adj.: Autonomous. Popularized by "cyber-punk," but nowadays used as a prefix to just about any word to signify its involvement with the digital or Net world. For example, cyberchick is a female Internet explorer.

Cyberspace
The online world.

FAQ
Frequently asked questions. Many Usenet newsgroups have a FAQ list that newcomers should read.

Flame
An intentionally nasty online message directed at an individual.

Flame War
Online cat-fight.

FTP (File Transfer Protocol)
A system which allows you to grab articles or documents from other computers. Many of these accessible articles come from universities and libraries.

Grrrl
Same as chick, except grrrls can be even tougher.
I'm a chick on some days, a grrrl on others.

Hacker
A clever computer user who comes up with original tricks to solve
computer problems and who explores cyberspace the way a
real-world explorer treks through the wildest of jungles.

Hit
People keep track of their Website's popularity through hits.
Every time someone visits a Website it registers as a "hit."

Home Page
The first page of a Website. A Personal Home Page is a site
someone creates to express themselves.

Hotlink
See Link.

Hotlist
A list of favorite links to Websites.

Hot Site
A Website that is coooool.

Hyperlink
See Link.

Hypertext
Text that is interactive. If you click on a highlighted word in a
hypertext document, you will be transported to another page or
site that pertains to the meaning of that word. For example, if
you're reading an online article about witches and you click on the
highlighted word "goddess," some article or definition related to
goddesses will pop up.

Image Map
A group of icons used as a map or a table of contents for a
Website. Instead of text, you click on a picture, which will take
you to a specific page of a Website.

Jump
Going from one Website to another via a link.

Link
A Website that is accessible from another Website. For instance, if you adore Nancy Drew, you could include a link on your own Home Page that would escort your visitors to Ms. Drew's Home Page. Also referred to as hotlink or hyperlink.

Log on/Log in
The act of revving up your modem and going to an online hangout.

Modem
A device that connects your phone line to your computer, allowing you to hop on the Internet (or at least visit a BBS).

Mouse Potato
Someone who's glued to her computer all day.

Net
The place where millions of connected computer users across the planet meet to communicate and express themselves.

Newbie
An online beginner. Newbies love to call other people Newbies. This usually starts a flame war.

Newsgroups (Also called Usenet Groups)
Areas where social Net gabbers add messages to ongoing conversations based on a particular subject. More than 5,000 of these groups are floating in cyberspace at the moment.

Nrrrd
See Hacker.

Online
When your modem is running and you've dialed in to cyberspace, you are online.

Online Service
A company you pay to provide you an email address, entry to all sorts of private online activities and services, and usually access to the Internet. Examples are the WELL and CompuServe.

Page

Each display file of a Website is called a page. If you click on a word which brings you to another display, you've jumped to a new page.

QuickTime

A software program that allows you to watch videos on your computer.

Shareware

Software that's made to be freely distributed to whoever wants it. Usually the creators ask that satisfied recipients make a donation. There's also freeware (no strings attached) and postcardware (if you like the software, send a postcard to the programmer).

Surfing

Jumping from site to site.

URL (Uniform Resource Locator)

The standard addressing system for the World Wide Web. When you see those long strands of characters that start with http://www . . . , it's not gibberish, it's a URL.

Webgrrl

A Chick who creates her own virtual pad on the World Wide Web. Coined by Aliza Sherman, aka Cybergrrl™.

Website

One of the thousands of virtual spots that comprise the World Wide Web. A Website can be made up of one or more pages.

World Wide Web (also WWW or Web)

A universe of full-color sites on the Net comprised of hyperlinked text, graphics, sounds, and videos that people can access using software called a browser (such as Netscape or Mosaic). These sites are created by people for various reasons, including self-expression, social awareness, and commercial outlets.

Zine

A small, independently owned, do-it-yourself publication.

Photo by Burns

Author Bio

Carla Sinclair is the empress of the pop-culture magazine *bOING bOING* and co-editor of *The Happy Mutant Handbook*, a guide to mischievous fun for higher primates. She also contributes to *Wired*. The two best ways to contact her in West Hollywood are by carrier pigeon or email (carla@well.com).

INDEX

Explore the NET CHICK
Clubhouse!

Psst! -- Over here! We're in the Net Chick Clubhouse, spreading gossip, telling secrets, relishing pop culture, luxuriating, and playing hard.

Come join us. Just click on the room of your choice the Entertainment Lounge, Map, Rumour Room, Office, or Beauty Parlor.

And hurry up - the party's already started!

(Brave boys may enter too.)

HEY, where are you going?

The Party's just begun! And we want YOU.

WHAT?	The Net Chick Clubhouse
WHERE?	**http://www.cyborganic.com/People/carla/**
WHEN?	Now

- Play with my Magic 8 Bra
- Win a key to my secret diary
- Kick back with some savvy words from the bookshelf
- Huddle around the chick-chat coffee table for hot gossip and grrrl talk
- Link to the sites I mention in my book, along with many new spots that I've just found

Plus there's even more, more, more games, secrets, updates, and smart talk awaiting you in the Clubhouse. Ignite your modem now!
RSVP not needed.

(Brave boys are invited, too.)